LANCASHIRE COUNTY CRICKET

1864–1953

A. N. Hornby 1847–1925

Lancashire County Cricket

THE OFFICIAL HISTORY OF THE LANCASHIRE
COUNTY & MANCHESTER CRICKET CLUB

1864-1953

A. W. Ledbrooke

WITH A FOREWORD BY
Tom Stone & J. Bowling Holmes

STATISTICS COMPILED BY
Charles M. Oliver

PHOENIX HOUSE LTD
LONDON

Printed in Great Britain by
Western Printing Services Ltd, of Bristol, for
Phoenix House Ltd, 38 William IV Street,

Charing Cross, W.C.2

First published 1954

Foreword

Tom Stone, *President*
J. Bowling Holmes, *Chairman of the Committee*

It is with much pleasure that the Committee has had this, the first official history of the Club, written.

It covers a long period from the origin of the Manchester Cricket Club through its transition to the Lancashire County and Manchester C.C. and to its arrival at a very eminent position in the world of cricket of to-day.

The Club has a great history which is well worthy the telling, and it has been well told. It includes descriptions and records of great personalities and matches and it is hoped that this book will therefore prove to be a valuable and permanent record as well as an interesting narrative.

We are indebted to the well-known journalist, Mr. A. W. Ledbrooke, for so ably writing and presenting this admirable work.

Tom Stone.

J. Bowling Holmes.

Contents

7

Chapter

Chapter

List of Plates

13

Introduction and Acknowledgments

IN COMPILING the first official history of Lancashire County Cricket Club—to give it its briefer and better-known title—I came immediately face to face with one difficulty: so much has happened since 1864 that one volume would barely suffice for the story. When I surveyed the task of covering 1,600-odd matches, discussing the administration of the club, and dealing with the lives of the greatest players, I came to the conclusion—very reluctantly—that feats of opposing players would generally have to be given scant attention. There simply was not space to do more than chronicle Lancashire achievements, and to give the Lancashire point of view. To have done justice to the players of other counties would have doubled the size of this book and I can only hope and assume that their own counties, in their own books, have done them honour. The exception is in the case of Yorkshire matches, so important a part of Lancashire cricket, and to these a full chapter has been given.

For the same reason of lack of space, I fear that much of the humour of the story has had to be overlooked. Those who wish to read countless off-the-field anecdotes should acquire a copy of William Howard's *Fifty Years' Cricket Reminiscences of a Non-Player*, published in 1928. Test matches at Old Trafford have been omitted since there are so many sources of reference available.

It was originally intended that this book should be written by the well-known Preston journalist, Mr. J. Arthur Brierley. When he became ill, I was invited to assist him, but unhappily he passed away before we could do little more than discuss the project. His widow has made available to me his library and a manuscript notebook kept up during the many summers he travelled the country with the Lancashire eleven and my first acknowledgment must therefore be to the generosity of Mrs. Brierley, still an enthusiast for the game and a frequent visitor to Old Trafford and to grounds farther afield. I have used Arthur Brierley's notes in dealing with the earliest officials; otherwise the work is my own, and responsibility for the opinions expressed is mine too.

For being given a free hand to express those views I owe a deep debt of gratitude to the Lancashire C.C.C. sub-committee charged with the duty of producing this book. Members of that sub-committee were: Dr. J. Bowling Holmes (chairman), Mr. R. A. Boddington, Major Rupert Howard, and Mr. Geoffrey Howard, and while they enthusiastically concerned themselves closely with the project, they never attempted to act as censors.

The general design of the book itself provides for a brief description of each season's cricket with interludes to discuss administration and the work of outstanding players. I have gone into greater detail for the championship years of 1879 (joint), 1881, 1882 (joint), 1897, 1904, 1926–7–8, 1930, 1934, and 1950 (joint) so that members of the club, for whom this book is primarily intended, should have a permanent record of the way in which those successes were achieved.

Reference to Appendix II will show the dates of each player's first and last appearance in the county team and it is suggested that readers should use this appendix, in conjunction with the chapter headings, as an index.

No cricket-lover needs to be advised to read all of Neville Cardus, and to him and his books I acknowledge my indebtedness. H. S. Altham's *History of Cricket*; R. G. Barlow's *Forty Seasons of First-Class Cricket*; Fred Reynolds's book of scores of the matches played from 1864 to 1882; Laurence Meynell's *Famous Cricket Grounds*; T. Swindells's booklet of statistics published about 1908; Roy Webber's books of records; and of course the yearly volumes of *Wisden's* without which we would all be helpless—these are among the sources I have consulted.

My thanks are also due to:

Mr. Geoffrey Howard, present secretary of the county club, for assistance in many ways;

Mr. Ernest Butler Rowley, the oldest surviving Lancashire cricketer, for a long and interesting talk and the loan of documents;

Major Rupert Howard, Mr. R. H. Spooner, Mr. Ernest Tyldesley, Mr. Frank Sibbles, and Mr. George Duckworth for answering my many questions;

Sir Francis Meynell for permission to reproduce Francis Thompson's beautiful poem;

The staff of the library of Kemsley House, Manchester, and

Mr. Percy Hoare, editor of the *Northern Daily Telegraph*, Blackburn, for aid in tracing old newspaper references and cuttings; and

Successive editors of the *Daily Dispatch* (Mr. Alexander Nicol and Mr. A. T. P. Murphy) for permission and encouragement to undertake this work in addition to my normal duties.

Finally, I should like to thank the following for their permission to reproduce certain of the illustrations in this book:

Associated Photo Services, Liverpool; Blackpool Gazette & Herald Ltd.: Central Press Photos Ltd.; Keystone Press Agency Ltd.; Manchester Guardian; Marylebone Cricket Club; Picture Post Library; Sport & General Press Agency Ltd.; D. C. Thomson & Co. Ltd., Manchester.

A. W. LEDBROOKE

Bramhall,
June 1952–September 1953

CHAPTER 1

Formation of the County Club

Manchester C.C. at Salford and Hulme; A match at
Lord's, 1842; A move to Old Trafford; Matches
against Yorkshire; Another move; The
first pavilion; County club formed
1864; Middlesex, the first
county opponents

THE FORMATION OF Lancashire County Cricket Club in 1864 was much more than the effort of a band of enthusiasts to broaden the scope of their fixtures. It was, and remains, a significant example of the development of the game in the middle of the nineteenth century represented elsewhere by the formation of county clubs, changes in the style of bowling, the first tours to Canada and Australia, the beginning of fixtures between Australian Colonies (now States), and by the appearance on the cricket field of W. G. Grace. It was a time of change in almost every walk of life, and cricket in Lancashire, as all over the English-speaking world, shared in the fine flowering.

There is ample evidence that the game flourished with local clubs in Lancashire from the earliest years of the century and by 1818 the Manchester Club had attained a position of importance, playing their matches first at The Crescent, Salford, and then at Moss Lane, Hulme. An interesting scorebook of 1826 records a match played between Manchester (with French of Liverpool) against Garrison (with Carter of Liverpool). The Garrison was made up of units from the Coldstream Guards and the Queen's Bays. In this match one man was given out 'foot before wicket'.

By 1842 members were ready to try their fortunes beyond the narrow field of fixtures against the clubs they knew, and a team was sent to Lord's to meet the Gentlemen of the M.C.C. They were overwhelmed and gave up the game after the M.C.C. had scored 220 in reply to their own meagre first innings of 59. A comment written at the time says: 'The bowling on the part of Manchester was very deficient, it being of the old-fashioned under-hand school, which afforded the Marylebone gentlemen much amusement in hitting it away.'.

As round-arm bowling had been legal since 1828, Manchester's cricketers were plainly a long way behind the times but we may guess that this visit to London spurred them to improvement and they met and defeated All-Yorkshire in 1844. They were shown a further example of high-class cricket when, in 1847, the touring All-England team came north. George Parr was just coming out, and in successive matches he made 100 at Leicester, 78 not out at York, and 64 at Manchester, and we may well imagine the effect on other players of their first sight of this new giant.

The ambitions of the Manchester club next took them to a ground at Old Trafford, still to be identified on the main Chester road as the subsequent site of the Botanical Gardens and nowadays as the White City greyhound track. And by 1849 there was a sufficient community of interest for a Lancashire team to be organised to play against Yorkshire, first at Sheffield and then in the return at Manchester. Two years later another game was played in Manchester and these three matches, though not regarded by Lancashire members of to-day as part of the official series of fixtures between the two counties, are so counted by Yorkshiremen.

Two events of 1857 must have been the talk of the Manchester cricketing world, and their impact echoes down to the present time. In this year the club side, with the assistance of Wisden, Lillywhite, and Tom Davies, defeated the all-powerful Surrey side by three runs, at Eccles, the only defeat suffered by the southern team in ten fixtures. The ball used in this match is now in the possession of the Manchester Tennis and Racquet Club, having been presented to it by the Western Club when the latter went out of existence. The ball carries the following inscription:

Manchester with Lillywhite and Wisden
v
The County of Surrey
Played on the Western Ground, Manchester
September 3rd, 4th, 5th, 1857
Manchester won by 3 runs.

The other event is one that has been described over and over again; a new ground at Old Trafford was obtained. An Art Treasures Exhibition had claimed the old site in 1856 and after officials of the club had vainly fought the threatened eviction, they set about finding fresh quarters. They had not far to seek; almost within a stone's throw they found a suitable spot, prob- ably already used for cricket, and there they pitched their wickets. Old Trafford, the ground now known to cricketers the world over, was established.

Bell's Life of 28 June 1857, reports the opening fixture— Manchester v Liverpool:

OPENING OF THE MANCHESTER NEW CRICKET GROUND.—The ground which, for many years, was occupied by the Manchester Cricket Club, at Old Trafford, is now covered by the Art Treasures Palace. The new ground is situated to the west of the Exhibition buildings, and consists of about eight acres of good, level, sandy land. The pavilion is erected on the north side; and while it is a great orna- ment to the ground, it is well adapted for the purposes for which it will be used. It consists of a centre compartment (intended for a dining hall) and two wings, a turret sur- mounting the centre. The dining hall is 36 feet long by 22 feet wide.

There was a residence for Thomas Hunt, the professional bowler (a Yorkshireman, by the way; when he died a benefit match was played for his widow, and this is the first benefit match on the ground of which record can be traced), and there was, of course, a bar. And the newspaper adds:

Underneath the building is an excellent wine cellar, no unimportant acquisition in a cricket pavilion. The entire front of the dining hall, which commands a view of the whole field, is composed of glass.

The cost of the removal was stated to be £1,100.

The start was auspicious. Manchester made 152 and 46, Liverpool 89 and 78, and so the home club won by 31 runs.

About this time opposition was provided by such clubs as Broughton, Sheffield, Liverpool, and Shrewsbury, and soon a pavilion was erected at a cost of £900. The players included members of the Rowley family, Joseph Makinson, the Rev. F. W. Wright, Middlemort, E. J. Bousfield, and H. W. Barber. The victory over Surrey was soon followed by another glimpse of high-class cricket when the All-England side played at Broughton and the bursting energy of the Rowleys and their friends reacted sharply to the news of the formation of the Yorkshire county club in 1863. The way was right for expansion and the decisive step was taken on 12 January 1864, at a meeting at the Queen's Hotel.

The *Blackburn Standard* of 20 January 1864, reported:

PROPOSED COUNTY CRICKET CLUB

Last Tuesday afternoon a meeting convened by circular and advertisement was held in Manchester to consider the propriety of forming a County Cricket Club, with a view of spreading a thorough knowledge and appreciation of the game throughout Lancashire. A good attendance of amateur cricketers from all parts of the county ... It was stated that matches would be held alternately in Manchester, Preston, Blackburn, and other places and it was hoped by this means to introduce other good cricket into every part of Lancashire. The recommended annual subscription is one guinea, the expenses would be trifling, and it was thought desirable that whatever surplus remained should be funded so that at some future day they might be enabled to secure a playing ground that would do them credit, and answer all the requirements of the County.

Those who attended this meeting were: S. H. Swire, E. B. Rowley, A. B. Rowley, H. W. Barber, D. Bleackley, A. Birley, T. Fothergill, E. Challender, J. Holt, jun., and Captain Ashton, of the Manchester club; R. Entwistle, J. Becton, R. K. Birkley, and H. Ashton, of the Western club; W. Horner, D. Long, H. Royle, and J. Higgins, Liverpool; E. J. Bousfield and J. W. Allison, Longsight; E. Whittaker and E. Hobson, Ashton; F. W. Wright, J. B. Payne, R. Crawshaw, and J. Whittington, Broughton; S. G. Greenwood and J. Yates, Blackburn; J.

Smith of Accrington; J. Swailes of Oldham; T. Wall of Wigan; A. Eccles, of Huyton; and H. M. Tenent, of the Northern club.

In forming the county club and building the ground they so keenly desired, the wishes of these enthusiasts were realised; the subsidiary aim of playing games all over the county was not. There was a growing disinclination to move fixtures away from Old Trafford and another potent factor was the establishment of the Lancashire League which not only catered for the wants of players and public but sometimes cramped the operation of the county in the engagement of the most desirable players. In later years there happily grew up a much greater degree of understanding.

With the necessary resolutions passed and a committee elected, all was ready and the first match in which a team officially labelled 'Lancashire' took the field was played at Warrington on 15 and 16 June 1864, against Birkenhead Park and Ground. An all-amateur eleven comprised J. Fairclough, J. White, E. B. Rowley, J. Becton, B. J. Lawrence, G. H. Grimshaw, S. H. Swire, J. Rowley, F. H. Gossage, W. Robinson, and T. T. Bellhouse. Thanks to 57 by J. Rowley and effective bowling by Lawrence, who took eight wickets, Lancashire gained a first-innings lead of 26 runs, but they were put out for 78 in the second innings and only time saved them from defeat, as Birkenhead Park were 90 for one wicket at the close.

For the return match at Birkenhead Park a month later Hickton, Holgate, and Nichols were called in to give professional aid; a heavy-scoring match was left drawn. All-amateur games filled in the fixture list against the Gentlemen of Shropshire at Liverpool and Shrewsbury, the Gentlemen of Warwickshire at Warwick and Old Trafford, and the Gentlemen of Yorkshire at Broughton and York.

The first inter-county match followed in 1865, against Middlesex at Old Trafford, and a remarkable event it proved. It gave Lancashire a capital send-off to a wider career with victory by 62 runs after a tie on the first innings, and the game has its sure place in the record books by reason of the feat of V. E. Walker, member of the famous Southgate family, who took all ten Lancashire wickets in their second innings.

In this and the return fixture at Islington, won by Middlesex by ten wickets, Lancashire included professionals, among them

Roger Iddison (who also played for Yorkshire) and Fred Reynolds, who thus began an association with the club that lasted until 1907 and who will be met again in these pages.

So the club was fairly launched. Lancashire were still indebted to Manchester for the use of the ground, and they had at intervals to ask for renewal of permission to play there, but the fixture list began to expand at once and we can now deal with the affairs of the club as it progressed under its succession of captains, pausing now and again to consider the most famous players and, not less important, the men who governed affairs in the committee-room and office.

CHAPTER 2

First-class Matches

1866–72 Captain: Edmund Rowley

*A wider fixture list; Iddison's first century; A record by
Ricketts; Arthur Appleby's début; Official matches
against Yorkshire; Hickton's all-ten against
Hampshire; Watson, Barlow and
McIntyre arrive*

IN 1866 THERE were four inter-county fixtures, and up to 1872
the programme, if it did not greatly expand, certainly did not
lack variety. To Middlesex, Surrey were next added as opponents. Then came M.C.C. and Ground and the matches with
Yorkshire that were to begin a rivalry keener than any other in
English cricket. Nottinghamshire, Sussex, Hampshire, Derbyshire and Kent, were all met in this period, to which an end
may be marked when a system of qualification of players was
drawn up and the county championship instituted in 1873.

That some general method of controlling the appearances of
players had become necessary may be seen from examples provided in Lancashire. In 1866 four Hornby brothers turned out
for the Gentlemen of Cheshire against the Gentlemen of Lancashire, at Chelford. Three weeks later, A. N. and E. K. were
playing for the Gentlemen of Lancashire against the Gentlemen of Yorkshire. Since amateurs are presumably free to
choose how and where they play in non-competitive sport some
justification may be argued for this peripatetic cricket; but in
a different category fell the professional Roger Iddison who in
the following season played for Lancashire against Surrey, was
then claimed by Yorkshire, and played for them in all three
matches against his old teams. In 1868 he was back again in
the ranks of Lancashire, and a very useful performer he was;
he scored the first century ever hit for the county (106 against
Surrey in a high-scoring match at the Oval in 1866) and his

complete record shows a batting average of 23 runs an innings (quite good in this period) and 56 wickets for 15 runs each.

Iddison's century was made after the side had followed on against a Surrey total of 422, the first innings of such magnitude hit off their bowling; they surpassed this themselves on the same ground a year later with a score of 429 and this ranks as one of cricket's most remarkable days. Sent in first for Lancashire was a new professional, James Ricketts, who carried his bat for 195, still the highest individual innings ever played by a cricketer making his début in an inter-county fixture. He played on and off for ten years but never bore out the promise of this sensational beginning.

Another splendid performance was by Arthur Appleby against Surrey at Liverpool. In his case a bowling analysis of six for 30 did not deceive for he was destined to become one of the finest amateur bowlers.

In 1867 the first three fixtures were played with Yorkshire and—dreadful omen—all were lost. Fred Reynolds, who published the first book ever connected with the County's affairs, gives first the Old Trafford match of June 27, 28, 29, followed by the return at Middlesbrough in September and then prints a Whalley fixture, played a week before that at Old Trafford, as an 'extra match'. But the scorecard of this game, preserved in the pavilion, bears the description 'The first Lancashire-Yorkshire match', and the evidence must be accepted that this great rivalry began at Whalley on June 20th of this year.

A useful player during this period was Cornelius Coward of Preston, who is said to have been an exceptional exponent of the cut. He played one fine innings of 85 against Middlesex in 1866 after five men had been dismissed for 16 runs. He played in several representative games such as North v South and England v Surrey, twice appeared for the Players at the Oval, and later became a first-class umpire as did his brother Fred, another early Lancashire professional.

Another who rendered good service was William Hickton, a fast round-arm bowler whose first big performance was in 1867 against M.C.C. Except for Cornelius Coward who had appeared there as a colt five years earlier, none of the team had ever previously played at Lord's and a depressing experience it must have been. The weather was vile, and mops and pails were used to clear pools of water from the pitch so that the match could be finished—one of the first recorded instances of artificial drying.

Some sixty years later, one may note here, Lancashire officials were prominent in urging the change of rules that led to artificial drying of pitches being permitted in first-class cricket.

Lancashire were beaten by fifty runs on this historic occasion though Hickton took 11 wickets for 91 runs. He surpassed this in 1870 when in the second innings of Hampshire at Old Trafford he took all ten wickets for 46 runs, with a match record of 14 for 73. A Derbyshire man, he too appeared for the Players at the Oval.

Gideon Holgate was another Yorkshireman who played for both counties, for Lancashire in the first of the three matches of 1867, and against them in the two following fixtures, and he kept wicket in the match at Lord's when Hickton bowled so well. A bird of passage from South Yorkshire, he was involved in the strikes which afflicted Yorkshire, among other clubs, in the early days of organised county cricket.

These, with Fred Reynolds, were the principal professionals for some time and the team was often predominantly amateur. E. Whittaker, the Rowleys, the Hornbys, the Hultons, J. F. Leese, E. Challender, F. Rutter, E. Moorhouse, E. Roper, F. W. Wright, A. Appleby, E. J. Bousfield—these are the names which recur in the matches and the averages, with A. N. Hornby gradually asserting himself so that he topped the batting figures each season from 1869 to 1872. The amateurs also had their own matches, and it was in one of these, against the Gentlemen of Yorkshire, that E. B. Rowley hit the tremendous score (for this was in 1867) of 219; he was also the first man to hit a ball right out of Old Trafford from a wicket pitched in the middle.

The Rev. Frank Wynyard Wright appeared intermittently from 1869. An Oxfordshire man, he played for Lancashire as one of the first of the great contingent from Rossall School, where his feats were such as to make him as remarkable a boy cricketer as A. G. Steel or R. H. Spooner. We remember him here because he was the first amateur to score a century for the county, 120 not out against Sussex at Old Trafford. He is said to have stood exceptionally close in when fielding at point. He settled down to scholastic work at Eastbourne and dropped

out of county cricket before his brilliant promise really had a
chance of fulfilment, though he continued to hit up huge
scores in club cricket.

These, then, were the men who put Lancashire on the
cricket map. In 1871 they received two remarkable reinforce-
ments in Alec Watson and R. G. Barlow, and another in the
following season when William McIntyre came from Nottingham. For some time—at any rate in first-class matches—Barlow
was principally a batsman, the attack depending chiefly on
Watson, McIntyre, and Arthur Appleby. These three became
regularly associated in 1872 and the effect was immediate, the
four county fixtures against Yorkshire and Derbyshire all ending in victory. The averages showed this remarkable record:

	Matches	Runs	Wickets	Average
McIntyre	3	232	41	5.65
Watson	4	178	20	8.90
Appleby	3	130	12	10.83

Barlow, who had taken a wicket with his first ball in county
cricket the previous summer (against Yorkshire at Sheffield)
must have been itching to share in the spoils, but besides the
three named no one else got a bowl, much less took a wicket.
The seven remaining batsmen of the eighty dismissed were all
run out.

CHAPTER 3

Championship Matches

1873–9 Captain: Edmund Rowley

Cricket under new rules; Lancashire against a Cup competition;
New players in Vernon Royle, A. G. Steel, Crossland,
Pilling, Briggs, and Nash; Other grounds refused
county matches; Hornby and Barlow go in first
together; W. G. Grace comes to Old Trafford;
The Australians' first visit to the ground;
Great crowds; The championship
shared with Notts, 1879

LANCASHIRE WERE WELL prepared for the change that came over county cricket in 1873 when rules were drawn up for the qualification of players. They had their band of skilful and enthusiastic amateurs, and in Watson, McIntyre, and Barlow they had three professionals whose services were now made secure by the limitations imposed on cricketers' wanderings. They had the verbal promise of security of tenure of Old Trafford, Reynolds to look after the Manchester Club's matches and generally to superintend the ground, and by extending their fixture list they had fairly won recognition as a first-class county to be accepted as worthy rivals in the field. Lancashire took, too, a full share in the management of the game, sending representatives to all the important meetings. They declined, however, to join in the proposed 'championship matches', a kind of Cup competition suggested at Lord's because 'county cricket has become more popular every year and requires no such encouragement'. It was also thought that the idea might encourage gambling.

The club set about improving their position. A new pavilion was planned as an addition to the structure already standing, and in the course of a few years several players of the highest class were recruited. Vernon Royle came out in 1873, Richard

Pilling and A. G. Steel appeared in 1877, Crossland in the following season, and Briggs and Nash in 1879, an accession of strength that would have been welcomed by any team at any time in cricket history. The sequel was that the championship was shared with Notts in 1879, and won outright in 1881, and though Edmund Rowley had by then ceased to be captain, the triumph came through the efforts of the men recruited under his leadership.

In viewing Lancashire's progress, it must be borne in mind that their chief rivals had enjoyed a start. Sussex had an unbroken organisation from 1839, and Notts had been sending out good players ever since William Clarke opened Trent Bridge in 1838. Surrey men had taken part in the development of the Hambledon club and the county played All-England every year between 1792 and 1810, with the county club formed in 1845. Yorkshire, though not formally organised until 1863, had the background of the famous Sheffield v Nottingham matches dating from 1771, and a county team was put into the field as early as 1833. Kent had been formed in 1859 with a history of big matches dating back a century earlier.

Starting level with Lancashire were Middlesex, who were established at Islington in 1864. Gloucestershire who, of course, had the inestimable gift of the Graces in the early '60s, were formed into a county club in 1871.

During Rowley's captaincy, the cricket, it need hardly be said, was on a small scale compared with the modern programme. Even when the championship was recognised (with the team suffering fewest defeats taking the title) Lancashire took part in only seven first-class games in the first season, and there was a certain amount of latitude in keeping engagements, as, for instance, when the Old Trafford fixture against Kent was not played 'owing to a misunderstanding in reference to a projected North and South Gentlemen's Match'.

Gentlemen's matches still formed a substantial part of the programme at Old Trafford, which continued to house all home games. Towards the end of Edmund Rowley's tenure of captaincy, Liverpool was pressing for county games, and applications were also turned down from Rochdale, Sefton Park and Burnley, though in 1876 the Kent match was allocated to Castleton.

Another point to be borne in mind when considering cricket

of this period, is the impact of the first Australian tour to this country in 1878. The discipline and the training, the resolution and smart appearance, of these men from overseas, made a tremendous impression; while their bowling, with its variations of pitch and pace, contrasted strongly with the somewhat mechanical methods of English cricketers. With this general background in mind, we can come to consideration of Lancashire's championship matches season by season.

1873: CHAMPIONSHIP MATCHES:
Played 7, Won 4, Drawn 0, Lost 3

Lancashire's first match under the new conditions was against Yorkshire at Old Trafford, the visitors winning in two days. The return at Sheffield was also lost but in between these two games Surrey were beaten by an innings and 113 runs in a fixture marked by Hornby's first championship hundred and destructive bowling by McIntyre and Watson who put the visitors out for 44 and 105. They bowled unchanged again at the Oval a month later when the double was duly completed and Surrey's 33 on this occasion remains the lowest total for which they have ever been dismissed by Lancashire. The match also saw the county try out a new first-wicket pair, Hornby and Barlow commencing their historic association with the prophetic entry: Barlow, run out, 0.

Vernon Royle, destined to attain lasting fame as one of the finest fieldsmen at cover-point, appeared for the first time in the second match against Yorkshire and so commenced a line of men who have distinguished Lancashire's fielding in this position through A. N. Hornby, Johnny Briggs, S. M. Crosfield, R. H. Spooner, Jack Sharp, Harry Makepeace, Eddie Paynter, and Cyril Washbrook.

At the end of the season Hornby, the only centurion, was top of the batting averages. McIntyre and Watson took 107 wickets between them; Appleby came next with five!

1874: CHAMPIONSHIP MATCHES:
Played 6, Won 1, Drawn 2, Lost 3

This season opened badly. A weak team was overthrown by Derbyshire at Old Trafford, for though Watson took nine wickets for 118 runs, Mycroft and Flint bowled out the home county for 38 and there was no recovery from such a set-back.

In the return at Chesterfield our old friend Hickton is found playing for the opposition and taking six wickets. Of the fixtures with Yorkshire, the home game was lost but ample revenge taken at Bradford where McIntyre, in tremendous form with 13 wickets for 66 runs, was well supported by Appleby.

The matches with Kent produced excellent cricket. At Old Trafford, Lancashire had five second-innings wickets down and still needed 87 to win when time was called. In the return at Maidstone, Barlow carried his bat for 26 in a total of 116, the first of many such feats standing to his name. With a century by H. W. Renny-Tailyour and some fine bowling by Capt. J. Fellowes, Kent won by ten wickets.

1875: CHAMPIONSHIP MATCHES:
Played 6, Won 4, Drawn 1, Lost 1

New ground was broken this year with friendly matches against Leicestershire and in the home game distinction was won by W. S. Patterson, who took nine wickets cheaply. Patterson was an outstanding Cambridge University cricketer. In the year following this bowling feat he hit a century against Oxford at Lord's—a very rare feat in those days—and in 1877 he took nine wickets and was in at the death with G. F. Grace when the Gentlemen beat the Players by one wicket in what has been called 'the Glorious Match'.

Two splendid matches with Yorkshire ended with a win apiece. At Old Trafford, Lancashire gained a first-innings lead of 71, then Yorkshire made such a recovery that a fourth-innings task of 148 looked as though it might be too much. But Hornby and Barlow, the latter batting much more freely than usual, together knocked off the runs to register the first three-figure partnership by a Lancashire opening pair. At Sheffield, Yorkshire batted consistently to win by an innings though Emmett, often such a big figure in these matches, was for once ineffective.

Barlow topped the batting averages with 388 runs in 13 innings (three times not out) and Hornby was close up second. McIntyre took most wickets (59) though beaten in the averages by Patterson and Watson.

1876: CHAMPIONSHIP MATCHES:
Played 10, Won 5, Drawn 0, Lost 5

This was McIntyre's season. Playing in all ten matches he

took 89 wickets for 11 runs each and he was so well backed up by Watson and Appleby that had the batting been stronger a really bold challenge might have been made for the championship.

Great names decorated the score sheets of the matches with Notts[1] when fixtures were resumed after an interval of some years. Daft, Shrewsbury, Barnes, Oscroft, Shaw, Morley were on the one side, and a new name on the other: D. Q. Steel, first of the famous brotherhood to appear, making his mark at once with an innings of 82 in the Old Trafford match which Notts gallantly won by one wicket after being outplayed for two days. At Trent Bridge Barlow carried his bat through the first innings and Lancashire won by six wickets.

A double win over Derbyshire was more than offset by Yorkshire's two victories, the first by nine wickets and the second at Sheffield by 18 runs. Two exciting games against Sussex ended with Lancashire beaten by three wickets on their own ground (D. Q. Steel bagged a pair) but victorious by 12 runs at Brighton.

1877: CHAMPIONSHIP MATCHES:
Played 10, Won 6, Drawn 0, Lost 4

A remarkable performance by W. S. Patterson was a feature of this season. He played in only two matches yet took 24 wickets for 232 runs—though when he captured 14 Notts wickets (in addition to making top score of 24 in the second innings) he was on the losing side. He had better fortune in his second game when with ten Yorkshire wickets for 130 runs he helped Lancashire complete the double over their neighbours. The first match at Huddersfield had already been won by nine wickets, thanks to the bowling of Watson and the all-round work of Appleby whose six cheap wickets were backed up by an innings of 69 not out.

It was no uncommon thing about this time for sides to be much more strongly represented at home than they were in away fixtures; Lancashire, for instance, sent a weak side to Derby and were beaten, and Notts met with a similar experience at Old Trafford, an eleven weakened by a strike failing against McIntyre and Watson. There was mixed fortune

---

[1] Where county names have been abbreviated, it has been done to make for easier reading and not with any wish to cheapen names proudly borne.

against the southern sides. Kent won both games but Sussex were beaten twice, the match at Brighton producing an exceptional bowling performance by Appleby who, in the follow-on, took nine wickets for 25 runs.

Outside the county games, the M.C.C. fixture was lost, and if the results were disappointing for a team possessing so much bowling talent there was one matter for congratulation. At long last a professional of the highest class was secured to follow the various players who had kept wicket. In preceding seasons this duty had been undertaken by Holgate, Perry, E. Jackson, E. J. Bousfield, J. R. Hillkirk, E. Moorhouse, R. Roberts, F. W. Wright, and occasionally A. N. Hornby and E. B. Rowley. Now in August of this year there arrived on the scene Richard Pilling, soon to be hailed as the only rival to Blackham.

1878: CHAMPIONSHIP MATCHES:
Played 10, *Won* 5, *Drawn* 2, *Lost* 3

Looking over Lancashire's rich and varied history, one finds certain seasons that stand out as critical, and this summer of 1878 was one of them. It witnessed the full development of A. G. Steel (who had played in the previous year and scored 87 against Sussex) as a great Cambridge University and Lancashire cricketer. It saw Gloucestershire appear at Old Trafford. It saw the first match ever played on the ground by an Australian team. It saw, too, the first overs of Crossland's long and controversial career. One ought to mention also the début of O. P. Lancashire, perhaps never more than a useful player but a splendid judge of the game who became a wise administrator.

Gloucestershire meant the Graces, and the visit of the Champion and his two brothers sent Manchester's interest in cricket soaring to new levels. More than £750 was taken at the gates, and on the third day, when the crowd was estimated at 16,000, hurriedly improvised extra turnstiles could not cope with the crush, so that 2,000 gained admission by climbing the fences. Once in, they encroached on the playing area and the game was repeatedly held up.

The quality of the cricket matched the occasion, most of the big men coming off with Hornby out on his own with a splendid second-innings century, and Barlow helping in a first-wicket stand of 108. A. G. Steel took nine wickets and he

Old Trafford in 1861

Mark Philips, president for forty years—
from 1833 to 1873.

A. B. Rowley, president 1874–9 and one
of the founders of the club.

In 1882 there was no better fast bowler in England than Johnny Crossland (*top left*) but his action was often in question. Arthur Mold (*top right*) who first played for Northamptonshire, also suffered in the 'throwing' controversy. The Rev. Vernon Royle (*below left*) was known as 'the policeman at cover-point', and another fine amateur of the '80s was Arthur Appleby (*below right*), a left-arm bowler of great accuracy.

might have won the match had not 'W. G.' stood fast in the crisis. When the match was left drawn, Gloucester were 111 short of victory with five wickets in hand, and the great crowd's pleasure was crowned by an innings of 58 not out from the greatest batsman of all.

The following home match was against the Australians and two stands, specially put up, were filled in spite of bad weather. Once again, more than £700 was taken, and if the crowds could not enthuse about cricket of the same quality as before, they saw Charles Bannerman in two characteristic bits of hitting and Arthur Bannerman run out by one of Vernon Royle's most dazzling pieces of fielding.

A new factor was the increase in value of Barlow in the attack. He met with particular success against Kent and Yorkshire, and with Steel often available, the gradual falling off in Appleby's powers was made good.

1879: CHAMPIONSHIP MATCHES:
Played 10, Won 5, Drawn 4, Lost 1

The team-building of preceding years now brought its first rewards, Lancashire sharing the championship with Notts as each side suffered one defeat in inter-county matches. The pair met in the opening fixture of the season at Trent Bridge where Lancashire had rather the worst of a drawn match but they must have been pleased with the form of their recruits, because Nash took five wickets and Briggs made top score with 36. Later in the season the weather disappointingly denied either side a chance of proving supremacy.

The single defeat which cost Lancashire the title was inflicted by Yorkshire at Sheffield where destructive bowling by Ulyett was followed by W. Bates's century—the first in one of these Roses battles. The five victories were scored in successive fixtures against Derbyshire (twice), Kent, Yorkshire, and Gloucestershire. The side afterwards fell away, perhaps missing the variety that was given to its bowling whenever A. G. Steel played, for the brilliant young amateur appeared only four times.

The home game against Kent was remarkable for the luck of Hornby, dropped seven times while scoring 61. When Gloucester came north, there was a big crowd to welcome them, but they saw nothing like the stern fight of the previous

c

summer, for after Lancashire had made 184, the visiting side were put out twice in four hours by Steel and McIntyre. For those who believe that modern cricket is slower than it ought to be, it may be remarked that in this match 277 four-ball overs yielded only 319 runs.

Barlow continued to figure regularly in the attack, McIntyre had another grand season, and they, with Steel, Watson, Crossland, Nash and Appleby, made up a formidable company, even if they could not all be accommodated in one eleven. Briggs occasionally gained a place because of his fielding ability and perhaps because of a vague feeling that he looked like a cricketer, but as a bowler he was still very much a rod in pickle.

CHAPTER 4

Championship Matches

1880–91 Captain: A. N. Hornby

A falling-off in form; A record season wins the championship,
1881; A great Cambridge University side; Another tie for the
championship, 1882; A demonstration against Crossland;
A record partnership by Robinson and F. Taylor; A
quarrel with Notts and Kent; The end of Crossland's
career; Briggs becomes a great bowler; G. M. Kemp
hits the first century against Yorkshire; A record
for the tenth wicket; A one-day victory at
Lord's, 1886; Fog in mid-June; Frank Sugg's
success; Lancashire beaten in one day, 1888;
Albert Ward and Arthur Mold arrive;
A. C. MacLaren's brilliant début

EARLY IN 1880 Edmund Rowley resigned the captaincy of
Lancashire; on the 29th of May A. N. Hornby was formally invited to take over the leadership. The enthusiasm of the Rowley
family and their friends had carried Lancashire so far; the time
had come for another step forward, and it was taken under the
guidance of one of the most remarkable men who has adorned
the cricketing scene. In another chapter an effort is made to do
justice to Hornby's many-sided genius: sufficient to say here
that he lacked nothing of the enthusiasm of his predecessor
while he added to it a will-to-win and an understanding of the
professionals under him that together represented captaincy
at its highest expression.

Hornby's period of captaincy has sometimes been stated to
have extended to 1899, but this is not correct. Illness and
absence from England broke into this long term. In 1892 and
1893 he appeared in only four of the first-class county matches
and the leadership generally fell on S. M. Crosfield, though in
Wisden's the captaincy is allocated between the two. In 1894

Crosfield was actually elected, but could not play in more than an occasional match, and A. C. MacLaren took over. In 1896 Ernest Rowley was in charge for half a season, with MacLaren playing in only ten of the twenty-two championship fixtures, and these three held the side until Hornby re-appeared to lead the eleven to its championship success in 1897. In the following season neither Hornby nor MacLaren played very often, though the former remained the official captain. In 1899 G. R. Bardswell was to have been captain, but as events turned out MacLaren, Hornby, and Alexander Eccles had to take turns in Bardswell's absence.

It is not, therefore, possible to sustain the claim so often made that Hornby's captaincy extended over nineteen seasons, though whether captain, president or merely onlooker, his influence was emphatic for an even longer span. To maintain the design of this book, his captaincy is taken to run from 1880–91. Taking the following eight seasons in a comprehensive survey, one may fairly say that Lancashire lacked a regular captain; even when 'the Boss' came back in 1897 he was then fifty years of age and able to appear in only fifteen of the twenty-six fixtures.

1880 : CHAMPIONSHIP MATCHES :
Played 12, Won 6, Drawn 3, Lost 3

The new captain did not allow the cares of leadership to affect his batting for he topped the averages and maintained his reputation as the only man to make a century. The team as a whole were not so successful as in 1879, and the reason is plainly written in the averages: a falling off in the bowling that had for so long sustained the side. McIntyre's decline was quite unexpected (he was only thirty-six) but it was so pronounced that after the first three games he was dropped, following eight successive seasons in which his name had never been missing from the eleven. Crossland had not yet fully developed and though Nash performed splendidly in his first full season and Watson took more wickets (79) than ever before, the loss of the consistent McIntyre was much felt.

The outstanding performance of the season was in August at the Oval. They had already beaten Surrey at Old Trafford but when in the return they followed on 110 runs behind, a second victory seemed quite out of the question. A typically dashing century by Hornby led the recovery and when Surrey went in again faced with the task of scoring 202, the bowling of Barlow, Nash, and Appleby was too good for them and Lancashire won by 60 runs.

A double defeat by Notts blotted the record though the second match at Trent Bridge produced a fine struggle and a stout effort by the bowlers to rescue the game. Lancashire made 72 and Notts 66 on a pitch described as 'heavy', and then Shaw and Morley bowled so well that Lancashire, all out 46, could set their rivals only 53 to win. Oscroft, Shrewsbury, and Scotton failed, but William Gunn and Barnes stopped the rot and the champions scrambled home with four wickets to spare.

When *Wisden's* summed up the season there was praise for Nash and the new batsman from Yorkshire, W. Robinson. Point was also made of the splendid fielding and the excellent wicket-keeping of Pilling.

1881 : CHAMPIONSHIP MATCHES :
Played 13, Won 10, Drawn 3, Lost 0

This was a season of triumph. Unbeaten in thirteen county games, Lancashire were undisputed champions by what *Wisden's* called 'A series of brilliant successes almost unparalleled in the history of County Cricket'. Six of their victories were obtained with an innings to spare and they were thoroughly in command in the three drawn games.

The batting was very strong with Hornby at the top with 50 runs an innings, three centuries, and the highest individual score of the season—188 against Derbyshire. He had a fair claim to be the batsman of the year, surpassing the performances of even W. G. Grace and W. W. Read. To support the captain's dashing onslaughts there were A. G. Steel, Barlow, Watson, Robinson, and Briggs.

In accordance with Lancashire tradition it was the bowling which really carried them through. Barlow jumped right to the front rank with 62 wickets for nine runs apiece and Nash, Steel, and Watson between them took 162 wickets at an average cost of about 11 runs. Crossland took only 13 wickets but ten of them were in a whirlwind match-winning display at the Oval.

The campaign began on a high note. At the end of the first day's play at Old Trafford, Derbyshire were all out 102 and Lancashire's score read :

A. N. Hornby not out	118
Barlow c Jackson b Mycroft	35
Extras	4
Total (for one wicket)	157

It was the great pair's biggest partnership to date; next day Hornby went on to score 188 and Watson and Nash did the rest.

Notts and Kent were beaten in turn and then came a wonderful match which must be described here though it was outside the championship. The Liverpool club could not have secured anything better for the opening of their new ground at Aigburth, for these were the halcyon days of University cricket, and the Cambridge eleven of 1881 was only a little less formidable than the great team of three years earlier, generally accounted best of all. Numbers 1, 2, and 3 were G. B., J. E. K., and C. T. Studd; among the later batsmen were three Lancashire men in A. G. Steel, O. P. Lancashire, and J. R. Napier. On a difficult wicket Cambridge scored 187, G. B. Studd carrying his bat for 106, and then Steel got to work. He took 11 wickets with bowling that was described as 'simply marvellous' and the University won with a day to spare.

Resuming their championship programme, Lancashire beat Surrey at Old Trafford, swamped Derbyshire at Derby where Barlow took six wickets for three runs, and then journeyed to Sheffield where they beat Yorkshire thanks to the bowling of an amateur, H. Miller, and a thunderstorm that spoiled the wicket on the last day. They returned to Old Trafford for McIntyre's benefit match featured by superb bowling from Watson and Steel, who put Gloucester out for 42 on a good pitch. Steel bowled 'W. G.' twice in the match, and he maintained his form by taking 13 wickets and making the winning hit in the return match with Yorkshire.

There were two drawn matches against Notts and Surrey and the winning touch returned at the Oval in a match which produced sensational cricket on the first day. Lancashire were dismissed for 78 in less than an hour and a half, an amateur named Parfitt taking seven wickets for 33 runs. This was immediately surpassed by Crossland with seven wickets for 14 runs and Surrey were all out in an hour for 36. Lancashire made no mistake in the later stages of the game; Hornby,

Robinson, and Barlow made the runs, and Watson and Crossland finished off the game with cold efficiency.

Bad weather stood in the way at Clifton where Gloucestershire were in a hopeless plight when the game was given up but not even the weather could prevent Lancashire from ending their season with a flourish worthy of champions. Almost the whole of the first day was wasted at Maidstone, then once they got on with the game Watson, Nash, and Barlow overwhelmed Kent by putting them out for 38 and 61, Nash having a match record of 12 wickets for 47 runs. Hornby scored only two runs but they were sufficient to give him a total of 1,001 runs in all Lancashire matches, the first four-figure aggregate for the county. Steel's record was 353 runs and 41 wickets in five matches, and no account of the season would be complete or just without reference to Pilling who stumped 16 and caught 30 in fifteen games.

Attempts have been made from time to time to compare this team with succeeding Lancashire elevens. As Crossland had not yet come to the peak of his powers the bowling appears to have lacked something in the way of pace though Barlow and Nash (left-hand), Steel (leg-break) and Watson (off-break) were so effectively consistent that it was remarked at the time that it did not seem to matter who went on first. The middle batting was too often changed to bear comparison with Lancashire's other championship sides, but in one respect at least the team stands second to none. With Hornby in charge, the fielding could hardly be other than good, and with Pilling behind the stumps, Briggs, Royle, and Barlow on the offside, Robinson in the deep, Watson at slip, and the captain enthusiastically skilful no matter where he chose to put himself, this team has claim to rank as one of the strongest fielding combinations of all time.

1882: CHAMPIONSHIP MATCHES:
Played 16, Won 12, Drawn 3, Lost 1

The programme was expanded this year so that all told twenty matches were played. Somerset came briefly into the select company of first-class counties, an extra fixture was arranged with Cambridge University, and the Australians were here again. It was a matter of argument at the time whether Lancashire or Notts were champions, and the decision now generally accepted is that they tied.

The feature of the season was the big advance by Crossland, who became not only the best fast bowler in England but the most controversial. Appearing in all twenty fixtures he bowled in all but one of them, taking 97 wickets for ten runs each, and his record would have been even better had there not been so many other bowlers capable of doing the work. Unfortunately, as we shall see, its triumph was qualified by criticism of his action and it may be as well to say at once that on the evidence that has come down to us it is impossible to disagree with the opinion that his action was probably the most questionable that has gone unchecked for any considerable period in first-class cricket.

The season opened badly enough with defeats by M.C.C. and Cambridge University, but the home game against Derbyshire gave the bowlers a chance to get into form and though a great match with the Australians was narrowly lost, the team soon began to deal effectively with less powerful opposition. Out for 29 and 51, Somerset yielded Nash a match record of 12 for 38 runs and Crossland, who could not get on in the first innings, took six wickets for seven runs. It has been stated that Nash took four wickets in one four-ball over, though the match reports of the time do not bear out the claim.

Barlow and Watson next put out Cambridge University (fresh from a magnificent victory over the Australians) for 31, Kent for 71 and 139, Derbyshire for 77 and 55, and then the team came to the critical match against Notts at Trent Bridge. Reinforced by A. G. Steel, the bowlers fulfilled their parts splendidly but their own batting was helpless against Shaw and Flowers, and Notts won by 37 runs.

After a draw with Surrey and a win at Lord's (where Hornby made 131 in his most dazzling style) came the return with Notts at Liverpool and a wonderful finish. Notts went in for half an hour with 118 wanted to win and apparently only a draw in prospect, but four wickets went down for next to nothing against the eager bowling of Steel and Watson, and it took all the patience of Shrewsbury to check the collapse.

Barlow played one of his monumental innings against Gloucester, staying till the total was 71 but scoring only 9 himself, and then in the following fixture against Yorkshire he showed he could play the other game with a fine, free innings of 68. Lancashire got home by 16 runs in this match, with a

couple of run-outs to add to the thrills of the close finish. The
next game at Clifton was even closer fought; all the great batsmen came off—Hornby, Barlow, and W. G. and E. M. Grace—
and Barlow specially distinguished himself by carrying his bat
for 58 in a total of 240, seeing all his team-mates out for the fourth
time in one season. A brilliant century by E. M. Grace almost
got Gloucester home but in the end Lancashire won by 13 runs.

The southern tour proceeded splendidly with victories over
Somerset at Taunton and Kent at Maidstone where Robinson
scored a fine century. Then came a dramatic match at the
Oval. As soon as Crossland went on the big crowd began a
hostile demonstration, but the fast bowler did not allow it to
affect his form because he opened with a spell of five wickets
for one run and had a match return of 11 for 79. At the end
of the first innings he had difficulty in making his way to the
pavilion between those spectators who variously offered con-
gratulations and abuse. The match was easily won and the team
returned to Old Trafford to beat Middlesex, so that they ended
the season with a string of seven victories. The effort was unavailing, however, because Notts, beaten at Sheffield in June,
stubbornly refused to lose again though hard pressed on at least
one occasion.

1883: CHAMPIONSHIP MATCHES:
Played 12, Won 6, Drawn 1, Lost 5

Everyone connected with the county must have been disappointed with the results of 1883. The history of cricket shows
few more remarkable upsets of form than provided by the team
this season for whereas they began with a string of victories,
the second half of the summer brought little but failure.

Derbyshire (twice), Kent, Notts, M.C.C., Oxford University
(twice), were all beaten at the start and among these victories
nothing was better than the recovery in the home game against
Kent. Following on 103 behind, Lancashire pulled the game
round with a typical display by Hornby who, unabashed by the
state of the game, added a brilliant 96 to his first-innings 88.
On the third day Kent collapsed on a worn wicket and were
beaten by 70 runs.

The second match against Oxford University (newcomers to
the fixture list) was featured by a partnership for the fourth
wicket between Robinson (154) and F. Taylor (96) who made

237 together, the professional receiving a collection of over £20 for his part in the stand. This was so far the highest partnership hit for any wicket for Lancashire and it was not beaten until twelve years later, A. C. MacLaren and Paul making 363 together when the former hit up his record 424 at Taunton. Taylor was a Rochdale man who had played for Clifton College and Gloucestershire. After leaving school he returned to Lancashire, playing intermittently from 1874 to 1888. He was a tall, hard-hitting batsman who fielded brilliantly in the slips.

Barlow and Watson went unchanged through the game at Derby and by the end of June it looked as though Lancashire would be champions again but defeat by Yorkshire at Old Trafford represented a turning-point in the team's fortunes. True, Surrey were beaten, thanks to all-round work by Barlow and splendid hitting by Briggs, but Yorkshire won again at Sheffield where 19,000 people applauded magnificent cricket by Ulyett who did the hat-trick and hit 61 in dashing style.

There was another demonstration against Crossland at the Oval and this time the scenes were so angry that there was a very real chance that the match would be abandoned because at the end of Surrey's first innings there was wrangling in the pavilion for half an hour before play could be resumed.

A glance at the averages shows the causes of the season's failures. The batting was generally only fair, the bowling was weakened by the inability of Steel to play in more than three fixtures, and Crossland was often freely hit though he had days of great effectiveness.

1884: CHAMPIONSHIP MATCHES:
Played 12, Won 7, Lost 4, Abandoned 1

In the winter of 1883–4 the question of Crossland's action brought a rift with Notts. A Christmas Card of more force than tact went from the Lancashire team to Trent Bridge and in reply came a New Year's greeting:

LANCASHIRE COUNTY CRICKET

The only rules necessary for players in the County Eleven are that they shall neither have been born in, nor resident, in Lancashire. Sutton-in-Ashfield men will have the preference.

There were two grounds for criticism. The first concerned

throwing, and it was not confined to the case of Crossland. Nash and Watson, though slow bowlers, were both suspect, and the Australians of 1882 had joined in the general condemnation. There was also some feeling against Lancashire's policy of seeking their players from beyond the county boundaries, and it was pointed out by critics in 1881, when they won the championship, that of the chief professionals only Barlow had a birth qualification.

Notts brought matters to a head by breaking off fixtures. They wrote:

Nottinghamshire declines to play Lancashire this season for the following reasons, that Lancashire have, during the last season, played in their eleven at least two men as to the fairness of whose bowling there is grave doubts.

Lord Harris was another opponent in this matter, and when the county chose the England team[1] to meet Australia at Old Trafford, the famous Kent captain took objection to Crossland's inclusion. The club wrote to Lord Harris and told him they had resolved to include their own fast bowler: 'Therefore we suppose under the circumstances the English team will lose your valuable assistance, which we regret very much.' As things turned out, Crossland was left out of the originally selected twelve and so he never gained Test match recognition.

Lancashire took their stand on the side of the fast bowler because umpires refrained from taking action against him and for a little while longer he remained an effective member of the team. This season he took 72 wickets for 13 runs each and with Watson and Barlow both taking over 100 wickets the attack was formidable even if Steel could only play occasionally. Briggs and Barlow each hit their first centuries for the county but Robinson lost his form and the batting generally lacked solidity.

With the expanding fixture list individual performances must now receive rather more brief notice and a broader survey undertaken. In addition to the championship programme there were fixtures with M.C.C., Oxford University, the Australians, and Leicestershire and Cheshire.

Beaten by Yorkshire at Old Trafford despite two fine innings

---

[1] England teams in those days were picked by the authority on whose ground the match was to be played.

by E. E. Steel (youngest of the brotherhood), Lancashire gained revenge at Sheffield where Barlow took 13 wickets and was responsible for a sensational collapse in Yorkshire's second innings when the first five wickets went down for 15 runs. The four Steels were seen together just once, when Surrey won an exciting match at Liverpool by 29 runs. An even closer verdict was the seven-runs defeat by Gloucester, sustained despite a grand innings by Vernon Royle.

Some dashing batting by H. B. Steel marked the games at the Oval and Maidstone. A useful change-bowler and quite adept at keeping wicket, he preferred club cricket or he might have made a bigger name for himself. It is said that few batsmen obtained such a high proportion of their runs by boundary hits.

The home match against Gloucester, generally included in the records as 'drawn' was in fact given up on the second day owing to the death of the mother of W. G. and E. M. Grace.

1885: CHAMPIONSHIP MATCHES:
Played 11, Won 6, Drawn 2, Lost 3

Lord Harris now revived the bowling controversy. Immediately after Kent had been beaten at Old Trafford he addressed a long letter to Lancashire.[1] He recalled that Lancashire, along with Sussex and Gloucester, had declined to fall in with the other counties when, in December 1883, they had agreed not to employ bowlers whose action was at all doubtful, and he then went on to refer to Nash and Crossland by name. He declared that though umpires had not no-balled them, they threw—in his opinion—and that he would ask Kent to allow the return fixture at Tonbridge to go by default. He added:

> 'I told your representatives before the match began, and I was but repeating what I have frequently said, that if there was one county in England against which I should have a disinclination to move, that county would be Lancashire. It is fourteen years since I first played on Old Trafford for Kent v Lancashire, and I think this makes the eleventh consecutive year that I have come up as captain of the Kent eleven.
> 'During all that time the relations between the two clubs,

[1] For the full text of the correspondence see *Wisden's* for 1886, pp. 241–4.

so far as I know, have been of the most cordial character. We always rejoiced when Lancashire was champion county. Kentish and Lancashire professionals have always been on the most friendly terms, the same amongst the amateurs; and if Mr. Hornby will forgive me for mentioning him last, or indeed at all, entirely divergent as are his opinions and mine, strong as they are on the question of the deliveries of these two bowlers, we have never allowed those opinions to interfere with our personal friendship, and, indeed, I believe each has no better friend on the cricket field, perhaps in a wider sphere than the other; and, lastly, I had the gratification on Thursday last of meeting with such a reception from the enormous company present at Old Trafford as I have never received on any cricket ground, in or out of England, in my life: only surpassed by the still more complimentary manifestation at my summary dismissal.'

Lancashire replied with vigour, not omitting to point out that Nash and Crossland had appeared at Lord's, had never been no-balled for throwing, and that Crossland had been selected by the M.C.C. only the previous season to play for North v South. They boldly sent a copy of the correspondence to headquarters with an implied challenge to the M.C.C. to take action.

However, the quarrel had a curious ending. Crossland's qualification had long ago been queried and now it was proved he had broken his residence in the county by going to live in Nottingham for four or five months from October 1884. The M.C.C. disqualified him and towards the end of June he played his last game against Cheshire at Stockport.

The hour produced the man. Lancashire had to go through the rest of the season and Briggs suddenly came out as a slow left-arm bowler of real quality for whereas 18 wickets had cost him 22 runs each in 1884, this year he took 79 wickets for ten runs each. From being a dashing batsman and a nimble fieldsman he became almost overnight a great all-rounder.

Two batting records were set up during the season. G. M. Kemp hit the first Lancashire century against Yorkshire, 109 at Huddersfield, and Briggs (186) and Pilling (61 not out) put on 173 together for the last wicket against Surrey at Aigburth. They took only 100 minutes over the feat, which stood as a world record until 1899, and even now it has not been beaten by any Lancashire last-wicket pair.

That the bitter feelings aroused by the Crossland affair could not be instantly relieved even by the more generous paragraphs of Lord Harris's letter was shown by the cancellation of the Tonbridge fixture, though the fast bowler had dropped out when it was due to be played.

1886: CHAMPIONSHIP MATCHES:
Played 14, Won 5, Drawn 4, Lost 5

Lancashire's bowling remained good, but the batting generally was very weak this season. Though Bennett Hudson made a remarkable début with 98 against Sussex and followed with 85 at Oxford a week later, he never repeated this form. Hudson was a Yorkshireman and a rover. He had professional engagements at Sheffield, Bacup, Batley, Grimsby, Sheffield again, and then Longsight, and he was one of the men tried by Lancashire in their search for a new fast bowler. His innings against Sussex was a furiously-hit affair which included sixteen fours and earned him the immediate award of a county cap tossed at him through the pavilion window by a grateful captain.

The event of the season was the one-day win at Lord's in the first fixture of the summer. After a blank first day, M.C.C. were bowled out for 30, Watson taking six wickets for 8 runs in fifteen overs. Lancashire's 53 was not much better and then M.C.C. scored 92. Lancashire thus wanted 70 to win and they accomplished it solely owing to the brilliant hitting of their captain. Not even in his long career was Hornby seen to much better advantage; on the treacherous pitch he hit away so well that in an hour he made 50 out of 60 and by six o'clock the match was won by six wickets.

Fixtures were happily resumed with Notts and Kent and it was the former county, champions in four successive seasons, who provided the opposition in Barlow's benefit match. It was watched by 27,000 people, of whom 11,000 on the first day were treated to the batting feat they had come to see, a century partnership by Barlow and his captain.

The home fixture with Kent deserves mention not only for the renewal of old rivalry but because (in mid-June) a dense fog held up the game on the first day! An amateur named Teggin took ten wickets for 87 runs in this match; like

Hudson he came from Longsight and it is curious that both should have achieved such immediate success and then so quickly disappeared from first-class cricket.

1887: CHAMPIONSHIP MATCHES:
Played 14, Won 10, Drawn 1, Lost 3

For the first time the championship was decided on a points basis, one point awarded for a win and half a point for a draw, unfinished matches now coming into the reckoning. From this year onwards it is possible to pin-point Lancashire's position in the table at the end of each season though, as every student of the game knows, changes have been made from time to time in the system of reckoning.

Lancashire finished second to Surrey in 1887, and the chief cause of the improvement was the stronger batting. It had been apparent for some years that the committee, after successfully inducing a number of great bowlers to play for the county, would have to turn their attention to the batsmen, and now they brought Frank Sugg, formerly of Yorkshire and Derbyshire, into the eleven. Not only was he immediately successful with 403 runs in seven matches, but he began a line of great professional batsmen unbroken to this day and his arrival at Old Trafford is therefore an important point in this history.

Power was also added to the batting by the improved form of Joseph Eccles who for three or four seasons scored consistently. There was still the need for a bowler of pace to support the efforts of Watson, Briggs and Barlow, though these rare stalwarts went on as though they could last for ever, even in a batsmen's summer—said to be the finest since 1869. Watson was specially effective early in the season and he vied with Attewell and Lohmann for the title of the best bowler in the country. The team had a brilliant spell in mid-season when in succession they beat Surrey, Gloucester, Notts, and Sussex. They were beaten on their own ground by Surrey (for whom Walter Read made 247) and at Nottingham, where J. A. Dixon did the hat-trick.

Lancashire came to the last fixture of the season with an outside chance of the title: they had to beat Yorkshire, and Surrey had to lose both of their remaining matches. Neither event matured and Lancashire in fact were easily beaten by their neighbours. Earlier in the season Yorkshire had scored 590 in a drawn match at Bradford and now they made 414 at Old Trafford, winning by an innings.

During a friendly match this season, Lancashire met their future team-mate Arthur Mold of Northampton and another incident worth recalling is the accident that befell A. C. M. Croome of Gloucester who, in attempting a catch, fell on the spiked railings at Old Trafford and hurt himself so badly that for some time his life was in danger.

1888: CHAMPIONSHIP MATCHES:
Played 14, Won 4, Drawn 5, Lost 5

Lancashire fell to fifth place this season, in spite of a personal triumph by Briggs. Robinson lost his form again, Watson fell off a little, some of the amateurs could not turn out regularly, and Sugg's rather rash methods often failed him. Amid the disappointments Briggs won great fame with 160 wickets and first place in the bowling averages to supplement his 800-odd runs.

One name comes into the list of Lancashire cricketers and then drops out never to recur: John Russell Napier, a Cambridge University fast bowler, who missed his Blue through injury. This season he turned out twice for Lancashire, first helping in a magnificent victory over the Australians and then taking four Yorkshire wickets at Sheffeld without conceding a run.

The fixtures with Surrey produced memorable cricket. At Old Trafford the visitors won the first championship match ever finished in a single day, putting Lancashire out for 35 and 63. In the return a fortnight later, the prospective champions were beaten at the Oval where J. Eccles hit brilliantly to score 184, making the most of seven or eight dropped catches.

Another eventful match was against Derbyshire who were put out for 17, still the lowest total ever made by a first-class team against Lancashire. Briggs had a match record of 13 wickets for 39 runs, and he had another splendid match against Sussex, taking nine wickets in an innings and then saving his side with a brilliant century. He had 13 wickets against Middlesex, 12 against Gloucester, and right at the end of the season 13 against the Australians at Scarborough. When *Wisden's* decided to inaugurate what was to become their famous series of portraits, they chose 'Six Great Bowlers', and Briggs was

Above: Lancashire, county champions (with Nottinghamshire) 1879. *Left to right*:
Standing to left: Rowbotham, J. Nash, R. Pilling. *Standing to right*: James Mac-
Laren, A. Watson, R. G. Barlow. *Back row*: J. Crossland, C. Haigh, A. N. Hornby
(capt.), F. Taylor. *Front row*: W. Robinson, V. K. Royle, J. Briggs.

Below: Lancashire, county champions 1881. *Left to right*: *Seated*: A. G. Steel,
Rev. V. K. Royle, A. N. Hornby (capt.), A. Appleby. *Back row*: G. Nash,
J. Crossland, Smith (umpire), R. Pilling, A. Watson. *Front row*: W. Robinson,
R. G. Barlow, O. P. Lancashire, J. Briggs.

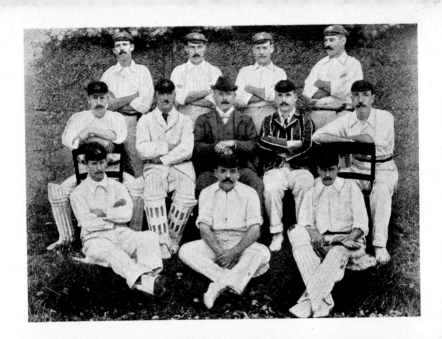

Above: Lancashire, county champions 1897. *Left to right*: *Standing*: A. W. Hallam, J. I'Anson, W. R. Cuttell, A. Mold. *Seated*: G. R. Baker, A. C. MacLaren, A. N. Hornby (capt.), S. M. Tindall, A. Ward. *Front row*: J. T. Tyldesley, J. Briggs, L. Radcliffe.

Below: Lancashire, county champions 1904. *Left to right*: *Standing*: J. Sharp, W. R. Cuttell, W. Worsley, W. Findlay, A. Kermode, L. O. S. Poidevin, Hallows, W. Brearley, J. S. Heap. *Seated*: J. T. Tyldesley, A. H. Hornby, A. C. MacLaren (capt.), R. H. Spooner, H. G. Garnett.

honoured along with Lohmann, Peel, S. M. J. Woods, Ferris, and Turner.

1889: CHAMPIONSHIP MATCHES:
Played 14, Won 10, Drawn 1, Lost 3

This season marked a turning-point in Lancashire's fortunes. Further team building brought in Albert Ward and Arthur Mold, the former bringing to the batting a solidity it had not hitherto known, and Mold making his mark at once as the most dangerous fast bowler in the country. The veteran Watson took on a new lease of life, and at the end of the season the county had three bowlers among the first four in the national averages:

	*Overs	Maidens	Runs	Wickets	Average
Attewell	1314.2	654	1555	140	11.10
Briggs	1040.3	447	1646	140	11.75
Mold	679.0	262	1207	102	11.83
Watson	850.3	438	1139	90	12.65

*The over was amended to five balls this year.

Albert Ward's arrival was little short of sensational because previously his few appearances for Yorkshire had brought him no fame. An aggregate of 822 and an average of 30 for this season does not look much judged by modern standards, but his style was so impressive that when *Wisden's* continued their sequence of portraits with 'Nine Great Batsmen of the Year', Ward was among them. Arthur Paul appeared with modest success, too, and now that they had a more settled eleven Lancashire were undoubtedly a fine match-winning combination. They shared in a triple tie for the championship with Surrey and Notts and though the others could possibly point to certain elements of good and bad luck, Lancashire certainly suffered sharply from an injury that limited Barlow's bowling so that he took only six wickets in county games.

A double win over Yorkshire, described elsewhere, was of course welcome, and there were victories over Sussex, Surrey and Kent in a triumphant southern tour but they could not quite make up the ground lost through defeats at the hands of Middlesex, Notts and Gloucester.

Middlesex won at Old Trafford because of Nepean's leg-breaks, and Notts were clearly the masters at Trent Bridge.

D

Lancashire had only themselves to blame for a three-wickets defeat by Gloucester at Liverpool because after a grip had been obtained on the game, three men were run out in the second innings. When Notts played the return the weather ruined the gate and the game, even though an effort was made to finish it by rolling a new wicket at right angles to the normal line.

The free hitting of Briggs and Sugg often succeeded in a wet summer but the opposite method sometimes paid, as Barlow showed at Maidstone when he carried his bat for 51 in an innings of 215. His feat was equalled by W. G. Grace at Bristol, the Champion making 37 not out in a vain effort to stem the Lancashire bowling. Towards the end of the season Leicestershire (not yet a first-class county) were beaten in one day, Briggs taking 15 wickets for 35 runs.

Following complaints about the pitch at Old Trafford, which had shown a tendency to 'go' on the second day, Walker of Nottingham was called in during the winter to give advice to Reynolds.

1890 : CHAMPIONSHIP MATCHES :
Played 14, Won 7, Drawn 4, Lost 3

This was a season of mixed fortunes for Lancashire, second to Surrey in the table. Under a new system of subtracting defeats from wins and ignoring drawn games Surrey won the title in clear-cut fashion and they emphasised their ability by twice beating Lancashire.

The first misfortune at Old Trafford was the loss of Pilling, who, after a severe illness, was sent to Australia in a vain hope of recuperation. Not only was his wicket-keeping missed, but it is significant that for the first time for many years there was reason to criticise the fielding of the side and it may reasonably be guessed that this followed from the loss of Pilling's brilliant example. As Briggs missed a month's cricket and Barlow's bowling did not return, the final record could really be considered quite satisfactory.

A. T. Kemble and Whiteside shared the wicket-keeping and another player to come to the front was Frank Ward who, after a few modest innings in 1889, now blossomed out with a brilliant 145 against Kent.

Yet all this was as nothing compared with the début of Archie MacLaren. Fresh from his feats for Harrow, he stepped into the Lancashire team at Brighton, and when Barlow, Sugg and Albert Ward had made only 23 between them, he hit a chanceless 108 in 130 minutes. The event heralded the arrival of something new in Lancashire cricket, a batsman neither in the utilitarian line of the professionals nor a hitter of Hornby's stamp, but a cricketer of irreproachable style and vivid imagination.

It was a great season for Briggs in spite of his injury for besides taking 86 wickets for the county, and 158 in all matches, he topped the Lancashire batting averages. Frank Sugg, erratic as ever, was seen at his best when he made 177 in three hours against Oxford University.

The home defeat by Surrey came in about seven hours' cricket. Watson and Briggs did wonders, but so did Lohmann, who had 13 wickets for 54 runs, and Lancashire were beaten by 61. In the return the champions were aided by the rain that left the batsmen at the mercy of Lohmann again. An outstanding all-round performance by Briggs was against Sussex when first he made 129 not out at a run a minute, and enabled Lancashire to declare at 246—2, and then with Watson bowled unchanged to dismiss the others for 35 and 24. The bowling analysis was:

	1st innings				2nd innings			
	O	M	R	W	O	M	R	W
Watson	27	21	7	5	19.4	16	6	4
Briggs	27	18	25	5	19	11	16	5

Mold had two great performances against Yorkshire and it was he who dramatically finished off Notts, so often stern antagonists, with a whirlwind performance just when stubborn batting seemed likely to save the game.

1891 : CHAMPIONSHIP MATCHES :
Played 16, Won 8, Drawn 3, Lost 4, Abandoned 1

Lancashire were runners-up again to Surrey, by whom they were beaten in the first important fixtures. They put one of their strongest sides into the field including MacLaren and A. G. Steel, but they lost the toss and with it the match. Worse still, Briggs was taken ill and Watson broke down with a strain; the former recovered and came back to bowl well but Watson was never himself and took only 29 wickets this summer. By the end of June the team had won only one of their six county fixtures; then they set about recovering the lost ground with such spirit that of the remaining ten games, seven ended in victory.

Besides Surrey, Middlesex (twice) and Notts beat Hornby's men. A great innings by A. E. Stoddart, whose 215 not out was scored against magnificent fast bowling by Mold, featured the Middlesex win at Old Trafford and he was again the most successful batsman at Lord's in a low-scoring match dominated by the bowling of Mold, Briggs, J. T. Hearne (who took four wickets in six balls) and Phillips. This was Hearne's first season and Lancashire had reason to remember his name because in the two fixtures he captured 21 wickets for 130 runs.

Mold scored a double triumph against Somerset with 15 wickets at Taunton and 11 in the return, at a total cost of 240 runs. He took 20 wickets (home and away) against both Gloucester and Sussex.

MacLaren played in only five games and did not score a century but he topped the averages with Albert Ward next, and there were one or two useful performances by a new professional, Albert Smith of Oldham. George Baker had his good days and so did S. M. Crosfield but Frank Ward played only once, while for Barlow the season brought nothing but failure and his career closed, as it began, in a match against Yorkshire.

CHAPTER 5

The First Great Players

*The Rowleys; Arthur Appleby; McIntyre, Watson,
and Nash; A Crossland story; The Steels; The
'Prince of Wicket-keepers'; Vernon
Royle, the policeman at cover-
point*

IF THE END of A. N. Hornby's first long period of captaincy
and the retirement of Barlow represented the end of a chapter,
it was a chapter with many bright pages, and Lancashire could
look back on twenty-seven years of splendid achievement. We,
too, can pause here, making a break in the season-by-season
narrative, to look at the records and personalities of the men
who had been responsible for placing the county among the
most powerful in the championship. We cannot do better than
take them in a broad chronological survey, and the Rowley
family, already mentioned in connection with the foundation
of the club, calls for further mention.

Alexander Rowley, one of the first great cricketers turned out
by Rossall School, a tall man and a free hitter as well as being
a clever left-arm slow bowler, assisted the club in the early days;
he had already played four times for the Gentlemen before the
county club was formed. Not only was he prominent with his
brothers in establishing the club, but from 1874 to 1879 he
served as its president.

Edmund, the first captain, was not formally elected to the
office until 1870, but there are good grounds for believing that
he frequently took charge of the eleven before then. Reynolds
certainly tossed for choice of innings in at least one match (at
Trent Bridge in 1868) and there is a note in *Bell's Life* in the
summer of 1869 that 'Roger Iddison's services both as executant
and captain were lost through injury', but the balance of evidence is that Edmund Rowley was Lancashire's first regular

53

captain, and he was so described in an obituary notice in the *Manchester Guardian*.

A fine natural hitter, he made a great reputation for himself in 1862 when he was only twenty years of age, by scoring 61 and 70 at the Oval for the Gentlemen of the North against the Gentlemen of the South. A further reference to the part played by the Rowley family in Lancashire's affairs, and an interesting link with the present committee, will be found in Chapter 8.

Arthur Appleby, who came from Whalley, was left-handed in both branches of the game. Hornby said that no finer bowler ever existed 'for with ease and grace and natural action no one could touch him'. He was decidedly fast, relying on accuracy of pitch rather than spin or swerve, and for twelve years he was right in the forefront of amateur bowlers. In twelve appearances for Gentlemen v Players he took 59 wickets, for Lancashire 220 wickets at an average cost of 13 runs a wicket.

With McIntyre, Watson, and Nash, we arrive at the first great professionals. Qualifying by residence, they began a long line of cricketers who, though not born within the boundary, have given distinguished service and loyal devotion to their county of adoption. Lancashire have never felt called upon to defend their policy of taking professional strength wherever it might be found but if justification be needed, it can be pleaded on two grounds; the loyalty of these 'outside' professionals and in the fame these men have achieved, and which might not have come to them had their activities been more narrowly circumscribed.

William McIntyre was a Nottingham man, brother of Martin McIntyre who had a briefly brilliant career for his own county. William played for Notts in 1870 and an interesting link through two generations is that his first match at Lord's was George Parr's last. He soon transferred to Lancashire and for ten seasons he was one of the most consistent fast bowlers in the game. Right-handed, he was very accurate and it is said that he never bowled a wide. For the county, he took 456 wickets at less than 11 runs each.

George Nash was a slow left-hander who afterwards played for Buckinghamshire. His 202 wickets cost just over 11 runs apiece.

Surpassing these three was Alec Watson, a Scotsman who was spotted by the Rusholme Club while touring with a team from Lanarkshire. Then fast round-arm, he had a spell with the Manchester club, afterwards playing for almost anyone who would give him a job, appearing sometimes for the crack touring sides, sometimes against them for local eighteens or twenties. His introduction to the county team in 1871 came by a curious chance because he only gained his place as they were short of a wicket-keeper. From one cause or another he was thus twenty-seven years of age before he bowled in first-class cricket.

Playing when the fixture list was considerably narrower than it is to-day, Watson took nearly 1,300 wickets for the county at 13 runs each and taking aggregate with average this is a record that will stand comparison with the best. When he dropped fast bowling and went in for off-breaks, he became very accurate, and there were few more skilful at keeping an end going for over after over. Though Watson's action was not beyond criticism he escaped much of the abuse that was heaped on the heads of others at this time because he was, in every other respect, a model professional. Those who thought that he threw, by the way, supported their argument by pointing out how well he could maintain his length against the wind. In 1898, when he was fifty-four years of age and had been four years in retirement, Lancashire invited him to play again, but Watson, perhaps wiser than the committee, declined the offer.

The fourth great professional bowler was John Crossland of whose fast bowling and ultimate disqualification something has already been written. His pace was described as 'tremendous' and Barlow told a story of a customer walking into his shop with the request: 'Wrap me up a bottle of arnica, a paper of court plaster and an arm sling, I'm going to play in a match this afternoon against Jack Crossland.'

Crossland took 278 wickets for Lancashire at under 12 runs a wicket. He and Nash died within a few weeks of one another in 1903 and their obituary notices will be found on facing pages in *Wisden's*. Both Crossland and Watson met with punishment appropriate to their offence in being denied Test match honours. Watson would certainly have gone on tour to Australia but for the fear that his methods might cause controversy though it is only just to record that not one of these early Lancashire bowlers was ever no-balled for throwing.

Some very able cricketers were unable to spare the time to

play regularly in the championship: among these were the
Steel brothers, though from 1876 when D. Q. appeared until
1903, when E. E. played his last game, one or other was often
in the eleven with all four turning out together on one famous
occasion. There were seven brothers altogether, members of a
Liverpool family related to the Studds, and six played cricket
well. The four who played for Lancashire were Allan Gibson,
Douglas Quintin, Ernest Eden, and Harold Banner, and of
these Allan was far and away the most gifted. Few cricketers
have shown such startling skill at an early age and it is no
exaggeration to say that he was good enough to play for England while still a schoolboy. When he came to play for Lancashire he was always able to overcome the handicap of lack of
practice and he invariably produced his best form against Yorkshire. All the same, the remark attributed to Tom Emmett:
'May as well go home, lads, Mr Steel's playing and Yorkshire's beat' sounds extremely unlike any conversation most of
us have heard at one of these matches. His 14 wickets for 112
runs in 1878 showed him up at his very best; he was still fresh
and had the assistance of a superb fielding side with Pilling in
all the pride of his youthful eagerness and quickness behind
the stumps.

Steel's bowling owed its success in part to its novelty, for
leg-breakers were scarce in those days, and this may account
for some falling-off as the years went by, batsmen being less
likely to be taken by surprise. When at school he seems to
have bowled at almost medium-pace with an occasional faster
ball, but later on he became slower as indicated by this note in
Wisden's: 'The compiler of this book once heard certain high,
slow, and twisting round-arm bowling described (he thinks
erroneously described) as "As readily and easily mastered as
the *A B C Railway Guide*"; but it seems the best of England's
batsmen find it difficult to master the ever varying pace, pitch,
and curve bowling of Mr. A. G. Steel, who makes his mark
in match records, against the cleverest of bats, on all grounds.'

As a batsman, he was great in every sense of the word, master
of all the strokes, able to score very fast because he hit at everything pitched off the stumps. He often succeeded when others
were failing against the wiles of Spofforth and he never bothered
much about taking time to play himself in. To these gifts was
added a serene temperament so that all told he ranked as an

all-rounder second only to W. G. Grace himself. For Lancashire he scored 1,929 runs, average nearly 30, and took 232
wickets at less than 13 runs each but it is for his splendid natural
flair for the game rather than for the matter-of-fact figures that
A. G. Steel takes his place in cricket history.

Of the other brothers, Douglas was a batsman and so was
Harold, who could keep wicket too. Ernest had a good record
for Lancashire as an all-rounder, scoring 982 runs, average 18,
and taking 122 wickets, average 21. He gave proof of some of
A. G.'s natural ability when in 1901, after an interval of thirteen
years, he was able to reappear in the side and to make himself
thoroughly at home.

Other names have already appeared in the review of the year-
by-year play; Ricketts, George Yates, the Coward brothers,
W. S. Patterson, S. S. Schultz, Bousfield, Edward Jackson,
Frank Taylor, Walter Robinson, F. W. Wright, Edward Roper,
Reynolds, and Iddison. A curious distinction belongs to Schultz
—he was out twice first ball in one innings! A college match
was started on the Christchurch ground at Oxford when a fast
bowler created havoc on the bumpy pitch, so the players moved
off to the Parks and started again. Schultz was out first ball
at each attempt.

Edward Jackson bore the brunt of keeping to McIntyre in his
early days with the county and it was recorded of one match
that he stood up to the fast barrage so well that long-stop had
only four balls to field. Jackson was followed by Pilling, a Bedfordshire man whose style was described as the perfection of
neatness and rapidity without the least unnecessary show—it
all sounds rather like W. A. Oldfield, the great Australian of
a later period. He was held in great regard and Lancashire
sustained a grievous loss when he died in 1891 after wintering
in Australia. He played in eight Test matches, and is still
remembered as 'the Prince of Wicket-keepers'.

George Kemp was a dashing off-side hitter who invariably
did well against Yorkshire whether playing for Lancashire or
Cambridge University. He dropped out of cricket because of
the claims of his Parliamentary career but he did not completely sever his connection with the club of which, as Lord
Rochdale, he became a vice-president.

Vernon Royle won unique fame for his fielding at cover-
point. He was ambidextrous, very quick on his feet, and

had a beautifully controlled throw. Unlike Jessop, who preferred to allow a batsman to be lulled into a sense of false security, Royle tried to keep batsmen pinned to the crease, perhaps hoping to tempt them to indiscreet strokes in another direction. Once again, Tom Emmett can be quoted for his reply when called for a sharp single: 'Woah, mate, puliceman's thur.' It is an interesting sidelight on changing batting methods that when Royle went to Australia, he caught five batsmen at cover-point in one match.

One of the several Yorkshiremen who played for Lancashire in these formative years was Edward Roper, a man of energy and enthusiasm who took a leading part in the affairs of the Liverpool club and who was tireless in urging that county games should be taken to Aigburth.

S. M. Tindall was a magnificent outfield and a plucky, hard-hitting batsman. His best, though not his highest, innings for Lancashire was 49 against Surrey in the tie match of 1894. He afterwards played for London County and then, on going to live in Australia, became secretary of Melbourne C.C. He was also an outstanding hockey player.

These, with greater and lesser men, were among the cricketers on whose deeds the fame of the county club was built. There were three who attained immortality—Johnny Briggs, of whom consideration may be left for the time being, and A. N. Hornby and Richard Barlow, to whom a special chapter must be allocated.

CHAPTER 6

'My Hornby and My Barlow'

It is little I repair to the matches of the Southron folk,
Though my own red roses there may blow;
It is little I repair to the matches of the Southron folk;
Though the red roses crest the caps, I know;
For the field is full of shades as I near the shadowy coast,
And a ghostly batsman plays to the bowling of a ghost,
And I look through my tears on a soundless clapping host
As the run-stealers flicker to and fro—
To and fro—
O my Hornby and my Barlow long ago!

FRANCIS THOMPSON

ALL FIRE, DASH, and daring. That was the description applied to Albert Neilson Hornby's batting, and it matched the man himself. He lives in Lancashire cricket history as its supreme expression of character, a fearless man known to all at Old Trafford as 'the Boss', a captain who understood his professionals and instinctively knew, as did Lord Hawke of Yorkshire, that benevolent despotism was the best possible kind of rule for them. He had the magic touch of the born leader and he used it, combined with his magnificent physical strength, to build for himself a position that has never been equalled at Old Trafford.

Because of his impetuosity and his short runs, and his vigorous treatment of those who ventured to disagree with him, Hornby has come to be regarded as 'a bit of a card', but this is not the whole truth and his merits as a cricketer must never be overlooked.

He was a punishing batsman with a forward style typical of the age and when he left the pavilion, soldierlike in his alert, brisk way, bareheaded (a rare thing in those days), hair neatly parted in the middle, rivals knew at a glance that an

59

opponent of rare mettle was walking out to meet them. No day was too long for him, he packed a *Wisden's* in his bag wherever he went, and through all the long years of his association with the county his enthusiasm never abated one jot. William Howard has related how Hornby once went off for a family holiday in the north of Scotland leaving the Old Trafford Jack-of-all-trades strictest instructions to telegraph the score twice a day, to write a full report each evening, and to forward press cuttings during an absence planned to last three weeks. At the end of the first week Hornby turned up at the ground just to see how things were going on and to watch an old friend play, a piece of enthusiasm involving a 600-mile round journey.

He was in the eleven at Harrow, where his six-and-a-half stone earned him the title of 'Monkey', and his delighted schoolfellows carried him off the field after a triumph over Eton at Lord's. It is said that he actually arrived at Oxford but, discovering that a certain amount of study would be expected, left in haste. So when he was twenty he played for Lancashire, and all told he scored more than 11,000 runs for the county. He twice played for England against Australia and was captain in the great match in 1882 when the home country were beaten by seven runs at the Oval.

Hornby also figured in the famous match of 1878 when M.C.C. were beaten in a day by the Australians. During the second innings he was hit by Spofforth and it was said that the injury would have put most men out of action for a week or so; but with the side faring so disastrously he insisted on resuming his innings.

It is literally true that he feared no man. He was in Australia in 1879 when, following a disputed run-out decision against Murdoch, the crowd broke on to the field. There was an ugly scene and Lord Harris was struck with a stick. Hornby never flinched; surrounded by the hostile crowd, shirt torn to ribbons, struck in the face, he seized the chief offender, marched into the pavilion, and had the final satisfaction of seeing him charged in court. He once chastised a newspaperman who had offended with criticism, and when in a club match one of his sons was barracked, Hornby senior held up play and went into the crowd to speak his mind.

His first-wicket partnership with Barlow is one of cricket's most celebrated associations, honoured in prose and poetry, and if it was often exciting with its half-way sprints and rapid retreats, its sudden collapses as one or other failed to get back in time, it was also a thing of high technical achievement with the dashing captain at one end, the stubborn professional at the other, a perfect alliance of master and man.

'First he runs you out, then he gives you a sovereign', was the complaint, but if he had a nod of comfort for Barlow and a gift as well, other men, less accustomed to his methods, did not escape the full force of his ire. George Yates, for instance, once went tearing down the pitch expecting Hornby to run for every hit. The captain had merely blocked the ball and when Yates, who had charged head down, arrived at the other end the greeting he received was: 'What the hell are you doing here, Yates?'

He had a genius for making friends, and his interests were wide. He was one of the best riders to hounds of his day, played rugby for England on nine occasions, was a member of the Blackburn Rovers team when they played their first match at the Meadows, was a first-class runner and hurdler, and—just for the fun of the thing—took on professional boxers in the booths which were a feature of fairgrounds in those days.

It naturally followed that he himself was a keen fieldsman, tireless through the hottest day, ready to stand anywhere in the service of his beloved Lancashire team. He was intolerant of anything less than perfection, and when S. M. Crosfield complained of feeling tired, Hornby told him he would put him in the long field at both ends next day. When the youthful MacLaren, fresh from school and perhaps rather full of himself, suggested going anywhere except point, that was where he was posted. W. B. Stoddart asked for anywhere except the long field—and he was told to go there!

Such men invariably have running through their make-up a streak of generosity, and in Hornby it was revealed in his gifts to professionals, his turning up at the ground once a week through the winter months to inquire concerning their welfare, and his quick recognition of skilful play by friend or foe. Caught on the boundary at Birmingham from a hit that looked like clearing the fence, he walked into the dressing-room not with any show of disappointment, but with cheerful praise for the fieldsman to whom he gave a sovereign. Similarly caught in the Gentlemen and Players match at the Oval by William Gunn who stood six feet three, he commented: 'No one but a demned giraffe would have got near it.'

His heart was big and it was made of the right stuff. A man of violent opinions, confident in everything he touched, obstinately clinging to his position as 'the Boss', he could yet wheedle when he wished. The year after Barlow had lost his place in the side, his old captain, holidaying again in Scotland, wrote to the secretary: 'Dear Sam—I hope you will play Barlow against Cheshire... Now do, to please me.' The committee, against their better judgment, deferred to Hornby's wish, so the old professional was given his last game of all for a team bearing the title 'Lancashire'.

If it could be said critically that the majority of the players in these early days had been imported, no such complaint held good against Hornby, born at Blackburn, or his most able professional Richard Gorton Barlow, born at Barrow Bridge, Bolton. No more enthusiastic cricketer than Barlow has ever walked the green fields; always careful to keep himself in perfect physical condition, he was more than just the partner of Hornby in those first-wicket associations that produced the short runs, the alarms, and the humour. He was sharp and skilful in the field, he was a successful and economical left-arm bowler, and he was above all the greatest of that party of stonewallers which included Scotton, Louis Hall, and Alec Bannerman.

We have seen how the visit of George Parr's team to Manchester may have quickened interest in the game in the North in the middle of the century; the same man was indirectly responsible for Barlow's introduction to big cricket. The latter's family had gone to live in Derbyshire and when in 1871 Parr's team played twenty-two of Staveley and District, Barlow (then twenty-one years of age) made a big impression. Hickton was in the touring side and he advised the young man to apply for a trial at Old Trafford where the authorities were soon convinced of his worth.

For anyone who can obtain a copy of Barlow's rather rambling reminiscences, the book holds a peculiar fascination. Self-sufficient, confident in his own abilities to such a degree that up to 1914 he was willing to play single wicket with any man in England of his own age, he could still see good in others and his story reveals keen powers of observation, put to good use first as a player and then as a first-class umpire.

Originally batting and bowling left-handed he took to batting right-handed—so he himself said—on the advice of his
father in order to avoid 'the awkwardness and stiffness which
left-handed bats so often display'. He was something of a boy
prodigy though there is no truth in the story, so often repeated,
that he was a railway porter who played a match with his work-
mates and was not dismissed over a period of six weeks. His
batting style was founded on forward defensive play, his judgment of length being so perfect that bowlers found it a terrible
problem trying to hit his stumps. He carried his bat twelve
times through a Lancashire innings, the most celebrated instance
being at Trent Bridge in 1882 when he saw the whole side dismissed for 69 while he himself remained undefeated for 5 runs.
Two weeks later he met the Notts bowlers again at Liverpool
and again he went in first and carried his bat for 44 out of 93.
In the second innings he again went in first and this time was
the last man to be dismissed (run out) for 49 out of a total of
188.

Sometimes he was dreadfully slow (his innings of 5 not out
occupied him two and a half hours) yet his batting must have
held an attraction all its own, and when he was allied with
Hornby or with anybody else who could keep the score moving
he must have looked the perfect barn-door to opposing bowlers.

For his bowling successes Barlow, left-arm about medium
pace, relied on accuracy of pitch but according to Sydney Pardon he never became mechanical, was full of resource, and was
quick to spot a batsman's weak points. He twice performed
the hat-trick and the second of these feats was a beauty, for his
victims were W. G. Grace, John Shuter, and W. W. Read in
a Gentlemen v Players match at the Oval in 1884.

Such an all-rounder could hold his own in the highest company and he played seventeen times against Australia in Test
matches, twelve times in succession. In these games he scored
591 runs and took 35 wickets and he won the distinction, unique
to this day, of being selected for England with the special intention of opening both batting and bowling.

Barlow took part along with his own county captain in the
1882 match at the Oval—the match that drew to such an exciting climax that one spectator dropped dead and another
gnawed through the handle of his umbrella; when one batsman went in literally speechless; and another could not face

the bowling until he had been fortified with champagne. Spofforth was the victor that day but Barlow mastered the great Australian two years later at Nottingham. The North of England had to go in a second time on a pitch so badly affected by rain that Spofforth exclaimed: 'Give me the ball and they won't get sixty.' They got 255, Barlow 101 of them.

Added to his skill was the tough fibre of the true professional cricketer and no one, surely, has equalled his performance of never missing a match on three Australian tours. He was a useful goalkeeper in good-class soccer and acted as referee in the celebrated Cup-tie when Preston North End beat Hyde 26—0. After his twenty-one seasons with Lancashire, he was a first-class umpire for an exactly similar period.

Barlow was the perfect underling, satisfied with that place in life to which God had been pleased to call him. When he retired, he took his cricket equipment to his home at Lytham where every corner and every ornament spoke of cricket and where he erected a stained-glass window with himself as the central figure. There were bats everywhere, even in the bathroom, and Barlow was a contented man as he surveyed the ample evidence of his life of service to the game.

CHAPTER 7

Championship Matches

1892–3 Captains: A. N. Hornby and S. M. Crosfield
1894–5–6 Captain: A. C. MacLaren
1897–8 Captain: A. N. Hornby
1899 Captains: A. C. MacLaren and G. R. Bardswell

*Briggs, Mold and Watson share the burden; Another one-day
finish, 1892; T. A. Higson in the Oxford team at Old
Trafford; Albert Ward's fine form; Bad starts to the
season; A tie with Surrey, 1894; MacLaren's 424 at
Taunton; Johnny Tyldesley's début; Bad luck
with injuries; Champions again, 1897;
Hallam and Cuttell in form; Briggs
breaks down; Jack Sharp and
R. H. Spooner arrive, 1899;
Trumper and Tyldes-
ley meet.*

THE LANCASHIRE CAPTAINCY became something of a problem to
the committee because, though elected to share it in 1892 and
1893, A. N. Hornby played only four times each season and the
leadership generally fell to S. M. Crosfield, for so long the devoted lieutenant of 'the Boss'. For three years A. C. MacLaren
held the post though he did not turn out regularly in either
1896 or 1897. Then came Hornby's return. In 1899 there was
a season when divided captaincy was tried again, and it was
not until 1900 that a settled leadership was possible. Inevitably
the work of the side suffered yet between 1892 and 1899 Lancashire were champions once, three times second in the table,
three times fourth and once sixth. Overall this looks a good
record; yet really the period was one of great individual achievements rather than of solid match-winning team-work.

1892: CHAMPIONSHIP MATCHES:
Played 16, Won 7, Drawn 4, Lost 5

E

The team played erratically this year. Not for the first time they began badly, then made a brave effort to pull themselves together, but taking the season as a whole the batting never seemed quite good enough to entitle them to be regarded as serious contenders for the championship. Arthur Smith topped the averages with 29 runs an innings, followed closely by Frank Ward, MacLaren, Sugg, Albert Ward, and Baker, all of whom had their good days but were unaccountably prone to failure.

The bowling was limited to three men—but what a trio they formed! In first-class county games Briggs took 85 wickets, Mold 104, Watson 52, averaging around 14 runs a wicket, and no one else took more than half a dozen. In match after match they bore the full brunt of the work in an association of left-hand art and artfulness, real speed, and sheer courage. They were supported by a very good wicket-keeper in A. T. Kemble.

The season opened with victory over Sussex in a match of interest to students of cricket history because Lancashire lost eight second-innings wickets against the lob bowling of Humphreys. Another curiosity came in the match against Middlesex, the sides hanging about on the third day until a quarter to six, which must stand as one of the latest starts on record. Middlesex were 226 behind with two wickets standing and Lancashire soon got one of them down; but they failed to dislodge the other, and so were foiled of victory after the long wait, and in spite of Mold's feat in taking 13 wickets and hitting the stumps ten times. Still a third memorable incident occurred at Liverpool where 'W. G.' was so lame that though he stayed an hour, he failed to score. The lion at bay!

When Somerset came north, Lancashire beat them in one day. Somerset made 88, Lancashire 116, and then Somerset again 58. Play was prolonged beyond the usual hour to allow Lancashire to knock off the runs and they won by eight wickets. Briggs took 12 wickets for 83 runs, and Mold eight for 40. It was Mold too who won the match against Kent at Tunbridge Wells, making the ball fly about after rain so that he had a second-innings analysis of nine for 29, and a match record of 13 for 91. He surpassed this performance at Brighton with 14 Sussex wickets for 159, all taken in one day in 53.3 five-ball overs unchanged with Watson.

The defeats were all met with away from home at the hands of Surrey, Notts, Somerset, Middlesex, and Yorkshire. Revenge was gained over Yorkshire at Old Trafford and the season finished with a similar reprisal against Notts with Mold in great form again.

When Oxford University came to Old Trafford they tried a new man in T. A. Higson, a rival who was soon to become more than a friend.

1893: CHAMPIONSHIP MATCHES: Played 16, Won 9, Drawn 2, Lost 5

Another in-and-out season ended with Lancashire second to Yorkshire. The wonder is that they did so well; the batting figures improved, it is true, with Albert Ward and Sugg doing much better but Alec Watson dropped out of the team and the bowling, already dangerously restricted, was now reduced to Briggs and Mold with a little help from G. R. Baker and William Oakley. Mold was just coming to his best and this season he was preferred to Tom Richardson in the Test matches while Briggs was established as one of the great all-rounders of his day. It is doubtful if any team has ever finished so high in the table when relying on only two bowlers.

Similarly the batting depended overmuch on two or three men. Albert Ward did especially well, scoring more than 1,000 runs in championship matches and standing third in the professional averages after William Gunn and Shrewsbury. He was selected for all three Test matches but stood out of the Lord's game against Australia to assist his county and the difference in pay amounting to £4 was made up by Lancashire.

A new wicket-keeper appeared this year in Charles Smith, a Yorkshireman who could not at first displace Kemble but who stayed on to render much useful service in his plucky, good-hearted way.

Towards the end of the season Lancashire had a chance of the title but they lost their last two games against Middlesex and Notts, whereas Yorkshire won their last three fixtures. Still, there was much cause for satisfaction, including the celebrated five-runs victory over Yorkshire when Ulyett was caught on the boundary, and a meritorious win at the Oval. Surrey had just beaten the Australians for a second time, but on this occasion they were overthrown by the all-round form of Briggs who scored 112 and took 11 wickets for 115 runs. There was another splendid match at Trent Bridge where after Notts had opened with 318 and a capital century by Shrewsbury, Lancashire gained a narrow first-innings lead thanks chiefly to a century by Sugg, and then rammed home this slight advantage when Mold and Briggs put out their rivals for 92. Then came a thrilling finish, Mee and Attewell bowling so well that six wickets went down for 55 runs. In this crisis Smith and Baker stood firm and knocked off the last 37 runs in twenty minutes.

In a season that brought him much glory Albert Ward did nothing finer than carrying his bat for 140 through an innings of 281 at Bristol.

The batting weakness has been mentioned; now the Committee, looking round for talent, offered an engagement at £2 a week to a young professional. His name: John Thomas Tyldesley.

1894: CHAMPIONSHIP MATCHES:
Played 16, Won 7, Drawn 1, Tied 1, Lost 7

S. M. Crosfield had been elected captain for 1894 but was unable to take on the duties so A. C. MacLaren took over. He was only twenty-two and his own batting for the county had so far hardly borne out the promise of his Harrow days and his brilliant first appearance for Lancashire, but he had played a lot of cricket, had the look of a great cricketer, and above all was devoted to the game.

His first two months of captaincy brought little but disappointment. Bad starts were notorious at Old Trafford but this one was the worst of all, seven fixtures in May and June bringing six defeats against a solitary victory.

While Mold and Briggs toiled, the leading batsmen simply could not get going and after many seasons of this sort of thing, strong comment was passed (and printed) concerning the necessity for pre-season practice. July brought the usual improvement—in five seasons only two games were lost in this month and over a period of ten years not more than one July match was lost in any one season. Towards the finish Lancashire, though beaten twice by Yorkshire, were playing as well as any team in the country but the lost ground was too much for them to be able to challenge for the title and they had to be content with fourth position in the table.

The averages for championship matches make remarkable reading. Mold had 144 wickets for 11 runs apiece, Briggs 97 for 15 runs each, and no one else took more than nine wickets.

The sensations of the season came in Briggs's benefit match (dealt with in the chapter devoted to Yorkshire matches) and at the Oval. Surrey were aiming for the championship and they had so little to spare over Yorkshire that they were specially keen to win this match. The first day was a wash-out and then when the match got going Briggs and Mold put their formidable adversaries out for 97. That Lancashire gained a first innings lead of 50 was almost entirely due to a spirited innings of 49 by S. M. Tindall and it looked as though this advantage, though slight, would be sufficient when Surrey could muster only 124 at their second attempt. But Lockwood and Richardson were there and they attacked with all the skill and energy at their command in a bold bid to save the match. Five Lancashire wickets fell for 9 runs, and seven for 26—among them MacLaren, Albert Ward, Sugg, Paul, and Briggs. Seventy-five runs, the number required for victory, began to look a long way off until Tindall and Charles Smith put on 39 with vigorous strokes and a little luck. With two runs still wanted Bardswell was caught by Wood, standing back to Richardson, and at the finish everything depended on the fast bowlers: Mold batting, Lockwood and Richardson bowling. Tinsley managed the run that tied the scores but Mold fatally snicked Lockwood's faster ball and the honours were fairly divided after an hour of terrific excitement.

Though not really an item of Lancashire history, an event in the home game against Sussex is worthy of mention. Qualified by residence for the southern county, the old Notts bowler Alfred Shaw, absent from the field for seven years and now almost fifty-two years of age, returned to the game and on a good wicket sent down 52 overs for 73 runs and four wickets—and that despite poor fielding! It was in this match that Mold gained one of his best returns, seven second-innings wickets for 17 runs. A few days later he had 13 for 114 against Middlesex who scrambled home by one wicket after making Lancashire follow-on. Derbyshire, returning to the first-class fixture list, also defeated Lancashire who were put out for 35 by Davidson and Hulme, though Mold again bowled finely and brought his record for three consecutive matches to 33 wickets, with the stumps hit twenty-seven times. And it was Mold too who figured as the destroyer-in-chief in another one-day match at

Old Trafford, taking 13 Somerset wickets (eleven clean bowled and a hat-trick thrown in) for 60 runs. Lancashire fairly rushed to victory, for Sugg came back to form after two months of ineffectiveness with a wonderful innings of 105, so hard hit that there were only eleven singles in it.

As the season went on, it was still Mold's year. He had 13 wickets against Gloucester (though Briggs played his part by getting 'W. G.' twice for 0 and 5), the same haul against Kent, and then surpassed it all with 15 for 87 at Brighton, where he responded magnificently to MacLaren's judgment in sending Sussex in to·bat.

1895: CHAMPIONSHIP MATCHES:
Played 22, Won 14, Drawn 3, Lost 4, Abandoned 1

This was one of the game's great summers. The championship was enlarged to embrace fourteen counties, W. G. Grace scored his thousand runs in May and hit his hundredth century, MacLaren smashed the individual record with his 424 at Taunton, and on to the cricket stage stepped J. T. Tyldesley, of whom *Wisden's* recorded: 'The general impression seemed to be that he had a good deal of cricket in him.' Lancashire had a splendid season, finishing second in the table, and they pressed Surrey so closely that the champions had to win their last fixture to stay on top.

The captain's great score calls for first consideration among the deeds of 1895. This innings, which beat the nineteen-year-old record of 344 set up by 'W. G.', was made in remarkable circumstances. MacLaren had been to Australia in the winter, travelled home later than the other tourists, and so missed the opening of the English season. He played in two fixtures without doing anything at all remarkable, and then, to the dismay of countless Lancashire enthusiasts, accepted a post at a preparatory school. So for seven matches the side played without their elected captain, and they were beaten three times. He rejoined the side at Taunton and after an absence of five weeks from first-class cricket, went in first and made his 424 out of the record total of 801.

MacLaren himself was batting for 470 minutes, hitting a six, 62 fours, 11 threes, 37 twos, and 63 singles, and the aggregate of 801, made in eight hours, was founded on two big partnerships. At the outset MacLaren and Albert Ward (64) put on

141, and then the captain and Paul (177) added 363 in 190 minutes. The record-breaker himself was seventh out at 792.

So the promising boy, after a year or two of doubt, at last grew up to be a great batsman; so far from exhausting himself with this one huge score, he finished the season with three centuries on successive slow, easy, and fiery pitches as though to demonstrate the complete command he now had of himself and his game. Yet not all the best batting is contained in record scores. Late in the summer Lancashire had to bat under atrocious conditions after being sent in at the Oval. MacLaren made 52 against Lohmann, Richardson, Lockwood, Hayward, and Brockwell, and thanks to this splendid performance Mold and Briggs were given the chance, gleefully taken, of winning the match.

After MacLaren the most successful batsmen this year were Albert Ward, Paul, Sugg, and Baker, though the fast wickets tried Sugg's temperament and technique alike, so that *Wisden's* remarked: 'Sometimes his cricket was such as to make the judicious grieve.'

Mold seemed better than ever, taking 182 wickets in championship matches alone at a cost of 13 runs each. He had 16 for 111 against Kent, 15 for 85 against Notts (including four in four balls), and 11 for 128 against Yorkshire. He astonished everyone (including himself) by helping Albert Ward to score 111 for the last wicket against Leicester at Old Trafford, the senior partner in this unexpected stand carrying his bat right through the innings. Briggs took 119 wickets including 12 for 49 at Leicester, and at last the overworked pair were given some assistance with the arrival of Hallam, qualified by residence.

In 1894 there had been reason for criticism of the fielding; now it returned to something like its old standard and Charles Smith, given a regular place in the side, kept wicket splendidly besides adding one or two useful scores to his 51 catches and 25 stumpings. Then there was Tyldesley, launched on his great career with an innings of 152 against Warwickshire in his second match, an innings so prophetic in every way.

The Manchester public responded to all this magnificence; on the first day of the game against Kent there were 20,000 people at Old Trafford, and 25,331 passed through the turnstiles on the opening day of the Yorkshire match in August.

1896: CHAMPIONSHIP MATCHES:
Played 22, Won 11, Drawn 7, Lost 4

Second again, Lancashire were this time runners-up to York-shire and they might have challenged the champions even more closely but for wretched luck with injuries. Mold had a dam-aged hand for most of the summer, Hallam missed five matches in mid-season, and Ernest Rowley, often captain in MacLaren's absence, also damaged a hand. It speaks volumes for Mold's stout heart that he kept going though undergoing treatment for his injury, taking 130 wickets. Briggs had 122 wickets, and for most men these would have been satisfactory totals but there was a rise in cost—to 17 runs a wicket in the case of the fast bowler, and almost 20 for the left-hander. Hallam took 58 wickets and Baker and I'Anson helped a little, but Lancas-ter, who had shown some promise in 1895, disappointingly failed to improve.

MacLaren played only ten times, scoring 713 runs with an average of 54, and the burden of batting fell chiefly on Sugg, Baker, and Albert Ward. Showing rather more self-control without losing his splendid punishing power, Sugg doubled both aggregate and average as compared with 1895. His greatest innings was 220, scored at a run a minute at Bristol.

The Yorkshire match was the first fixture on the card this year. It was nearly no fixture at all because Lancashire thought their rivals' correspondence, following a proposal for Bank Holiday games, lacking in courtesy, and there was a definite threat from Old Trafford of a break in the series. Lancashire fixed a holiday game with Kent, and sent the correspondence to the *Manchester Guardian* and the *Sporting Chronicle*; for some seasons Kent continued to provide the opposition at Whit-suntide and August Bank Holiday.

Lancashire lost this opening game, then won eight off the reel and with MacLaren still to join the side ambitions of the title must have run high. Then came the injuries, some bad luck with the toss, and hopes were finally extinguished by ill-fortune with the weather.

The big triumph was represented by a double victory over Surrey. In the first match bowlers had things all their own way and imagination tingles at the thought of Mold and Richard-son in all their fiery splendour. Lancashire wanted only 83 to

Edmund Rowley, captain 1873–9   S. M. Crosfield, captain 1892–3

A. N. Hornby, captain 1880–91, 1897–8   A. C. MacLaren, captain 1894–6, 1899–1907

Above: A. H. Hornby, captain 1908–14
Above left: Jack Sharp, captain 1922–5
Below left: Myles Kenyon, captain 1919–
1922

Above: Col. Leonard Green, captain
1926–8 *Above right*: P. T. Eckersley,
captain 1929–35 *Below right*: W. H. L.
Lister, captain 1936–9

Above left: Nigel Howard, captain 1949–53 *Above right*: J. A. Fallows, captain 194
Below: Kenneth Cranston, captain 1947–8

win but five wickets went down for 35 runs against superb bowling and fielding. Then came a dropped catch and with it a second chance for Baker, and with Briggs hitting bravely for a few minutes, victory was won by three wickets. Later in the season there was a very similar finish at the Oval, where the task this time was 60 to win. Tom Hayward bowled so well that six men were out for 30 runs but MacLaren hung on and again the nerve of Briggs proved good enough in the crisis so that Lancashire got home by four wickets.

MacLaren was the central figure in a different kind of incident against Gloucestershire. He had scored only two when he trod on his wicket but on appeal the umpire decided that he had completed his stroke and was starting to run and was therefore not out. The Lancashire captain stayed to make 56.

Derbyshire's Davidson and Storer set up an Old Trafford record with a partnership of 308 in a drawn game, but in the return at Derby, Mold and Briggs carried all before them.

1897: CHAMPIONSHIP MATCHES:
Played 26, Won 16, Drawn 7, Lost 3

After taking second place five times in the seven seasons 1890–6, Lancashire became champions in 1897 and though the finish was close, they deserved their final triumph. It was won because of better bowling; for years Mold and Briggs had laboured almost alone but now Hallam took his full share of the work and an astonishing success was achieved by Willis Cuttell. To the pace and artfulness of the old hands, this pair brought steadiness and variety in a nice proportion, so that the attack became one of the most complete to take part in the championship, not surpassed until Yorkshire produced the historic alliance of Haigh with Hirst and Rhodes. The son of a Yorkshire professional, Cuttell had also played for his native county. He took an appointment at Nelson and so qualified for Lancashire, embarking on his first full season at the age of thirty-two.

Briggs had 140 wickets this season, Cuttell 102, Mold (again afflicted by injuries) 88, and Hallam 90, their averages varying from 16.54 to 18.31. There, in a paragraph, is the strength of the team.

The batting, it must be confessed, was hardly in the same class though there was MacLaren, of course, with his inevitable suggestion of quality and his average of 50 for the third year in succession. Ward and Baker each scored a thousand runs, Sugg was brilliant on his good days, and the young Tyldesley scored well after the disappointments of the previous summer. A. N. Hornby was back in the field, directing the team with all his old vigour, while Charles Smith was brilliant behind the wicket until he met with injury, when a new star was discovered from the ground staff in Lees Radcliffe who played in only four matches but at once evoked memories of Pilling because of a similar neatness of style.

Comparisons with the 1881 side should only be made with this in mind: that Lancashire's first championship side played only thirteen games, whereas the 1897 team had an exacting programme of exactly double that number of fixtures.

The team got off to a good start by winning at Derby where Mold took 12 wickets and Ward and Paul shared in a first-wicket partnership of 171, Ward making the most of his luck in being dropped five times to carry his own score to 162. Hampshire were well beaten, the Trent Bridge game was drawn, and then came a row of three victories against Leicester, Middlesex, and Derbyshire, the third by one wicket in a splendid finish at Liverpool. Frank Sugg's benefit match with Kent was ruined by rain after a successful first day, and following this check came a heavy defeat from Surrey, who batted brilliantly on a difficult pitch.

Of the next seven games three (against Somerset, Gloucester, and Essex) were won and four (against Warwick twice, Sussex and Yorkshire) were drawn, so that by the third week in July the team's record, though good, hardly suggested championship possibilities. Meantime Notts had enjoyed a fine run and Yorkshire and Essex had both been showing good form.

Of Lancashire's remaining eleven fixtures, however, eight were won, with one drawn and two defeats sustained against Essex and Surrey. One reason for the abrupt change of fortunes was the bowling of Briggs who in three successive games took 36 wickets for 323 runs. MacLaren, too, found his best form in an innings of 244 against Kent, made in five hours with brilliant pulling bringing him most of his 38 fours.

Defeat at Leyton in spite of two glorious innings by Sugg was a sharp set-back which gave Essex themselves a chance of the title, immediately squandered against Surrey. So the finish of the season was wonderfully exciting as Lancashire and Surrey pressed forward, and when the pair met at the Oval, the ground was filled and all sporting England waited for the result. The visiting side had all the bad luck, having to take the field without Mold and then having Sugg hurt when, in the second innings, the game stood very level and the famous hitter was just opening out. Surrey won by six wickets and it looked as though they must win the title, but it was Lancashire who stayed the course better. They drew with Middlesex and beat Notts, Cuttell taking a dozen wickets, whereas Surrey first lost to Somerset and then only drew with Sussex. So it was Lancashire's title at long last, and the general verdict was that on all types of pitches, they had a team worthy to be called champions.

1898: CHAMPIONSHIP MATCHES:
Played 26, Won 9, Drawn 11, Lost 6

After the triumphs of 1897, there were disappointments this year. Hallam's health broke down so that he did not play at all, Briggs was stale after an Australian tour, Mold's suspect knee kept him off the field in August when three matches were lost, MacLaren played only occasionally, and the new all-rounder Hallows strained his bowling arm, a sorry story of misfortune that plunged the champions of the previous summer to sixth place in the table.

Up to the end of July things went fairly well, nineteen matches yielding nine victories and only two defeats, but afterwards success eluded the side and the bowlers—or at any rate, those who were left—underwent heavy punishment. Essex scored 339 for six wickets in a fourth innings at Old Trafford, a record for a county match at that time, and at the Oval, with Mold absent, Lancashire had to field out while Surrey scored 634, Tom Hayward making 315 not out to compile the greatest individual innings ever recorded against the county.

There were compensations amid the failures. Cuttell became the first Lancashire cricketer to complete the 'double' of 1,000 runs and 100 wickets, C. R. Hartley batted well on occasion, Lees Radcliffe confirmed his reputation as a wicket-keeper, and W. B. Stoddart and Tom Lancaster bowled well once or twice. Best of all was the success of Tyldesley—not so much because he scored 1,918 runs in all first-class matches but because of the manner in which he obtained them. An innings of 200 against Derbyshire when Lancashire scored 464 for seven wickets in 270 minutes on the opening day, and a partnership with MacLaren at Canterbury that put on 155 runs in two hours—these were hints of what was to come in succeeding summers. From these and similar performances stemmed the superb batting of the Lancashire team about and after the turn of the century.

1899: CHAMPIONSHIP MATCHES:
Played 26, Won 12, Drawn 7, Lost 6, Abandoned 1

At long last A. N. Hornby gave up the captaincy. It was the end of a chapter, for a wider world than the cricket field—the Victorian Era, with its fascinating mixture of dignified leisure and greedy excitement—moved to its appointed end, and as we look back it seems peculiarly appropriate that the great captain should have gone out as the motor-car came in. There was to be an occasional appearance in the side, but it was time to look for a fresh and younger captain and to appoint someone who could reasonably look forward to some years in the office. The obvious choice was A. C. MacLaren though for a little while there were difficulties so that in 1899 G. R. Bardswell was elected joint captain with him. As it turned out neither could play very often, and Alec Eccles sometimes had charge of the team, at others A. N. Hornby himself consented to play again. It was an unsatisfactory arrangement and the work of the side suffered.

The team continued to be dogged by bad luck, too. Hallam came back to the game, played for a month, and then broke down while bowling against Hampshire at Old Trafford. Worse still was the illness of Briggs, so skilful this season that he actually displaced Rhodes from the England team to play against the Australians at Leeds. He had taken three wickets for 53 runs when, on the evening of the first day, he collapsed and had to be detained in a mental home. His cricket for the year was finished, and, as things turned out, there was but one more great season left to him.

So once again we have to turn to the consolation rather than the prizes. There was the further progress of Tyldesley so that he played twice for England, one of the few professionals who could match up to the brilliant amateurs of the day. There was the arrival of Jack Sharp, entering on a unique career, and there was the appearance of Reginald Spooner, whose style is held to this day to be the perfection of the classic method. Sharp first made his mark appropriately enough at Liverpool with some good bowling against Essex, and other good performances emphasised his worth before he was recalled to the Everton club for training for the new football season. The editor of *Wisden's* commented: 'It seemed something like Nemesis that Everton . . . should have lost every one of their first three League engagements.'

Spooner had distinguished himself at Marlborough and had already made a century for the county second eleven when he was selected to play for the first eleven against Middlesex at Lord's. The match was lost, but it made his reputation. Against J. T. Hearne and Albert Trott he first hit 44 in eighty minutes, then 83 in less than two hours.

There were other new faces in the side. Sidney Webb, newly qualified from Middlesex, took 30 wickets, and there was Albert Hornby with an occasional appearance—once with his father against Leicestershire. There was J. L. Ainsworth, an amateur slow left-arm bowler who had been on tour to America with success and who for Lancashire now took 18 wickets in three matches and then dropped out of the game.

In such a season there were bound to be experiments; one of them brought out Albert Ward as a bowler, very slow and sometimes very expensive, but at such a time every man had to lend a hand.

When the Australians came to Old Trafford there was a meeting between Trumper and Tyldesley, perhaps never surpassed as brilliant stroke-makers on difficult pitches. Trumper made 82, Tyldesley 56 out of 102 and then 42 out of 81. In that second innings the next best score was six by Ward, Cuttell made four, there were five ducks, three men hit a single each, and extras helped with 16! Truly the sky was filled with portents.

CHAPTER 8

Administration 1864-98

Early losses soon made good; Reynolds goes shooting; Experiment with four stumps; A system of fines; First attempt to purchase the ground; New buildings and an office in Manchester; Lacrosse and lawn tennis at Old Trafford; Snobbery at Liverpool; A new pavilion planned; The clubs amalgamate; The ground purchased for £24,082; S. H. Swire and his colleagues

WE HAVE SEEN how the cricketers won fame for the club and can now survey in greater detail the work in the pavilion and office.

When the county club came into being, there was a pavilion in existence that had cost the Manchester club £900. In 1868 a proposal to admit the public free of charge was defeated by a very large majority and it would seem that such a gesture could hardly be afforded, because in at least one year there was a loss of over £100 on the county games, made good by a subscription list to which the chief contributors were members of the committee. Evidently things improved rapidly because in 1873 a new public pavilion was approved at a cost of £160, a wooden structure fifty feet long with a 'stranger professional' dressing-room, a small bar, and a long room. It was completed two or three years later.

Formation of the county team did not at once deny the public opportunities of watching the touring sides of great professionals which about that time were doing so much to popularise the game and improve technical standards. The United All-England team played the All-England eleven, for example, at Old Trafford in May 1867.

The committee had problems of greater and lesser import. There was, for instance, the matter of Reynolds shooting pigeons; not only did he take out his gun but he invited friends, not members of the club, to indulge in the sport; a minute

78

records that the secretary was to tell Reynolds that such irregu-
larities could on no account be countenanced, and in due course
the groundsman promised it would not occur again. Then
there were complaints of trespass from a neighbouring land-
owner and the club agreed that on certain occasions 'such as
races, etc.' (presumably athletic meetings) they would station
a policeman at each end of a footpath.

Another difficulty arose with the Royal Agricultural Society
who had been erecting tents and diverting a road and as early as
1869 the question of the lease was much in mind. In February
1870 the steward to Sir Humphrey de Trafford refused to renew
it but promised that the club should not be disturbed.

An interesting experiment was tried in 1872 when at Birkenhead Park's suggestion a game was played with four stumps.
Manchester made 212 and Watson and Reynolds bowled out
Birkenhead Park for 84 and 46. About this time, the growing
status of the two clubs, Manchester and Lancashire, is indicated by a minute noting that Anfield C.C. (as subscribers)
asked for help in finding a bowler.

There is to be seen a rather earlier minute providing for a
fine of five shillings for any member who 'having engaged in a
match shall quit the same without the consent of his side'.
The same fine applied if a member smoked in the pavilion
before dinner or while fielding or batting in a game. In 1870
Fred Reynolds extended his duties; hitherto a professional
cricketer, he now became responsible for 'collecting subscriptions, managing the cricket department, keeping the ground in
order, attending to the comfort of members, being present on
the ground on all necessary occasions'—all for £60 a year with
cottage rent free.

The entrance fee to the Manchester club at this time was one
guinea, annual subscription two guineas, 'young gentlemen
under the age of twenty-one to pay one guinea a year during
minority'. The Lancashire subscription was ten shillings. The
two clubs worked in harmony from the beginning and soon
S. H. Swire was empowered to engage two good extra bowlers;
we may guess there was a dual purpose here.

In January 1878 a big decision was taken though it could not
be implemented; an approach was made to Sir Humphrey de
Trafford with a view to purchasing the ground or, failing that,
securing a permanent tenancy. Meantime, Mr. A. B. Rowley pro-

posed making improvements to the pavilion at his own expense.

The new lease cost the club a bonus of £2,250, but despite this outlay the committee forged ahead with plans for a new dining-room, a public refreshment pavilion, and new offices in Manchester.

An official union between Manchester and Lancashire clubs was agreed in 1880, and the joint organisation entered upon a period of special prosperity that lasted for fifteen years with every season yielding a financial gain. A new stand ('no smoking') and A. N. Hornby's vigorous captaincy added to the popularity of the club with the general public. Apparently members were well content to leave matters in the hands of a few efficient officials because in the year of amalgamation a serious suggestion was made that in order to secure a better attendance of members at the annual meeting, a dinner should be provided.

Lacrosse was sometimes played in the winter and there is reference in the minutes to an application for use of Old Trafford for All-England lawn tennis matches, permission being granted with the condition 'not during cricket matches'.

The visit of the strong Cambridge University eleven to open Liverpool's new ground at Aigburth has already been noted as a feature of the 1881 season; but later in the summer Hornby wrote to the committee: 'I write to you on behalf of the County Eleven (and in the interest of cricket) to allow the match Lancashire v Yorkshire which is advertised to take place at Liverpool on July 28, be transferred to Manchester as we all think the ground is in such a dangerous state, and not fit to play a bona fide County match on at present.' The match was transferred in accordance with the captain's request and the committee were of a mind to play all games at Old Trafford but members overruled them at the annual meeting of 1883. Aigburth soon became a first-class ground in almost every respect and matches there have become a feature of every summer, with Neville Cardus extolling its lovely lawns.

Such items as the absence of the scorer on the last day of the 1881 match with Notts, and an allegation by Hornby that the umpire for Notts was drunk, came before the committee, and there was a decision to appoint a new scorer (Mr. Slater) with a ban on his reporting the matches at the same time. The purchase of a horse and dog cart is, one assumes, the record of an acquisition of a minor luxury for the committeemen.

When the North played Australia at Old Trafford in 1882, the players were given £12 a man, with an additional £3 if they won, one of the earliest references to a winning bonus. The pay for members of the ground staff was usually about twenty-five shillings a week in winter, £2 a week in the summer, with match pay extra.

The great throwing controversy broke around the county and is dealt with in the chapter including matches of the period. Another dispute concerned the behaviour of the crowd at Derby, and here Lancashire seem to have been justified in declining to play there following scenes in the 1886 match. It must have been a lively occasion in more than one respect because Briggs absented himself for two days after this game and had his wages cut in proportion to the time lost.

Older members may remember the card-seller, Whittham. He paid £35 for the rights, while the caterers had to pay £200 annually for their privileges—clear proof of the size of the crowds and the air of general prosperity.

Rivalry between Manchester and Liverpool was unceasing. W. S. Patterson, who died in 1939, is quoted in *Wisden's* as saying, in reply to a question as to whether he had ever been president of the county club: 'Lancashire had rather a strong amateur representation, two or three Steels, two or three Hornbys, as well as Vernon Royle. The management was always jealously retained at Manchester. I lived in Liverpool!'

Another sharp comment about the conduct of the club was passed by the Rev. R. S. Holmes, who suggested that Lancashire's need to import professionals in their early years was due to the high subscriptions to local clubs, barring working men from joining. He wrote:

'Working men cannot afford two guineas a year for the privilege of being snubbed by their social betters, and that is the condition of things in the best clubs around Liverpool. In Yorkshire I know several clubs every whit as good in every way as those just referred to, where the "sub" is only half a guinea and even less, and where the banker, lawyer, parson, and mechanic stand on precisely the same level.'

Another item breaks into the serious business: 'The Hon. Sec. to write to the Manchester Hiring Co. (they did the cater-

F

ing) asking them to inform the committee, who ordered champagne for the players for the occasion of the Australian match?'

In 1888 membership stood at 1,850 plus 60 life members and 600 ladies. It was in this year that Mr. A. B. Rowley showed his keen foresight when he declared that the club ought to adopt the Surrey and M.C.C. method of having young bowlers on the ground, and choose the best for the county. He also suggested formation of a second eleven. Reynolds had by now increased his responsibilities so that he was ground manager and assistant secretary at £200, rent free, with coal, gas, and water.

The club did not allow their dispute with Kent over Crossland's bowling to rankle; when Lord Harris left England and a representation was organised, Lancashire sent £30. They gave a clock to Oxford University for their new pavilion, offered Essex £50 if that county could first pay off their liabilities, donated £100 to Cheshire on condition their neighbours raised £500 by their own efforts, and promised help to Somerset 'if in any serious financial difficulty'.

The committee often showed remarkable anticipation in cricket matters; for instance, in the early '90s there was a general discussion among the counties about the declaration rules and Lancashire suggested that a first-day closure ought to be permitted. They failed to carry their point at the time, but more than fifty years later it was agreed that a side should be allowed to declare on the first day at 300, and it was a Lancashire captain, N. D. Howard, who first took advantage of the rule.

Negotiations for the purchase of the ground were re-opened, with a price of £10,000 suggested, but again the talks broke down. Every season now ended with the treasurer able to report a surplus and though they could not buy the ground the committee obtained use of extra land (now the practice ground) and it was soon in use for minor matches.

If the members desired one thing more than another it was a new pavilion and at the annual meeting in 1894 it was agreed to go ahead at a cost not to exceed £6,000. But it cost at least half as much again, and almost immediately the committee were faced with their biggest task of all; the problem of finding the money to buy the ground, now at last within their grasp. The price was £24,082 for an area of just over eighteen acres and the conditions included the certain use of the ground exclusively for thirty years. As the banks' terms were not considered sufficiently liberal, 200 bonds of £100 each were issued at four per cent. and the purchase was completed in November 1898.

These problems were faced as they occurred with unflinching courage; the long-drawn-out negotiations, the financing of different schemes, the maintenance of the county eleven at a high standard—every step was taken with great skill. Succeeding committeemen and officials knew when to proceed warily and when in turn to launch out on some ambitious scheme or other. Most of them were connected in some way with the cotton industry and they knew whether trade was propitious for their plans.

Of the men who set their hands to all this work, the first to be mentioned is Mr. Edwin Whittaker, already noted as one of Ashton's representatives at the 1864 meeting. At his own expense he had a boarded fence erected to replace the original one that enclosed the ground and in the late '60s he occupied the office of honorary secretary for two of the three years that broke the long tenancy of office by Mr. S. H. Swire.

Sam Swire, as he seems to have been known by everyone, was honorary secretary of the Manchester club from 1862, took similar office with the county club on its formation, and with a brief interval (1866–8 inclusive) held the office until his death in the last week of 1905. With his passing, a paid secretary was appointed.

He has been described as a typical Lancastrian—bluff, kindly beneath a sometimes forbidding exterior, and absorbed as few men have been by his constant view of the play from his personal seat in the north wing of the pavilion which nobody else was privileged to occupy. When A. N. Hornby became a member of the eleven in 1867 there began a unique association of two strong-fibred figures which guaranteed firm guidance of affairs of the club in the middle and in the office.

In the earliest days committee meetings were held at the Queen's Hotel or at the business offices of one of the members. The link between cricket and cotton was a strong one and eventually it was suggested at an annual meeting that the club should open an office in Manchester 'near the Royal Exchange, connected by telephone to the ground'. The Barton Arcade premises were taken at a rent of £42 (in 1885, so we are anti-cipating a little) and many present-day members will recall the rather dark approach to the club's administrative headquarters. They were vacated in 1937 when everything became centred on the cricket ground.

Swire attended the office every Tuesday and Friday to oversee the work of Fred Reynolds the ground manager; William Howard, the general factotum who became known to countless cricketers as dressing-room attendant at Old Trafford; and the clerk Tom Irving who had originally come from Cumberland to qualify as a left-arm bowler. Irving seems to have been a some-what irresponsible character, and he and Howard used to leave the office for a game of billiards or for refreshment. If the secretary turned up while they were away, they would find on their return that he had chalked on the door: 'Out again, no fire. x x x—S. H. Swire.' The three crosses indicated marks of censure and the promise of a lecture when he eventually caught up with them. He had a rooted objection to publicans becoming members (he said it was the wives he really minded) but the office staff conspired to defeat his scrutiny of nomination forms by describing would-be members who were 'in the trade', as wine and spirit merchants.

No doubt the staff played him up, but he had quiet ways of reprimanding them for their misdemeanours or the theft of his cigars; one way was to turn up at the office unexpectedly when there was a big mid-week football match on, and staying all day, so that the others could not slip away.

First president of the county club was Mr. Mark Phillips, already president of the Manchester club since 1833. He car-ried on until 1873, to be succeeded by Mr. Alexander Butler Rowley, member of one of the most remarkable of all the famous cricketing families. Seven brothers were prominent in Manchester cricket and athletics in the '50s, so it was natural that A. B. and his brother Edmund Butler Rowley should attend the inaugural meeting. Both played for the Gentlemen against the Players at Lord's.

As player and captain 'E. B.' has already been mentioned; it must be added that he served on the committee for forty years. His son, Ernest Butler Rowley—at the time of writing this history, still alive and keenly interested in the game and everything connected with Lancashire cricket—also played for

the county and led the side for half a season in 1896 when
A. N. Hornby was taken ill. Elected in 1888, he is the oldest
surviving county and playing member, and it may be noted
here that the family connection is maintained through his two
sons who are life members, and with Col. Hugh Kennedy who
is a great-nephew of Edmund Butler Rowley and has served on
the committtee since 1936.

Joseph Rowley, who hit the first half-century for the club in
its opening fixture, lived for a time in Paris where he became
friendly with Whistler, Leighton, Poynter, and du Maurier,
the last-named taking him as the original for 'Taffy' in
Trilby. He was a great all-round sportsman excelling at
wrestling, throwing the hammer, and boxing, and all golfers
must envy the natural talent that enabled him to take up the
game at sixty and to become a scratch player. After studying
French in Paris he settled in Flintshire to live the life of a cul-
tured country gentleman and magistrate and to maintain a close
connection with Lancashire cricket.

James MacLaren was hon. treasurer from 1881 to 1899, following E. Challender in the office, and the period was one of
unsurpassed prosperity. It was during these years that the
greatest improvements were carried out or planned and the
negotiations for the purchase of Old Trafford brought to a
conclusion. He and Swire differed over the purchase of the
ground, the secretary considering the price too high, but the
alliance of MacLaren and A. N. Hornby carried the committee.
William Howard and other members of the staff extracted
some enjoyment from watching the manœuvres of the principal
executives to avoid each other during the busy time as the deal
was carried through, for if one was expected at the office, the
other would stay away. Quick-tempered and unable to tolerate
interruptions when at work, MacLaren was at the same time
generous and kindly. He gained greater fame outside the
county as the father of a great cricketer and as president of the
English Rugby Union.

Chairman of the committee at an early date was T. T.
Bellhouse, and a close associate of his and the secretary's was
A. H. Wolff, vice-president of Manchester club from 1876 for
three years. Recently there fell from an old minute-book, perhaps not disturbed since the hand of S. H. Swire placed it there,
a faded note echoing something of the '70s: 'Dear Sam,—I am

sorry I shall not be able to attend the meeting ... If I can manage to get back in time for a rubber, will do so'.

Joseph Makinson was a great cricketer who was also a first-class administrator. Educated at Huddersfield College and Owen's College, he won the 1856 University match for Cambridge by sterling all-round play. He took eight wickets and then in the second innings, when Cambridge were set 123 to win, he hit 64, the next best score being 16, and his team got home by three wickets. He hit a century against Jackson and Willsher of the All-England touring side at Broughton in 1860 and repeated the feat against the United South of England on the same ground seventeen years later. He was associated with Lancashire from the beginning, took part in the first county game at Old Trafford, and played on and off till 1874, meantime maintaining his connection with Broughton too. A fast bowler and a splendid batsman of the forward type who earned praise from Richard Daft and W. G. Grace, he became chairman of the Lancashire committee, a post for which his legal experience (he was Stipendiary Magistrate at Salford) eminently fitted him. Another figure of the early days was Sir Joseph Leese who became M.P. for Accrington, and Stipendiary of Manchester. He and Joseph Makinson died within a few weeks of each other in 1915.

Another member of the committee who has a sure place in this history is Mr. A. G. Hulton, one of the large contingent of Old Rossalians who have played for the county. We recall him here because it was he who at the annual meeting in January 1880 proposed that the Manchester and Lancashire clubs be amalgamated. At this meeting the accounts of the two clubs were presented jointly for the first time, and though at a subsequent meeting of county members some slight opposition to the fusion was voiced, a general meeting two months later confirmed the union.

CHAPTER 9

Championship Matches

1900–7 Captain: A. C. MacLaren

*The Golden Age of cricket; Briggs back in the team; Mold no-
balled; Briggs breaks down again; Johnny Tyldesley's great
year, 1901; South Africa beaten; MacLaren resigns; then
changes his mind; S. F. Barnes plays for two seasons;
Walter Brearley arrives; The championship
triumph of 1904; Kermode's influence; Two
huge totals, 1905; Brearley—17 wickets in
a match; A great duel with G. L.
Jessop; Trouble with the crowd at
Lord's; Dean's first 100 wickets*

IT MUST EVER be Lancashire's proudest boast that during
cricket's most brilliant period, nothing surpassed the dashing
batsmanship of MacLaren's team. The promise of 1899 was
now abundantly fulfilled in summers of achievement that are
part of cricket's richest history; and while for season after
season dazzling stroke play and rapid scoring entertained the
crowds, style went hand in hand with efficiency. During the
eight years now to be reviewed the side won the championship
once, twice finished second, once third, and twice fourth.
These were eight exciting years, tinged with drama on the
field and in the committee-room.

As the twentieth century dawned, cricket basked in its
Golden Age; and when, twenty years later, the game's already
splendid literature was ennobled by the appearance of its
greatest writer, it was Lancashire cricket played at Old Trafford
which provided the splendid spur to inspiration and it was to
the age of MacLaren, Tyldesley, and Spooner that Neville
Cardus turned again and again for his finest expression:

'A. C. MacLaren ... lighted a fire in me never to be put
out. He had an aristocratic face; he walked the grass as

87

though he lorded it; when he was setting his field he waved
the players here and there with far-reaching gestures...
As I watched him my young eyes saw him robed in glory.'

Those, indeed, were the days. When R. H. Spooner, back
from the wars, joined the team, the order often began with
MacLaren, Spooner and Tyldesley. Yorkshire had their great
all-rounders, Hirst with his spendthrift energy, and Rhodes
with his tight-lipped assessment of every situation. Sussex had
Ranjitsinhji and Fry. There were others too, yet amid all this,
nothing bettered the superb method of the three first batsmen in
the Lancashire team; even now it evokes the highest praise
from those who recall it, the most vivid dreams of those who
were born too late.

MacLaren was still a young man, not quite thirty, when he
took over the side again. He had already succeeded 'W. G.'
in the captaincy of the English Test match team, he had printed
his name boldly in the record books with his score of 424 at
Taunton, he had already hit his Test centuries at Melbourne,
Adelaide and Sydney, he had been through the testing fire of
'standing in' for A. N. Hornby. This was the man, so well
equipped, who now became captain in his own right.

1900 : CHAMPIONSHIP MATCHES :
Played 28, Won 15, Drawn 11, Lost 2

May 1900 arrived with everyone's hopes high at Old Trafford.
Briggs had recovered his health, and so had Hallam, and the
only disappointment was that Spooner had been sent to Ireland
with the Militia. Along with Briggs and Mold, there were
Sharp and Webb to make up the attack, so that even such a
good cricketer as Hallam could find a place in only four games.
Not surprisingly he decided to seek his fortune elsewhere and,
returning to the county of his birth, he gained greater fame
with Notts than he had done with Lancashire or Surrey. To
supplement the powers of the leading batsmen, C. R. Hartley
hit his first hundred and H. G. Garnett appeared on the scene,
and it is surely not the distance of time that lends enchantment
to these names. Here was something more than mere talent,
and Lancashire fought out the championship with Yorkshire,
every other county falling far behind.

Nine times out of ten Lancashire's record would have secured them the title, but this was their neighbourly rivals' year, for Yorkshire went through the season unbeaten. Up to the second meeting between the pair (played at Old Trafford as early as 19 July) the teams had identical records, but following this drawn game, Lancashire were defeated on their own ground by Gloucestershire (thanks to Jessop's batting and bowling) and later they were severely beaten at the Oval.

Among the individual performances may be mentioned Mold's 12 wickets for 46 runs at Hastings, Hartley's 109 in 110 minutes at Glossop, and MacLaren's 102 in 75 minutes at Southampton. Pride of place, however, was claimed by Briggs, who, in Worcester's first innings at Old Trafford, captured all ten wickets.

There was a curiosity at Leicester: during a light-hearted second innings every Lancashire man went on to bowl, just as every Sussex man had done a few days earlier on the same ground.

Albert Ward just topped the batting averages, playing rather more consistently than Tyldesley and MacLaren. Of the bowlers, Briggs and Cuttell took more than 100 wickets, Mold 97, Webb 72, and Sharp 53 at averages ranging from Mold's 14 to Sharp's 23, but their joint success was qualified by the disaster that overtook Mold. The fast bowler was no-balled for throwing by the Australian umpire Phillips, at Nottingham on 25 June, and after being 'called' he sent down only one more over during the game. He went on playing for the remaining months of the season, but his time was almost up; the county captains met, Sydney Pardon thundered in the pages of *Wisden's*, and Mold's days in county cricket were numbered.

1901: CHAMPIONSHIP MATCHES:
Played 28, Won 11, Drawn 12, Lost 5

Blows fell heavily on the county this season. Mold, no-balled again, did practically nothing in the second half of the year, Cuttell was disabled by a broken bone in the hand, and Briggs broke down again, his career coming to an end after his recovery in 1900 had given rise to high hopes for the future. To lose three such men, all bowlers and all Test match cricketers, would have crippled many teams, and it speaks volumes for the spirit of the team and the strength of the batting that a final position of third place in the championship was attained.

Big scores by opposing sides were answered by brilliant Lancashire batting and the remaining bowlers laboured to make good the losses. Sharp and Webb each took their 100 wickets, the former making the most of the bad wickets at Old Trafford and often making the ball fly about with his great pace.

During the close season some dressing had been applied without being properly sieved and small stones were consequently rolled into the turf. MacLaren is said to have bounced into the committee-room and flung a handful of pebbles on to the table: may one hazard a guess that this was directly after Hirst had skittled the side for 44? It took a period of wet weather and much hard work to put the pitch to rights.

Johnny Tyldesley asserted himself as never before, scoring 2,605 in championship matches and 3,041 in all games. He played one of his finest innings for the Players at Lord's where the professionals fielded this team: Abel, Carpenter, Tyldesley, Hayward, Braund, Storer, Lockwood, Hirst, Gunn (J.), Trott, and Rhodes, an eleven good enough to represent England against Australia. P. F. Warner was making his first appearance for the Gentlemen and of Tyldesley's 140 he wrote: 'Tyldesley played superbly, his play on the off side and his hooking of any short ball approaching perfection.'

With H. G. Garnett jumping to the front rank in his own dashing way, Lancashire now had three left-handers; Hallows was an established all-rounder, and there was a useful new man in Hibbert.

An association of Tyldesley and Garnett produced one of the brightest bits of batting this season when the team embarked on the task of scoring 307 in four hours against Sussex. They went for the runs and the second pair put on 148 in eighty minutes; the bid for victory failed, but failed gloriously, maintaining the tone of a match that had already yielded Garnett 110 in the first innings, and Ranji 69 and 170 not out. Lancashire had not seen the last of Ranji; they met him again five weeks later at Hove: Sussex, sent in to bat, made 457 for seven. Ranji was dropped when six, Killick ought to have been run out before he scored, and they rubbed in the mistakes by scoring 204 and 119 respectively.

Broughton made 99 on his first appearance for the county in Harry Carpenter's benefit match at Leyton, Sharp took 13 wickets at Worcester, and Tyldesley took tremendous toll of the Notts bowling with 13 and 221 at Trent Bridge and then 161 and 46 not out at Old Trafford where the side fought an honourable draw from an apparently hopeless position.

Incidents crowded thick and fast: South Africa made their first appearance in Manchester and were beaten. A. E. Lawton, afterwards prominent in the sporting world of Manchester, won the toss for Derbyshire and putting Lancashire in to bat at Derby, rued the day when his team were beaten by an innings and 184 runs. At the Oval, MacLaren and Garnett scored 116 in 56 minutes for the first wicket, though the cheers changed to jeers when the captain, with no chance of a finish, preferred to let his batsmen practice rather than tire his bowlers. This was not the only occasion during the season when his judgment was queried, for he placed his side in jeopardy in the home game with Derbyshire by an eccentric declaration. Doubtless there was criticism again when he brought in S. F. Barnes to play in the last fixture of the summer and then, on the evidence of six wickets for 70 runs, took him to Australia. But this time MacLaren was right!

Mold bowled for Lancashire for the last time at Lord's in a match ornamented by the beautiful batting of Garnett and Warner, and made curious by the failure of Middlesex to include a regular wicket-keeper, so that Lancashire were given 74 byes.

At the close of the season MacLaren, about to sail for Australia with his team, announced his intention of going to live in the south (for the benefit of his wife's health) and of playing for Hampshire. Alexander Eccles, an occasional member of the side after scoring a fine century in the University match of 1899, was offered the captaincy and he was prepared to take on the position. The manner of the announcement of MacLaren's decision—a letter to the Press by the county secretary— and its curious timing led to a good deal of pointed comment, but all ended well. As soon as he returned from Australia, without the Ashes but with Barnes's reputation made, MacLaren changed his mind—a form of somersault that came easily to him.

1902: CHAMPIONSHIP MATCHES:
Played 24, Won 7, Drawn 11, Lost 5, Abandoned 1

The year opened sadly with the death on 11 January of beloved Johnny Briggs, not forty years of age but with a career of more than twenty years during which he had attracted admiration for his skill, affection for his jovial pugnacity. So Lancashire had lost both Mold and Briggs, the two great professionals who had sustained the attack for so long, and without them MacLaren's hopes centred on Barnes. It is history that these hopes were not fulfilled; he had his great days during the two seasons he played for the county but both he and Sidney Webb were criticised from the same viewpoint: that they lacked the power to produce their best form when things were running against them. Eighty-two wickets for Lancashire in his first full season, at an average of 21 runs each, was certainly something below Barnes's potential worth.

Since Barnes's reputation depends on the unique combination of feats for England and phenomenal averages in league cricket, and not on year-by-year work in the county championship, his place in Lancashire's history is a modest one and his brief connection with Old Trafford can be dealt with at once. After his first disappointing year he showed an improved record in 1903 with 131 wickets in championship matches at 17 runs each; then he sought a long-term financial guarantee and as club and player could not come to terms, they parted company. By common consent there has never been a finer bowler on all types of wickets and when, in the '30s, Barnes returned to Old Trafford to undertake a coaching engagement, he showed that it was possible for a genius to defy sixty years and to bowl with a superb high action that produced a remarkable 'bounce' from the pitch. Lancashire were unable to keep him in the game as a player, but it was during the two seasons 1902-3 that he developed his famous leg-break; it is his own statement that he first really exploited it on a soft wicket at Derby when Webb failed to take advantage of the conditions.

We have gone ahead a little. The disappointing form of 1902 did not bring the compensation of finished games, one being given up without a ball being bowled and as many as eleven of the remaining twenty-three being left drawn. There were some new faces in the side, and among the four players who shared the wicket-keeping was W. Findlay, later to become secretary of Surrey and then of M.C.C., a wise administrator, president of Lancashire and finally, as the crown to his career, president of M.C.C.

There was a glimpse of Kermode, qualifying, in the match

against the Australians at Liverpool, where he marked his début with seven wickets. And there was a new fast bowler who turned out at Brighton, by name Walter Brearley, whose modest start gave no hint at all of the brilliance that was to carry him to immortality among cricketers.

Still, there were the bright days. At Trent Bridge MacLaren and E. E. Steel hit up 180 together in a couple of hours, and Steel had another good match against Worcester with eight wickets for 32 runs. Best of all was a swashbuckling performance at Tonbridge where victory was secured in about six hours' actual cricket. Kent made 84 and then on the last day, with only two hours left, MacLaren declared at 146 for nine. Hallows and Cuttell answered the call, putting Kent out for 54 in 90 minutes. They bowled unchanged through the two innings, Hallows having 13 wickets for 71 runs, Cuttell seven for 50.

Lancashire saw two of the great old players at Lord's, 'W. G.' and Murdoch making 120 together, and this match is remembered for another reason, a transgression of the rules. Barnes broke down after bowling a few overs, and his substitute, Boughton, was later permitted to bat.

The wet summer did not allow Tyldesley to score so well as in 1901, but he again topped the county averages and in the table for the whole of England he was beaten only by Shrewsbury, Ranji, Abel, and Quaife.

1903 : CHAMPIONSHIP MATCHES :
Played 26, Won 10, Drawn 11, Lost 5

This year brought another wet summer, said to be the worst up to this point since the championship had been inaugurated, so in gaining three more victories from a slightly longer programme, and sustaining only the same number of defeats as in 1902, Lancashire showed some improvement. But they did not touch the form of their best years and they were again fourth in the table. On figures, indeed, the team looked rather stronger. There was the improvement in the record of Barnes, MacLaren had a better season, Brearley played in fifteen games, and Spooner was regularly available. There was a new wicket-keeper in Worsley, beginning an association with the club and with MacLaren and Brearley that led to a good deal of humour on and off the field.

Brearley's early-season form was excellent, but as the weather broke, so he fell off; not yet was he the man who became so eager to bowl at both ends, all day, in any weather. Still, the promise was plain and even so early in his career he was given a place in the Gentlemen's eleven at Lord's, where he did fairly well, though everything else in the match was overshadowed by the famous partnership of MacLaren and Fry who, on a pitch that was never perfect, hit up 309 in under three hours.

With Spooner's four-figure aggregate, Brearley's bowling, and the appearance of Worsley, there were hints of good things to come, and another lay in the promise of L. O. S. Poidevin who, while qualifying, produced good form against London County.

Though Barnes and Brearley shared all the twenty Surrey wickets at Old Trafford, and Cuttell had 12 for 73 against Leicester, and despite the wretched weather, it was the batsmen who wrote their names in the books in the boldest style. There was Tyldesley's 248 against Worcester at Liverpool, scored in less than four hours; there was Spooner's chanceless 247 at Trent Bridge, with almost every ball struck firmly in the middle of the bat; and there was on the other side of the score-book an innings of 168 by Jessop that made light of opposition provided by Barnes, Brearley, and Cuttell. Finally, there was the first-wicket partnership of 368 by MacLaren and Spooner against Gloucester at Liverpool. The reports say that neither batsman was quite at his best, but imagination boggles at the thought of these two supreme stylists surviving to make the highest stand ever recorded by a Lancashire opening pair.

The year ended sadly with the death of two of the old stalwarts. Crossland died in September, and Nash in November.

1904: CHAMPIONSHIP MATCHES:
Played 26, Won 16, Drawn 10, Lost 0

When the season of 1904 opened, the captain and the Lancashire committee may well have wondered what they were going to do about the bowling. Since MacLaren had taken over he had lost Mold and Briggs, he had seen Barnes come and go, and Hallam had departed for Nottingham. Sharp had done very little in 1903, Webb and Littlewood would never be great cricketers. Yet suddenly the team found a match-winning quality that carried them through the season with a record so far in advance of any of their rivals that the championship struggle soon ceased to be a struggle and became a runaway triumph. Lancashire were not only unbeaten, their sixteen victories were six more than won by Kent, who finished third, and seven more than Yorkshire, who were second.

How did such brilliant success emerge from such misgivings as must have been felt before the season started? The averages tell part of the story. Tyldesley once again a heavy scorer after the slight set-back in 1903; Spooner, after a modest season on his first return, now a great batsman judged by any standard, blending his remarkable style with run-getting efficiency; Hallows, the true all-rounder, completing the double event; Cuttell back to his best in an astonishing revival that brought him 100 wickets as compared with 70 the previous summer and 37 in 1902; Brearley showing increased staying power and a better average; almost everyone scoring runs in a summer that brought much fine weather and many fast pitches; and above all the reinforcement of a fresh cricketer, coming into the team with all the eager enthusiasm of a man whose energy has been bottled up and who is just waiting for a game and an opportunity.

Qualified by residence, Kermode joined the side in June and in a season of hard wickets, the acquisition of a pace bowler was just sufficient to give the final razor-edge to the attack. Sixty-five wickets for 23 runs each is not an impressive record judged by itself but he came into the team just when the weather was coming to its hottest. Poidevin, too, was able to play and he scored more than 800 runs. The finishing touches were added by MacLaren's captaincy and the all-round fielding ability of the team in which Spooner stood out at cover-point.

It was Spooner who gave the season a significant send-off at Leicester, sharing with Garnett in a stand of 137 in 80 minutes; then I'Anson took part in a flurry of hitting that raised the score by 113 in under an hour, and Cuttell's bowling completed the job so well begun. An innings victory gave Lancashire a convincing start to the new season.

Brearley's 12 wickets for 144 runs marked the side's first game at Old Trafford, Warwickshire going down by nine wickets when Spooner and Tyldesley hit off the last 80 runs in three-quarters of an hour, the professional being the dominant partner on this occasion. A draw against Yorkshire was followed by another innings win, this over Kent who were put out for 42 in the second innings by Hallows and Cuttell, the latter coming out with a match record of nine for 34. Surrey were the next victims, dismissed for 82 and 56 to provide Cuttell (ten for 51) and Hallows (nine for 71) with another triumph.

The side went on tour, beginning at Bath where Somerset were beaten by ten wickets. Brearley sent down more than 60 overs and, if expensive, took ten wickets; the batting was sustained by Tyldesley, at his very best in making 210 in three hours and a quarter. On to Gloucester and another innings victory, helped in the early stages by Gloucestershire's wretched fielding (they dropped nine catches) and devastatingly finished off by Hallows's nine wickets for 37 runs. Next stop Birmingham, and at last the bowlers were checked by a total of 426 that heralded a drawn game. Lancashire, indeed, followed on after rain, but Cuttell, 18 not out in the first innings, kept his pads on and went in again with Spooner to take part in a stand of 157 that saved the game with honour. Even in such a tight corner Cuttell made his 128 in three hours.

Back at Old Trafford, Lancashire had all the better of the early stages of the fixture with Sussex and on the Saturday the crowd saw a wonderful display of batting by MacLaren and Spooner. Here was the cream of cricket, 200 going up inside a couple of hours; but the winning position could not be maintained, Brearley going lame, and a century by Fry saved the game for Sussex. Three centuries by the masters in one day ... and then at the finish half a hundred by Ranji: could sport offer anything better?

Going south, MacLaren's men won two more games. The toss helped at Tonbridge, and when the wicket went towards the finish Lancashire had just the man for the occasion in Tyldesley, who hit bravely for 82. At the Oval it was a rather closer finish, Surrey making a bold bid to get 337 in the fourth innings. Tom Hayward was well set when rain and sunshine alternated to the bowlers' benefit and Huddleston (seven for 72) and Hallows seized their chance, getting Lancashire home by 70 runs.

When Kermode joined the side, the double was completed over Somerset. He took five wickets on the first day, and then came MacLaren and Tyldesley with a century each and a partnership of 187 in 105 minutes to be followed by hundreds from

Sharp and Cuttell and a total of 580. At Trent Bridge it was MacLaren and Tyldesley again; after Notts had made 447 (Iremonger 197) the great pair scored 324 together and a total of 586 was reached in spite of A. O. Jones's tactics when he placed all his field on the leg side and bowled wide of the stumps.

This game finished on 2 July, drawn of course, and now came the sequence of victories that fairly settled the championship. By the time the game with Yorkshire at Leeds fell due, six consecutive victories had been recorded, two in a single innings, three by ten, nine, and eight wickets, and the sixth by 192 runs.

Tyldesley's 196 and Kermode's nine wickets were the match-winning factors at Worcester, and then two days sufficed for the game at Derby where the fast bowlers Brearley and Kermode shared fifteen wickets. Here again the speed of scoring in the early stages made the road easy, 172 runs coming in the first two hours. Next Middlesex were overthrown at Old Trafford where Kermode, whom most of the batsmen were meeting for the first time, broke the back of the batting before lunch. Tyldesley hit 102 in two hours, Hallows made a century that was slower but equally valuable, and then Kermode made his total of wickets twelve so that Lancashire's second innings task was to score only 103, accomplished for the loss of two wickets.

Then Essex were beaten and again dashing batsmanship opened the door for the bowlers: Spooner and Tyldesley made 166 in 100 minutes, and Sharp and Hornby added 177 at the same rate. The remainder of the match belonged to Brearley; the pitch was fiery, he was in the mood to bowl at both ends if permitted, and 14 wickets fell to him for 151 runs.

Rain interrupted the fixture with Gloucestershire at Liverpool but Lancashire would not be denied. They made 222 for five wickets in three hours on the first day, increased this to 346 and then bowled out their rivals twice with Hallows taking 12 wickets for 90 runs. Later in the week he followed up this splendid piece of work with 11 wickets for 144 runs at Old Trafford where Worcestershire were crushed . . . though Spooner bagged a pair.

That made fifteen wins in nineteen games and we need not wonder that the pace was too hot to last. Hallows was feeling the strain, and there was a check in Hirst's benefit match though Lancashire showed one of the essential qualities of champions by wriggling out of a tight corner. Some of the

G

men were very tired, and they were rested in the game against South Africa; a young man named James Heap was given a chance, gleefully taken with five wickets captured and so earning an extended trial later in the season.

Sussex at Brighton avoided defeat, owing everything to Ranji who made 99 and 207 not out with all the facility of his own peculiar genius, and then the team moved on to Leyton. The first day was limited to less than two hours by rain, yet Lancashire made 163 for two wickets. Next day Spooner went on to 215, giving one of his best exhibitions of driving and taking part with Hallows in a partnership of 296 in under three hours. Here however the pitch was master of all, Lancashire's 505 for six drawing 559 for nine in reply, Spooner's lobs yielding 110 runs in 19 overs.

For a time the winning touch quite eluded the side and at Lord's they were fortunate to escape defeat. Albert Trott's bowling was too much for them and they had to follow on, but rain on the third day let them off. Another draw at Old Trafford, this time against Notts, saw the side in trouble before a patient century by Poidevin saved the situation. The Leicestershire fixture at Liverpool was ruined by the weather but happily the champions were able to finish their county games with a flourish on their headquarters ground, beating Derbyshire in a game marked by splendid fielding, good batting by Spooner and Tyldesley, and effective all-round work by Hallows.

The summer's cricket ended with a game against the Rest of England at the Oval, drawn though four days had been allocated. Jessop and MacLaren batted with superb dash, and there was an all-too-brief association of Spooner and Tyldesley.

Looking back one may surely learn a lesson for all seasons, the value of runs quickly scored on the first day, in preference to a scramble and possibly a false declaration on the third day. In match after match Lancashire had seized the initiative at once because, as we have seen in this journey up and down England in the company of this brilliant band of cricketers, they scored at eighty, ninety, or even a hundred runs an hour.

Unfortunately the year ended with a minor domestic squabble. Brearley was left out of the team for the big match Champions v the Rest and he promptly announced his retirement. However, the breach was healed, and when cricket was next played at Old Trafford in the following summer, Brearley was there bowling with all his old energy, optimism, and skill.

1905: CHAMPIONSHIP MATCHES:
Played 26, Won 12, Drawn 10, Lost 3, Abandoned 1

Lancashire were not able to hold on to the title in 1905 but they made a good fight for it and they finished second, close up to Yorkshire. This was an Australian season and the Test matches played a big part in the fortunes of the two principal counties because in June, Yorkshire were hard hit by the loss of their best players and were beaten by Derbyshire, and then in August, Lancashire went down to Gloucestershire when their own eleven was similarly weakened by the absence of Mac-Laren, Spooner, Brearley, and Tyldesley, and at a time when a draw would have enabled them to tie with the champions.

For the first two months of the season Lancashire played up to their 1904 reputation, winning game after game with only a brief check from the Australians. However, to the discerning eye there must have been ominous signs, and the one big difference was that while in the previous year everyone had done something, this time almost all the effective bowling was being done by two men, Brearley and Kermode. Cuttell's decline was so marked that he lost his place, Hallows fell off too, and Poidevin's adoption of the new-fangled googly did not solve the problem. Still, if the finish was a trifle disappointing, their cricket was most attractive; they remained the best batting side in the country with nine of their regular players averaging over twenty runs an innings—Poidevin, maker of five centuries, at the top.

Twice the 600 mark was passed. At Trent Bridge the total was 627 with every Nottingham man bowling, Spooner reaching his century before lunch, and Tyldesley hitting 250 in under six hours and giving nothing like a chance. Three weeks later at Brighton the score was 601 for eight wickets, Hallows going in to flog tired bowling for 130 runs in 110 minutes. And there was fast scoring too, on a slightly reduced scale at Taunton, where it took the team only 225 minutes to run up 401 runs.

Even as the season wore on, and the bowling was stretched to its limits, and the whole side becoming perhaps a little jaded, the scoring was phenomenally fast. At Canterbury, in Fred Huish's benefit, C. H. B. Marsham sent Lancashire in to bat on a pitch soaked by the previous day's rain: at the close of play the score was 467 for seven wickets! Brearley and Kermode finished off the match, which was a financial success for Huish.

Brearley's great day was against Somerset at Old Trafford, when he took nine wickets for 47 runs before lunch. This must have been one of the most startling first days in the history of county cricket because Somerset were dismissed for 65 and when stumps were drawn Lancashire were 424 for eight. Brearley went on to join the select company of bowlers who have taken four wickets in four balls and seventeen wickets in a match, though even here the batsmen would not allow the bowlers to snatch all the glory. In the last 40 minutes of the opening day 139 runs were hammered on the anvil of the Somerset bowling, A. H. Hornby making 93 of them. In completing his century next day he carried his partnership with Findlay for the ninth wicket to 113 in half an hour.

It was Lancashire's turn to field out to some hard hitting when Gloucester came north, and this was one of the matches that are still talked about whenever someone says 'those were the days'. There was banter about Brearley's batting, and a joke misfired. Tempers which had begun the game so serenely became ruffled; and in the second innings, when Jessop and Board launched a savage attack on the bowling, the cricket became rough and tough. Gloucester had been hopelessly outplayed, and three wickets were down for 47, so that they had nothing to lose and everything to gain. The hitting was magnificent, and Brearley set about quelling it; his method was to bowl full tosses, some of them head high, and the two great cricketers stood opposed much as Larwood and Bradman did twenty-seven years later. While it lasted, the battle was white-hot. In four overs, 57 runs were plundered, and Jessop and Board put on 98 in 40 minutes. Brearley got them both out and Lancashire won, but controversy raged for some weeks.

Jessop himself criticised his rival in print, and is said to have threatened never to appear at Old Trafford again; but the sores soon healed . . . or was there some slight infection left and was this the origin of body-line bowling? The match was Billy Cook's first, and in taking eleven wickets he made a wonderful début; but perhaps he went home to Preston wondering was this really first-class cricket!

Poidevin's bowling was not often successful, though he pulled out one magnificent all-round performance at Worcester when he took eight wickets in an innings and scored 76 run out and 168 not out. His fellow-Australian Kermode had ten wickets in the game at Leicester.

An extra fixture against an England XI at Blackpool had an exciting climax, time being called when the county, with three wickets to go down, wanted one run to win. Cook was caught in the long field trying to obtain the winning run, but under the rules then in force there was no time for another batsman to go in.

1906: CHAMPIONSHIP MATCHES:
Played 26, Won 15, Drawn 5, Lost 6

The Lancashire team was gravely weakened in 1906 by the fact that Brearley, by now the best fast bowler in the country, could play in only five matches. MacLaren, too, was often away. On the credit side, the fielding was first-class right through the summer and Willis Cuttell, in his last season, played in something like his old form. All the batting averages were lower, but the old facility of scoring fast remained; for instance, when Tyldesley hit 295 against Kent (the eventual champions) at Old Trafford, the team scored their 531 at the rate of a hundred an hour.

This game marked the first appearance of Frank Woolley. He missed a couple of catches, and a duck and bowling figures of 1—103 made his début, up to a point, a sorry occasion; but he hit away beautifully on the last day to foreshadow all that was to come during the next quarter of a century.

Even a drawn match at Birmingham was enlivened by Tyldesley's 102 in 80 minutes, and Spooner and Heap made 114 in an hour for the first wicket at Worcester. All was overshadowed, though, by a wonderful innings from Spooner who came to a hard wicket at Bath after a succession of soft pitches. He hit a century before lunch and went on to make 240 in 260 minutes.

Besides Cuttell's good form, there were other compensating features of this season, just as there had been in the promise of 1899. So long kept in the background, Huddleston appeared in nine matches and proved his worth on anything like a helpful pitch, Harry Dean came into the side for the first time and showed much promise with his left-arm swervers, and Frank Harry looked worth another trial. Even more startling was the appearance of W. R. Gregson, a fast bowler who in his second match against Leicester at Blackpool, took nine wickets and achieved a hat-trick by dismissing V. F. S. Crawford, R. T. Crawford, and C. E. de Trafford.

Other good things this season were a capital win at the Oval due to Sharp's bowling and one of Spooner's most charming innings, and a sixty-runs win over Notts at Old Trafford in a game that was all over in six hours of actual cricket. Tom Wass had 16 wickets for 69 runs, and Huddleston 13 for 41. Kermode had 13 wickets at Derby, Harry 15 against Warwick at Old Trafford, Cuttell ten against Sussex. There was, too, Worcester's first-ever win over Lancashire and they were to prove quite a nuisance during the succeeding seven or eight years. This first victory was achieved in spite of another of Spooner's great innings, a century on a rain-affected pitch.

James Heap was tried as an opening batsman, and high up in the batting order came another new name; it was that of Harry Makepeace, commencing an association with the club that was to extend over forty-five years.

1907: CHAMPIONSHIP MATCHES:
Played 26, Won 11, Drawn 7, Lost 7
(One abandoned on the second day)

And so we come to 1907, the last season of MacLaren's captaincy, a summer of variable form so that the side fell to sixth place in the table. Brearley still could not play, Spooner turned out in only five games. Cuttell had gone to Rugby School, and Findlay left to become secretary of Surrey. The loss of Brearley was emphasised when he turned out for the Gentlemen and took ten of the Players' wickets.

This was a season, too, of close finishes, though the real sensation came from a match that was not played out. When Lancashire went to Lord's, heavy rain limited play on the first day when Lancashire scored 57 for one wicket. There was no cricket at all on the second day and when play was given up after the umpires' final inspection, a handful of spectators decided to look at the pitch for themselves. Following a general discussion between captains, players, and umpires, MacLaren handed the following statement to the Press:

'Owing to the pitch having been deliberately torn up by the public, I, as captain of the Lancashire Eleven, cannot see my way to continue the game, the groundsman bearing me out that the wicket could not be again put right.—A. C. MacLaren.'

Needless to say, arguments raged furiously, and the Middlesex president, Mr. R. D. Walker, brother of the V. E. we met in 1865, addressed an indignant letter to the Press. It was stated that when the pitch was rolled the following morning, for the regulation ten minutes, the damage was largely obliterated and amounted, in fact, to one rather deep heel mark.

Several close finishes showed that Lancashire's team, whatever their technical limitations, could fight to the end, for though they lost to Essex by four wickets, they beat Kent by six runs, Somerset by two wickets, Northants by 36 runs, and then right at the end of the season in successive games, they overcame Derby by one wicket and Leicester by two wickets.

Dean took more than 100 wickets for the first time, even if he was still a natural bowler without much resource when the ball would turn, and both Harry and Huddleston worked hard. Lawrence Cook, brother of Billy Cook, appeared on the scene, and soon he would be known as 'Lol' and a great favourite with the crowds. The whole side, indeed, strove manfully to falsify the gloomy forecasts made when the season opened, and it was not always the much-maligned bowling that let the side down. There were four successive innings against Middlesex at Old Trafford and Notts at Liverpool that failed to reach a hundred, J. T. Hearne doing the damage for Middlesex and Wass and Hallam for Notts. In the second of these matches Sharp bagged a pair and the second innings came only to 37. Amid the crash of wickets there was one curiosity, MacLaren being twice run out at Liverpool, and again in his next innings against Derby.

Yet the batsmen were capable of almost anything on their day. Tyldesley was wonderful on bad wickets, Sharp was constantly chipping in with useful scores, and at Chesterfield on a difficult pitch, MacLaren and Hornby indulged in a brilliant first-wicket partnership of 162 in 105 minutes. It was here that Dean recorded an outstanding bowling performance with nine wickets for 46 runs.

The last fixture of the season was against Leicester at Blackpool, and when Dean and Harry knocked off the last 21 runs, it was the end of MacLaren's captaincy. He would play again, he would captain England again—but this match at Blackpool must be the end of a cricket chapter. For us, it is the time for another retrospect.

CHAPTER 10

A. C. MacLaren, Johnny Briggs and Arthur Mold

*MacLaren's noble style; From Alec Watson to W. W. Arm-
strong; A double century at fifty-two; Briggs the
all-rounder; Great bowling in Test matches;
Mold and the campaign against throwing; Frank Sugg, Albert Ward,
S. M. Crosfield, Willis
Cuttell, James
Hallows,
etc.*

IN CHAPTER 5 we discussed some of the earliest of the great Lancashire players. We now come to consideration of another
batch of splendid cricketers—and the first to be named must be
Archibald Campbell MacLaren, captain of Harrow, Lancashire, the Gentlemen, and England, and maker of the largest
individual score ever hit in this country.

MacLaren is one of the game's immortal figures, an aristo-
crat among cricketers as much for his imperious captaincy, his
swooping slip catches, his delight in cricket conversation, his
feats at home and abroad, as for noble batting based on an
admirable combination of the classic forward style (with its
accent on the drive) and a modern method with vivid hooking
and pulling.

MacLaren was a Manchester man by birth. He went to
Elstree, where Vernon Royle coached him, and on to Harrow
where he distinguished himself by scoring 55 and 67 against
Eton when only fifteen years of age. In his fourth year (1890)
he won even higher praise, scoring 76 of a total of 133 when
only one other boy reached double figures.

His father was already a leading official of the Lancashire
county club, so that there was no danger of the brilliant

youngster's being overlooked; a month after his splendid performance for Harrow he appeared in the county team and hit a century at once, taking less than two hours and a quarter about it. From then until 1907 he was a great Lancashire and England cricketer, held in such esteem that two years after he had given up the county captaincy he was recalled to lead the Test match eleven. For England against Australia he scored 1,931 runs, hit five centuries, and established a special reputation for his mastery at Sydney.

He began to play with Lancashire when Alec Watson and Richard Barlow were still in the side; thirty-one years later when Armstrong's 1921 Australians were carrying all before them, he repeatedly proclaimed his belief that he could raise a side to beat them, and he did it at Eastbourne. Even then the final flourish had not been applied; that came when at the age of fifty-two he took an official M.C.C. team to New Zealand and hit a double century in a match then described as a Test but since robbed of that status. Has any other veteran batsman ever played such an innings, provoking other members of the touring side to exclaim that they did not know the game could be played with such style?

In 1896 he hit 424 in one innings; later in the season he made three consecutive centuries in eight days, and the county recognised the feats by election to life membership and the gift of a gold watch. He took the side through the grand seasons of 1900–7, and in one of them, 1904, they were unbeaten and indisputable champions.

His figures—22,000 runs, average 33—look modest by comparison with those of modern masters; he made those runs, however, on pitches of variable quality, and he played his best innings against the best bowling, as for instance his 728 runs, average 45, against the Players. Of batsmen who began playing in 1890 or earlier, only Grace, Shrewsbury, Abel and Hirst have finer records.

MacLaren has been described as an optimist in his private life, a pessimist in his cricket. His captaincy of England—he led the team in twenty-two Tests, a record—was often open to criticism, and he was probably a difficult man for the selectors to deal with; he himself thought a committee of one was the ideal arrangement, and after he had given up the game he wrote vigorously about the sins of omission and commission of various selection committees. Ambitious schemes were constantly in his mind; pneumatic pads, bats from Spanish willow (which proved too heavy), and so on; and if they disappointingly came to nothing—why, then, there was always the horse that was certain to put things right.

Off the field he was perhaps inclined to follow the whim of the moment; he was wrong to have given up the match at Lord's when the pitch was cut up by the crowd—but his instinct did not let him down when he chose Barnes for his Australian tour. On the field, he was cool, calculating, not easily flustered. MacLaren was born to be a commander in action, not a staff officer at base, and his coaching appointment at Old Trafford in 1921 was not a success.

His temperament made him impatient of regular hours and of anything approaching to routine, and when early in 1923 an injured knee caused his resignation, there could have been few regrets on either side. The passing of the years has not dimmed MacLaren's reputation as a cricketer, however; we honour him for his brilliant conception of batsmanship, effulgent even in the Golden Age. So long as there is an Old Trafford, so long will his name be revered.

So, too, will that of Johnny Briggs—the little man, the cricketer perennially young, the boy who so quickly found his way into the hearts of Manchester people and stayed there. He first played in 1879, and he must have shown remarkable promise because he held his place even when his batting and bowling figures were modest. Perhaps his fielding saved him; as a cover-point he has hardly been excelled with his buoyant movement, his artful stratagems, and his unflagging zeal through the hottest day.

His batting developed first, on aggressive lines with a special fondness for a slash in the direction of cover-point.

Then came his bowling, on the slow side of medium, and though it has been said that he became a great bowler almost overnight with his eleven wickets against Australia at Lord's in 1886, we have seen that it really developed as soon as the need arose through Crossland's disqualification. Like MacLaren, he became an international figure, yet above all he was a Lancastrian—not by birth, it is true, but by upbringing; his family moved from Nottingham when he was still a child and he spent the remainder of his life in the county.

Briggs played in a benefit match at Liverpool when he was only fourteen and Barlow, spotting his promise, recommended him to S. H. Swire. An engagement on the ground followed, Briggs went to live at Barlow's house, and the older man's judgment was abundantly justified. In due course they appeared together in the county side and for England, too, and after one great match at Lord's when Briggs bowled so well, Shrewsbury played a particularly fine innings of 164, and Barlow bowled steadily, the following appeared in a London newspaper:

'Thanks to you, we're dancing jigs,
Shrewsbury, Barlow, and Briggs.
Who'll call England's cricket star low,
Briggs, and Shrewsbury, and Barlow.
Here's your health, ye glorious three!
Barlow, Briggs, and Shrewsbury.'

There can be no two views about his class as a bowler. He had a simple, easy action, so that he could stand up to the longest day; he had plenty of spin; he had a good flight; and above all he had the genius for pitching the ball up to the bat, a gift that was exemplified in the great game against Yorkshire when, with everything turning on one hit, he lured Ulyett to destruction.

He took 97 wickets in Test Matches against Australia, and in two matches against South Africa in the winter of 1888, he first took six wickets for 73 runs and then, at Cape Town, fifteen wickets (fourteen of them bowled) for 28 runs. There has never been a match analysis like it in representative cricket, and probably there never will be. He is one of the three English bowlers to have performed the hat-trick against Australia, he hit a century against them, and he played a prominent part in the match which is still regarded as furnishing the most sensational victory in all cricket. It was at Sydney in 1894 when Australia, after causing England to follow on, had to go in again to score 177 to win. They began the last day with the score 113 for two, but on a sticky wicket Peel and Briggs bowled out the others so that England got home by ten runs.

In first-class cricket he took 2,200 wickets at just over 16 runs each, and of those who have taken a comparable total of wickets, only Alfred Shaw and Schofield Haigh have a better average. Add his 14,000 runs, and his fielding, and there is one of the most complete all-round cricketers who ever graced the field. He was, incidentally, a good rugby footballer, playing half-back for Widnes.

The comedian, they say, is never far from tragedy. It was one of life's ironies that Briggs, who loved being alive, who was full of quips and pranks, should be stricken by a mental breakdown. He recovered, played again, took all ten wickets in an innings, but soon afterwards there was another collapse, and he died at the early age of thirty-nine.

Arthur Mold was born near Banbury, just within the border of Northamptonshire, and he played a few times for his native county before making his name with Lancashire, having qualified by residence. He first played in 1889, making his mark almost at once with 13 wickets against Yorkshire, and by 1892 he was sufficiently to the fore to be selected as one of *Wisden's* 'Five Great Bowlers'.

We can have no doubt that he occasionally threw. Mr. Ernest Rowley recalls that now and again fieldsmen would look at one another and nod knowingly, as much as to say: 'Arthur threw that one', and Harry Makepeace related how, when taken to Aigburth as a boy, he exclaimed in wonder that Mold, with all his great pace, could bring the ball back from the off so devastatingly.

By the turn of the century, a campaign against throwing was in full swing and Mold was no-balled at Trent Bridge in 1900. During the following winter a meeting of county captains agreed on a list of bowlers who should not be employed, and another list of those to be warned, though Lancashire queried with the M.C.C. the authority of the captains to come to such a decision without reference to their county committees. Those to be barred were: C. B. Fry, Captain Hedley, Captain Bradford, Griffin, Mold, F. Davidson, Roche, W. G. Quaife, and Geeson. Those warned were H. G. Bull, W. Low, Tyler, Bland, and Lockwood.

In defiance of the ban, Lancashire included Mold in their side in 1901, and in July came the dramatic incidents of the game against Somerset at Old Trafford, described by William Howard:

'Several weeks before the date of the match I was informed of what was likely to happen ... I had almost dismissed the matter from my mind, never thinking that an umpire would take upon himself the action of no-balling a player who had been bowling in first-class cricket for so many years, including Test and Gentlemen v Players matches, with precisely the same delivery.... There were other umpires in the country quite as competent as he was, and who considered Mold a fair bowler....

'The first few minutes of the game were marked by the dead silence round the ground as the voice of the umpire rang out: "No ball"....

'As the no-balling continued the crowd resented Phillips's decisions by shouts and groans.'

Poor Mold took it pretty well, complaining chiefly that he should have been stopped at the beginning of his career since it took away the credit of his performances. He also stated that he could not throw a ball fifty yards if he tried. We must give him credit that throughout this match, which of course virtually closed his career, he kept his temper.

Leaving aside the question of his action, he was a great asset to Lancashire. He took 16 wickets against Kent at Old Trafford in 1895, three times 15 wickets in a match, and seven times (six with Briggs) he bowled unchanged through a match with one partner. He took four wickets in four balls against Notts in 1895, did a hat-trick against Somerset, twice took over 200 wickets in a season, and when he bowled Lohmann at the Oval in 1887 he sent a bail 63 yards. On anything like a helpful pitch he made the ball get up very sharply and this characteristic, combined with his great speed and break-back, made him a terror even to the greatest batsmen.

Something quite different in the way of cricket talent was contained in the strong frame of Frank Howe Sugg who played for the county after appearing in turn for Yorkshire, Durham, and Derbyshire all in the space of five years! A big man, he was apt to be rather rash, but on bad wickets his hitting was often of priceless value to his side, and he scored more than 10,000 runs for the county.

He was a remarkable all-round player of games; when he died in 1933, *Wisden's* recorded that he had played soccer for Sheffield Wednesday, Derby County, Burnley, and Bolton Wanderers, being captain of the first three teams; excelled as a long-distance swimmer and joined with Burgess and Heaton in swims; held the record for throwing the cricket ball; reached the final of the Liverpool amateur billiards championship; won prizes all over the country for rifle-shooting, bowls, and putting the shot; and was famed as a weight-lifter! It is not therefore surprising that he takes high rank among the country's best outfielders. He proved a fine accession of strength to the team as he came in just when Walter Robinson was finishing.

When we come to Albert Ward, we are dealing with a batsman of the front rank, a player distinguished not only in his county's records but in those of his country too, because some of his finest performances were accomplished against Australia. Here was another Yorkshireman who joined Lancashire when the county were building up their playing strength, and his aggregate of almost 15,000 runs, average over 30 runs an innings, shows how well the county chose their men. He possessed the ideal temperament for an opening batsman—'cool, patient and persevering' said *Wisden's*—and four years after crossing the Pennines, he achieved Test match recognition. In the winter of 1894–5 he went to Australia and in the last Test match, on which the rubber hinged, he and J. T. Brown took part in a great stand of 210 which virtually settled the issue.

Apart from his batting, he was a magnificent fieldsman in the deep, and now and again he was successful with his very slow bowling, sometimes turning the ball the wrong way before the term 'googly' was invented.

In 1899, Ward was the victim of a curious dismissal. Batting against Derbyshire at Old Trafford, he had his bat broken by a ball from Davidson; a piece of wood knocked off a bail, and he was out for 72—hit wicket.

During thirteen seasons in the Lancashire eleven, George Baker scored almost 7,000 runs and took 155 wickets. He hardly ranks among the giants of the county's list of cricketers, but he was a player who repeatedly chipped in with a useful performance and who was often the junior partner in a big partnership. A Yorkshireman, noted as a sprinter and rugby footballer, he was very popular, and his genial disposition as much as his all-round skill made him a great success as coach at Harrow, where he stayed for twelve years. Baker never achieved Test match status, though he was twice selected for the Players. His big year was in 1897 when he scored more than

1,200 runs and so played his full share in winning the championship.

S. M. Crosfield played for Cheshire as well as Lancashire. His record on paper is a modest one, but he gained a reputation for scoring runs when they were most wanted. He was coach at Old Trafford for three years.

Crosfield was the staunch friend and lieutenant of A. N. Hornby. He was a splendid captain himself, yet was content to serve as the second man to the little genius who stood at the head of affairs. A solicitor by profession, he was noted as a fine shot, frequently winning prizes in England and abroad. It was he who made the critical disputed catch in the Yorkshire match of 1893 when Yorkshire, needing only 57 to win, were put out for 51.

Willis Cuttell was a Yorkshireman, born at Sheffield, and like his father he played for the county of his birth. It was an engagement in league cricket that brought him to Lancashire and after qualifying by residence, he played for his adopted county from 1896 to 1906. On the slow side of medium, he turned the ball a little either way but it is as an all-rounder that Lancashire chiefly remembers him, because he was the first of their players to accomplish the cricketer's double. Besides Cuttell, only J. Hallows and Hopwood have taken 100 wickets and scored 1,000 runs in one season. As Cuttell was an excellent field, he was a very complete cricketer. He was coach at Rugby for twenty years and then, for two seasons, acted as a first-class umpire.

James Hallows was born near Bolton, within that small area which has given so many splendid cricketers to Lancashire. He was twenty-five before he had anything like a full season in first-class cricket and though he scored more than a thousand runs in 1901, he did not make any great impression. However, he had meantime changed his bowling style from fast to medium, and he deserves high rank among the county's men because his best work was done when it was most needed. As soon as Barnes went, and when the outlook was darkest, Hallows jumped to the forefront. He was left-handed at both batting and bowling, and he shared with John Tyldesley, Spooner, Cuttell, and Brearley the honours of 1904 when the team went through the summer unbeaten. His career was cut short by the ill-health that constantly afflicted him and he died

W. Findlay and Walter Brearley photographed together at Lord's during the annual coaching of schoolboys

J. T. Tyldesley

A. G. Steel

J. Briggs

S. F. Barnes

R. H. Spooner

when only thirty-four years of age. What the county lost may be best judged from his 1904 ranking in *Wisden's*—level with Hirst, Rhodes, and John Gunn.

Albert Hallam's best work was done for Notts; he also played for Leicestershire, held a position on the ground staff at the Oval, and was with Lancashire for six years. He had three good seasons and then returned to his native county, where his bowling, always marked by great accuracy of pitch, earned him wider fame than he had so far won in his rather curious career. His best summer at Old Trafford was in 1897 when he took 90 wickets.

Doctor L. O. S. Poidevin was an Australian who came to England to study medicine after already making a name with New South Wales and taking part in what was then the record score of 918, to which he contributed 140 not out. For a time he played for London County and then with Lancashire with varying success. His two good seasons were in 1904, when he scored 865 runs and helped the team to win the championship, and 1905 when, with 1,376 runs and an average of 44, he came out top of the averages above even such men as Tyldesley, Spooner, MacLaren, and Sharp. He was a good orthodox batsman, patient and watchful, and once or twice he bowled his googlies with effect. He returned to Sydney, where he died in 1931.

Another Australian of the same period was Alexander Kermode, a fast bowler brought back to Lancashire after MacLaren had seen him bowl for New South Wales. Curiously, he too met with most success in 1905, taking over a hundred wickets, but his form went off suddenly. A big man with a somewhat ungainly action, he figured in league cricket with some success.

Playing about the same period as Albert Ward was Arthur Paul, another tall batsman. Born in Belfast, the son of an Army colonel who became Chief Constable of the Isle of Man, Paul qualified while with Nelson as club professional. He is perhaps now best remembered for the service he put in at Old Trafford as coach, so that his fine batsmanship has rather been forgotten; but he was a player of great skill and when MacLaren hit his record 424 at Taunton, it was Paul (177) who stood with him in the outstanding partnership of the innings—363 for the second wicket.

H

Besides being a cricketer of first-class ability, Paul was a fine footballer. He appeared at full-back and threequarter for Swinton, and played in goal for Blackburn Rovers. In 1888 he went to Australia with a football team promoted by Shrewsbury and Shaw.

Two of Lancashire's good wicket-keepers after Pilling were Arthur Kemble, a member of the famous theatrical family, and the professional Charlie Smith. Together they formed a link spanning from 1885 to 1902; and they died within a few weeks of one another in 1925. Kemble, who stood up to Mold at his fastest, was also a rugby international. Smith was one of the several Yorkshiremen who first played for their native county and then crossed the hills to Lancashire. A plucky wicket-keeper who did not mind the hard knocks of the job, he occasionally made runs going in late.

Another Smith was Arthur, from Nottingham, a roving cricketer who went to Detroit and Brooklyn to coach, and was for a time professional at Oldham. He was a steady and patient batsman.

John I'Anson was a useful all-rounder—a medium-paced bowler and a steady bat. His career lasted from 1896 to 1908, and he was rather unfortunate in being overshadowed by so many great Lancashire players of that period. He has a place in cricket history for his splendid début: ten wickets (seven for 72 and three for 77) against the M.C.C. at Lord's.

It must in fairness be added that many of the cricketers who qualified by residence were not specially imported but arrived in the county either with their families or through taking club engagements. They are in a different category from the star performers who were admittedly attracted to Old Trafford with the idea of strengthening the side, such as Mold, Albert Ward, Frank Sugg, and Kermode.

CHAPTER 11

Championship Matches

1908–14 Captain: A. H. Hornby

*Brearley's great efforts; Ralph Whitehead's sensational début;
Alfred Hartley's success; Ernest Tyldesley appears; The advance of Makepeace; Two fourth-innings feats, 1910;
A. H. Hornby in at the death; First-innings points
awarded in the championship, 1911; A grievance
against southern counties; Victory over Hampshire by an innings and 455 runs; A wet
season safely negotiated; A disputed
catch in a close finish; Brearley
leaves the county; Parkin's 14
wickets in his first match*

In 1908 A. H. Hornby, already a familiar figure at Old Trafford, took over the captaincy. Though his first joys were those
of the hunting field, he could not help being a great cricketer,
bearing such a name, and he proved to be a fearless and tireless
fieldsman, a dashing batsman, and an energetic and able captain once his first rather impetuous manner had been softened
by contact with, and appreciation of, the senior professionals.
His period of captaincy did not bring the opportunity of a cele-
bration for a championship triumph, and for the seven seasons
the average position in the table worked out at about seventh
place, but the true picture was brighter than might be thought
from that overall record. Several new men of distinct promise
appeared, some of the men already in the side made advances,
and frequently the batting asserted itself in such a style that the
great days of MacLaren's time were recalled.

The weakness of the side was the lack of supporting bowlers.
Walter Brearley (for a time) and Dean did great things but
another bowler of Test-match calibre was badly needed; he
was not forthcoming until the dramatic appearance of Cecil

Parkin in 1914 and then the break in cricket due to the war meant that his genius could not fully flower until some years had passed.

1908: CHAMPIONSHIP MATCHES:
Played 26, Won 10, Drawn 6, Lost 9, Abandoned 1

There was much incident the first year of the new leader's captaincy, beginning with the welcome reappearance of Walter Brearley. The fast bowler did not allow the memory of past squabbles to affect his cricket; he flung himself into the game with unabated energy, and even if he was helped by some fiery pitches at Old Trafford, his record of 148 wickets in seventeen championship matches, at 15 runs each, restored him at once to a place among the leading bowlers of the day, and earned him a place among *Wisden's* 'Five Cricketers of the Year'.

With Dean taking 124 wickets, the two leading bowlers did their part splendidly, but after Huddleston (56 wickets) no one else did anything of note. The policy of including Huddleston only when a soft pitch was assured, limited his chances, and the degree to which this extraordinary plan was carried out can be assessed from an occurrence at Tunbridge Wells; the side travelled south without him, but once it was seen the pitch might help, he was telegraphed for in great haste. He arrived in time to take four first-innings wickets for 38 runs, bowling unchanged with Dean.

The return match against Kent produced another curiosity. In the first over Blomley was injured, and he was replaced by Phillips who was allowed to keep wicket, but neither this concession nor Brearley's 13 wickets saved Lancashire from a heavy defeat.

The two games with Nottinghamshire were even more interesting. The unbeaten champions of the previous season maintained their invincibility until the first week in June, when Lancashire overcame them at Trent Bridge with a day to spare. With the pitch soft on top but firm underneath, Brearley made the ball fly about and in the second innings Dean, I'Anson, and Harry joined in the work of destruction. In a low-scoring game, Hornby's brilliantly-hit 59 was the highest individual innings. The return game at the end of the month was also won, by three wickets, but it was not the exciting finish that caused most discussion: that centred on the experience,

unique in first-class cricket, of Ralph Whitehead. He was playing in his first big match, and on the first day he made 131 not
out, only to have his triumph dimmed when he was no-balled
for throwing.

Another exciting game was at Glossop where the end came
with Lancashire—attempting to score 66 in 75 minutes—two
runs short of victory and with only one wicket standing. A
dropped catch cost Derbyshire victory almost secured by the
superb bowling of Cadman and Warren.

The value of having a fast bowler to match one on the other
side was shown at Lord's; Brearley was away, and on the worn
pitch Mignon demoralised some of the Lancashire batsmen. In
the following week Brearley rejoined the side, which he captained in the absence of Hornby, and he celebrated to some purpose, taking 14 Essex wickets for 111 runs. He was in form
against Somerset too, taking five second-innings wickets for
14 runs and with Dean dismissing the side for 33 in 50 minutes
after the batsmen had made good a first-innings failure with a
score of 400 made at the rate of 100 an hour, Sharp, Tyldesley,
and MacLaren all hitting with wonderful certainty.

Tyldesley comfortably topped the county's averages. He hit
105 in 100 minutes against Cambridge University, and his 243
at Leicester, gathered in 310 minutes, was the season's highest
innings. Sharp came next, and the only other Lancashire man
to top the 1,000 mark was Alfred Hartley, who made a
big advance on his form of 1907. Kermode and Harry gradually dropped out, MacLaren was in poor form, and Spooner
turned out but once. Poidevin played in only nine games, and
with these uncertainties, a heavy burden fell on four or five men.

Though there is not space to chronicle many of the feats
of other sides, it would be ungenerous not to mention here the
performance of Worcester who scored 235 in 150 minutes to
beat Lancashire by nine wickets, a capital effort even though
Dean and Brearley were away.

At the close of this season, after complaints about the variable
quality of pitches, Apted from the Oval was called in to advise
on the maintenance of the ground.

1909: CHAMPIONSHIP MATCHES:
Played 24, Won 14, Drawn 6, Lost 4

This season witnessed an upward surge in the table. As

against nine defeats, there were only four, and Lancashire finished second in the table; they challenged Kent boldly for the title until the end of July when successive defeats by Yorkshire and Worcester ended their hopes. To lose twice to Yorkshire was a disappointment, but otherwise it was quite a brilliant season and the victories included one over Kent.

A considerable factor in their team's success was that fewer players were called upon, and the slight falling off in the form of John Tyldesley was hardly noticed. Huddleston was at last given a regular position, and Alfred Hartley went in first with such success that he was acknowledged as the fit successor to the immortal Albert Ward. And though the sensational recruit Ralph Whitehead was laid aside with scarlet fever, there was another newcomer to the eleven, welcomed not only for what he was but because of the proud name he so modestly bore: Ernest Tyldesley, beginning that long and honourable career which forms one of the happiest of all the many splendid episodes in the county's history.

The bowling was very strong. Brearley took 115 wickets for 15 runs each, Heap eagerly seized his few chances, Huddleston and Dean each took more than 80 wickets in championship fixtures, and Jack Sharp and Lol Cook had their useful days. The six bowlers returned averages ranging from Heap's 12.97 to Cook's 19.29, so it is little wonder that the team was a finer match-winning combination than in the previous year.

The batting averages were less convincing, with Sharp at the head of those who played regularly, but Makepeace's nine-hundred-odd runs represented a big advance and offset the poor form of MacLaren who, again captain of England, played a lot of cricket this summer yet never really touched his old form.

The great triumph of the season was the double victory over Surrey. At the Oval, a brilliant century by Sharp put Lancashire on the right road and Brearley and Dean made the most of the opportunity with help from the weather. They had the luck in the return match, too, when injuries to Hobbs and J. N. Crawford conspired with rain and sunshine to complete the task begun by Lancashire's consistent batting. Huddleston here came out as an all-rounder, following up his 78 not out with five cheap wickets. In Surrey's second-innings collapse Heap had five wickets for 16 runs.

Dean had two wonderful matches. At Liverpool, Hornby

sent Warwick in to bat and Dean responded to his captain's
spur by taking nine wickets for 35 runs. In the second innings
he had four for 46, and Huddleston six for 19. This match,
played early in June, marked Ernest Tyldesley's first appearance with an innings of 61 and the old and the new were fittingly linked when, in partnership with MacLaren, 128 runs
were added in 90 minutes. Right at the end of the season Dean
surpassed his 13 wickets at Aigburth by taking 14 against
Somerset at Old Trafford, at a cost of 77 runs. In a game of
low scores, Heap took five wickets for 35 runs to lift himself
to the top of the Lancashire averages.

John Tyldesley was not his old self but he had his good days,
as when he and Sharp scored 237 in 150 minutes at Worcester.
At Eastbourne, Spooner and Hartley made 208 together for the
first wicket, and K. G. McLeod unexpectedly came out as
bowler, taking 12 wickets for 172 runs. McLeod was concerned
in an unusual 'double' at Bath where he and John Daniel, both
rugby internationals, each made a century. Lancashire won
by 9 runs, five minutes from time, and had reason to thank
McLeod for the rapid progress he made on the first day—128
in 95 minutes.

1910: CHAMPIONSHIP MATCHES:
Played 29, *Won* 14, *Drawn* 10, *Lost* 5

This year a new system of reckoning in the championship
was instituted at the suggestion of Lancashire. The new
method, though it retained a percentage figure in the final
column, had the merit of simplicity as the result was determined by the percentage of wins to matches played. So, neither
for the first time nor the last, Lancashire were to the forefront
of what was intended to be a progressive scheme, one designed
to encourage lively cricket with victory always in mind. Yet,
curiously enough, Lancashire themselves suffered by the change,
for their record was little inferior to that of 1909; under the old
system they would have finished second, but as it turned out,
they slipped down to fourth place behind Kent, Surrey, and
Middlesex.

Even so, a better record would have been possible but for
the team's wretched luck with the weather; of the twenty-nine
championship fixtures (the odd number is accounted for by
the fixture against Kent at Old Trafford being limited to two

days by the funeral of King Edward), ten were drawn, and it was not through any lack of enterprise because nine of the unfinished games were directly affected by rain. The tenth, against Middlesex at Lord's, would have been won had the catches been held on the last day.

There were three outstanding games this season and the general work of the side must be quickly summarised so that the victories over Hampshire and Notts may be given adequate treatment. That over Yorkshire is dealt with in a separate chapter.

The team suffered from an injury that limited Brearley's appearances to three games, but Dean rose to the occasion in fine style, taking 133 wickets for 15 runs each and Huddleston, Heap, Whitehead, and Cook were all effective. Among the batsmen, Johnny Tyldesley came back to his old form after the disappointments of the Test matches of 1909, and he not only scored more runs than anyone else in England but headed the first-class averages. Two centuries against Hampshire at Old Trafford and a fine forcing innings on a slow pitch at Lord's were among his six three-figure scores.

It was against Notts at Old Trafford that Lancashire became the first side in the history of the championship to score 400 runs in a fourth innings to win a match. For two days Notts outplayed the home eleven. A century by Hardstaff and consistent batting by others built up a first-innings total of 376, and good bowling by Wass, Clifton, and Iremonger put Lancashire out for 162. Despite his big lead, A. O. Jones declined to enforce the follow-on and Notts cautiously set about making victory secure. Their slow batting recoiled on their own heads, however, because on the third morning they had to take risks in an attempt to make good the wasted hours. Eight wickets went down in 45 minutes, so Lancashire went in again with five and a quarter hours left for play, exactly 400 runs wanted. A. Hartley and W. Tyldesley did not accomplish much, but John Tyldesley (91) and Sharp (102) proceeded to score 191 together in 150 minutes. Ernest Tyldesley and Whitehead kept it up with 80 runs in 40 minutes and when Whitehead was bowled by Riley, only 42 runs were required with 50 minutes to go.

But while this exciting cricket had been delighting the spectators, there was drama behind the scenes. In the words of William Howard:

'Mr. Hornby for some months had been troubled with a loose cartilage, which had come out of place while fielding. Being unable to walk, he altered the batting order, putting himself in last. . . . Going to the bar for a small soda or something to relieve the excitement, I met one of our old members, John Allison, who seldom came to see a match, and, judging by his appearance, was celebrating this occasion. He was the proprietor of a nursing home in Manchester, and was well respected by all who knew him. Answering his inquiries about Mr. Hornby, I informed him of the state of affairs, and to my astonishment, Mr. Allison insisted on going into the dressing-room, determined to make the Lancashire captain fit to bat.

'It was useless to remonstrate, so I reluctantly took him up. Five minutes later Mr. Hornby had his pads on, ready to go in at the fall of the next wicket. Our friend, who was responsible for the transformation, looked quite elated with his success.

'It was a most lucky thing for Lancashire, especially as it happened at an opportune moment; two wickets falling quickly about this time had made the prospects of victory look very bad. When Mr. Hornby went in, still suffering from pain, over 80 runs were wanted and the clock against us. Eight men out, thirty-six to win, when Lol Cook joined his captain—excitement intense. Two minutes from time Lancashire won a magnificent match by two wickets, Mr. Hornby scoring 55 not out. . . . He was carried shoulder high off the ground, the crowd singing "For he's a jolly good fellow". Long after the match was over, Mr. Allison called me to the refreshment bar to confirm what he had repeatedly told his friends : that it was he who had won the match.'

Some six weeks later Yorkshire were beaten in Sharp's benefit match, and soon afterwards came the famous match with Hampshire at Southampton. For a time it followed the pattern of the game against Notts: the opposing side batted with splendid consistency, Lancashire found themselves 106 behind on the first innings, and the home team then made 296 for nine before declaring and setting Lancashire the task of scoring 403 to win—exactly the number obtained against Notts, this time with five hours available. The task was accomplished and on this occasion it was fulfilled with something to spare both in time and wickets. The big difference was that the team had a good send-off, Hartley and W. Tyldesley scoring 100 in an hour. Johnny Tyldesley failed for once but then came the match-winning stand, Sharp and Makepeace, so often partners on two fields of sport, putting on 242 in 160 minutes. Sharp's 150, made in under three hours, included 22 fours and only 28 singles, and though both he and Makepeace (95) missed being in at the finish, it was perhaps fitting that Hornby should be there again when the winning hit was made and victory achieved by five wickets with half an hour to spare.

These were striking reminders that the old touch had not quite deserted the side, and there were other instances too, as for instance when MacLaren, on one of his rare appearances, hit a century in 80 minutes on a rough wicket at Birmingham. And the old captain joined hands with Ralph Whitehead in a brilliant burst of hitting at Worcester that yielded 260 runs in 150 minutes.

The two matches against Somerset produced wonderful cricket and wide margins of victory. At Old Trafford in May the home county made 558 runs for six wickets and won by an innings and 248 runs. Hartley made 234 without a chance, and Johnny Tyldesley's 158 was even finer, the great batsman rising to the peak of his form, hitting 27 fours with splendid driving, and sharing in a partnership worth 295 runs in 130 minutes. Sharp followed with a century at a run a minute and all told Lancashire put together their big score in under five hours. The return at Bath was equally remarkable. Dean began by taking nine wickets, Hornby, Hartley, and Johnny Tyldesley scored rapidly, and Dean completed the work with seven more wickets to give himself a match record of 16 for 103 and Lancashire victory by an innings.

Heap's best match was at Northampton, where he had nine wickets in an innings and a complete return of 14 for 93. Huddleston had eight for 31 against Derbyshire at Glossop and another fine bowling performance was in the home match against Worcester, Dean and Huddleston going through the match unchanged with the visiting side out for 48 and 62.

It had been a wonderful season even if the championship title had proved beyond reach. The batting had shown its old fury, the professional bowlers had put their shoulders to a task made heavy by Brearley's absence, and only the lack of a first-rate wicket-keeper formed ground for criticism, William Worsley's pluck and good humour not quite masking his technical limitations. Nothing had been more pleasing than the progress of Alfred Hartley, honoured in the season's summing-up by a place among *Wisden's* 'Five Cricketers of the Year'.

1911: CHAMPIONSHIP MATCHES:
Played 30, Won 15, Drawn 8, Lost 7

The summer of 1910 had been rather wet; in 1911 the sun shone almost without interruption and cricketers responded to the conditions by finishing 145 of the 180 championship fixtures. Another method was tried in reckoning the championship, with points awarded for the first time for a first-innings lead. Under the new system Lancashire, who had another eventful season, finished fourth to Warwickshire.

On the field, Lancashire certainly had little reason to feel dissatisfied with events because though hard hit by injuries to Johnny Tyldesley, Hartley, and Hornby, they won fifteen matches. But it must have puzzled the committee that in such a year attendances should fall off, so that a sharp financial loss was incurred. They had a grievance that some of the southern counties travelled north with weak teams.

One of the most pleasing features of the year was that Dean at last won for himself a prominent place in the cricket world. After several years of hard work and of selfless willingness to bowl in two styles, he now came right to the front, taking 183 wickets in all first-class matches, more than anyone else in the country. With Brearley playing in only ten games L. Cook had more opportunities and took 85 wickets but some of the change bowlers were costly and Huddleston was again victim of the policy that left him out of the side when the pitches were hard.

If Dean stood out among the bowlers, so did Spooner among the batsmen. Able to play regularly for about three months, he scored more than 2,300 runs; in championship matches for Lancashire he scored 1,700 runs, average 56. He delighted crowds everywhere and at the Oval, when he made 224 out of 360 and the next best score was Sharp's 35, he played the fast bowling of Hitch without losing anything of his perfect style.

Johnny Tyldesley had a modest season by his own standards,

yet all the same he averaged 40 for the county, and so did
Sharp. Makepeace made further progress, and so did W.
Tyldesley, while K. G. McLeod and H. G. Garnett were once
again seen in the cricket field. The latter kept wicket service-
ably though the county continued to look for a professional to
fill this position regularly.

The season opened dramatically, with Warwickshire giving
a broad hint of their new powers by winning at Old Trafford.
In their third game Lancashire found themselves engaged in a
desperate struggle at Leicester where the home side, set to get
318, were 273 with only three men out. Then Dean and Cook
brought the game back to a precarious balance, and finally Lancashire won by 13 runs. Three days later there was an even
closer finish, Derbyshire winning by two runs at Old Trafford
and so recording their first win over their neighbours since
1895. A heavy defeat at Lord's (in spite of Brearley's heroic
bowling) and a drawn match at Trent Bridge brought May to
an end and already all hope of winning the championship—
not an unreasonable expectation on the form of 1910—had to
be given up. A brief interlude at Liverpool, where Brearley took
14 Somerset wickets, only raised false hopes for in Whit week
both Yorkshire and Kent won at Old Trafford.

But then the tide turned. Of the next ten matches (including
one against the All-India touring side) eight were won, one
drawn, and only one lost, and in securing the eight victories the
team had such margins as an innings (three times), ten wickets,
nine wickets (twice), 372 runs, and 228 runs. A run of drawn
games followed, and there was another defeat by Warwickshire,
but Lancashire finished the season splendidly with four victories
in their last five fixtures.

So much for the bare results. They came from cricket of a
type that made this a vintage year, Lancashire and their rivals
playing as though they wished to give everything they had, as
though they must hasten to glorify the cricket scene, as for
instance when Kent, in Whit week, scored 222 for seven
wickets, making the runs at one a minute to win with only
a couple of minutes to spare. And when Hampshire came
north, with the record feat of the previous year much in mind,
no doubt, Spooner, Sharp, McLeod, and Johnny Tyldesley
were in such form that Hornby allowed them to go on and on
so that 676 runs were scored in six and a half hours, still the

second highest total ever recorded by Lancashire. Spooner's 186 led in every sense of the word.

As though jealous of the cheers for the batsmen, Dean and L. Cook pounced on the unhappy Hampshire men, put them out for 102 and 119, and left the home county winners by an innings and 455 runs, the easiest victory ever recorded for Lancashire and third biggest margin in the history of the championship. It surpassed by three runs the winning margin of the Taunton match in 1895.

1912: CHAMPIONSHIP MATCHES:
Played 22, Won 8, Drawn 10, Lost 2, Abandoned 2

This was the season of the Triangular Tournament, and like all the other counties, Lancashire had a smaller championship programme. They were again fourth in the table but as they lost only two championship matches, beat the Australians twice, and were the only county to defeat the South Africans, the record was very satisfactory. Moreover, after one of the wettest summers on record, they were one of the few counties to come out with a financial profit.

The many soft pitches suited Dean and Huddleston. The former was able to exploit his natural spin, relying less on the swerving style he had learned from George Hirst, and he well earned his selection for England and his part in the victory at the Oval which gave England first place in the international tournament.

Even if Johnny Tyldesley's Test match career was ended, he was still good enough to score more runs than anyone else in the side in championship matches. Spooner proved that he could shine on soft wickets, Sharp maintained his high place, Makepeace continued his sure advance, and Hornby had one of his best seasons. Ernest Tyldesley hit his first century, the first of more than a hundred that were to flow from his bat in succeeding summers.

For two months the team made a good showing in the championship race, but then they were beaten by Kent at Tunbridge Wells and thenceforward the winning edge seemed blunted. Kent's victory was sweet to the winners, sweet revenge for defeat at Old Trafford a month or so before, when the home side got home in what would in any case have been the last over, by means of a disputed catch when Blythe returned the ball to Dean, who had 15 wickets in the game.

It was Dean, too, with 13 wickets for 49 runs who had most to do with Worcester's double collapse for 47 and 41, and he had another good match at Derby with 12 for 163. At Leicester he bowled unchanged with Huddleston and they shared the wickets equally.

A win at Lord's was specially welcome, representing as it did Lancashire's first victory over Middlesex there since 1900. There was excellent entertainment in the game with Surrey at Old Trafford for both Spooner and Hobbs made centuries, and Whitehead performed the hat-trick. At Trent Bridge, Hornby and Makepeace opened the match by making 141 together and in the second innings they scored 193 for the first wicket, though this double success did not give the team victory. It was well into the summer before Johnny Tyldesley really got going and then in one week he made 174 at Brighton (Ranji making 176) and 143 at Leyton.

The arrival of a first-class amateur wicket-keeper in F. R. R. Brooke was quite an event in the season's cricket, though Alfred Hartley's batting fell off so much that he asked to be dropped, while Walter Brearley indicated his final break with the county by appearing for Cheshire.

1913: CHAMPIONSHIP MATCHES:
Played 26, Won 7, Drawn 8, Lost 11

This was one of the least successful seasons in the history of the club, and just when everyone must have been thankful that the sorry summer was drawing to its close, there was a controversy concerning the management of the club; it is dealt with elsewhere in this book. On the field, the team lost eleven matches, and dropped to eighth place in the table, a result that might have been even worse had not Hornby enjoyed phenomenal luck with the toss. The brightest thing about the year's cricket was that in three games against Yorkshire (the extra fixture was to mark the visit of King George V to Liverpool), two ended in victory for Lancashire.

An accident in the hunting field meant that Spooner could not play cricket this year, and the chief batsmen were Johnny and Ernest Tyldesley, Makepeace, and Hornby. The Tyldesley brothers enjoyed one remarkable week in June; first of all they each scored a century at Leicester, where C. J. B. Wood carried his bat for 38 in a total of 179, and then they went on to the Oval where John made 210 and Ernest 110. This was the match in which Hayward became the second batsman after W. G. Grace to complete a century of centuries.

Adversity brought the best out of Makepeace, by this time one of the best professional batsmen in the country. At Maidstone, where Lancashire met with one of their sharpest defeats, he scored 88 in the first innings of 158 when the next best score was 17, and in the second innings he carried his bat for 39 in a total of 88.

Among the bowlers Heap, Huddleston, Dean, and Whitehead all had good records, and Huddleston had an outstanding match when he took 12 Leicestershire wickets at Old Trafford for 89 runs.

Lancashire had for long been in the forefront with schemes for improving the game and making it more attractive to the spectators, and in August they tried the experiment of beginning the Derbyshire match on a Friday, but the weather broke and there was no real opportunity of obtaining a correct assessment of the value of the idea. In the following fixture Middlesex were at Aigburth; Heap had one of his best performances with eight first-innings wickets for 28 runs and there was a liberty with the laws of the game when P. F. Warner, who had fielded for a few overs, was taken ill and H. W. Lee was allowed to take his place in the team.

1914: CHAMPIONSHIP MATCHES:
Played 26, Won 6, Drawn 11, Lost 9

Things were no better in 1914 than they had been the previous summer. Indeed, though the number of defeats was fewer, the overall record was worse in that Lancashire finished eleventh in the table, and the bowling was described as weaker than at any time in the existence of the club. The misfortunes began with Dean's breakdown with a bad knee, were continued in a difference he had with the committee, and—so far as the bowling was concerned—were only relieved by the appearance of the inimitable Cecil Parkin, then professional with the Lancashire League club, Church. His first match was against Leicester at Liverpool when he took 14 wickets for 99 runs and altogether in six matches he took 34 wickets. Unhappily it was to be several years before he could be put to the test of a full season's cricket.

Another new player who appeared and who was ultimately also to make his mark, was Charles Hallows, originally a left-arm bowler (to the end of his career with the county he was known to his brother professionals as 'Flight') but who was to prove, for an all-too-brief period, one of England's best batsmen.

Returning to the field this season was H. G. Garnett, in specially good form against Notts with a not-out century at Trent Bridge and 96 in the return, and these and other feats were recognised by selection to play for the Gentlemen at Lord's. Less happy was the return of MacLaren, who made only four runs in two innings.

Spooner was able to play again in a few games, and in point of style his 67 at the Oval overshadowed other and bigger innings by the Surrey cracks. Here four bowlers (Whitehead, W. Tyldesley, Huddleston, and Cook) bore the full burden of an innings of 402 in 108 overs. Johnny Tyldesley was back at the top of the county's averages, making 253 at Canterbury and 122 not out in a total of 228 against Hampshire at Liverpool, when Dean took 13 wickets.

Best of the six victories was against Kent at Old Trafford when Huddleston (11 for 107) and Heap (eight for 134) supported a solid batting display. Twice the team felt the full force of the erratic genius of Frank Tarrant. At Lord's he made 198, sharing a stand of 380 with the younger Hearne, and in the return he pulled out a quite exceptional all-round feat in scoring 101 not out and taking 16 wickets. Northampton beat Lancashire by an innings, and they strove until 1953 before they gained their next success. A large crowd acknowledged the experiment of playing a fixture at Lancaster where Quaife, Baker, Jeeves, and Foster swept Warwickshire to victory.

Towards the end of the season, as fighting in Belgium began the war, reality fell away from cricket. The season died before it had run its full course and the championship was awarded to Surrey when first-class cricket, after pursuing its splendid way for so long, closed down—to use the language of the times—'for the duration'.

The Liverpool C.C. ground when Lancashire played the New Zealanders there in 1949

Lancashire v. Worcestershire on the ground of Blackpool C.C., in 1953

CHAPTER 12

The First World War 1914-18

*A hospital at Old Trafford; Members maintain
their support; Lancashire v Yorkshire in
a prison camp; Gloomy outlook
not justified*

THE OUTBREAK OF war finished cricket at Old Trafford for four
years. The pavilion, and later all the buildings on the pavilion
side of the ground, became a hospital with accommodation for
eighty sick and wounded men. During four years, 1,800 patients
were treated there.

Most of the players joined up. Johnny Tyldesley, too old to
serve, was prominent in arranging matches in various parts of
the county for war charities.

Just before the outbreak of war a special appeal for funds
had been launched and the committeee were faced with the
complex problem of maintaining interest in this fund, per-
suading members to keep up their subscriptions and meeting
obligations due under the pre-war contracts with players. In
1915, subscriptions were paid by 1,667 members, and though
as the war dragged on, interest not unnaturally fell off a little,
the number of members who maintained their payments never
fell below 1,100 in any one year.

The club sent out kit to the prisoners of war at the notorious
Ruhleben camp, and in due course there came back a score
sheet of a match played there: Lancashire v Yorkshire.

By 1916, the club's liabilities to players under the pre-1914
contracts had been fulfilled, and the financial statement showed
a small surplus for the year.

Lancashire officials took a rather gloomy view of the prospects of re-starting the county championship, and they were
foremost in urging two-day matches. The experiment was
tried, but was given up after the one season of 1919.

The pavilion closed as a hospital on 8 February 1919. The

I

committee formally decided to adopt 'a bold policy' and fixed fees for the professionals at £5 a match home or away, with expenses £1 at home, £3 away, and with a bonus of £1 for a win. By May 1919, first-class cricket was being played again on the famous ground, the championship was in full swing, and the gloomy forecasts were proved quite unfounded. But in the long room of the pavilion a tablet told its sad tale: Harold Garnett, Alfred Hartley, J. A. Nelson, W. K. Tyldesley, and Egerton L. Wright had all given their lives in the fight.

CHAPTER 13

Johnny Tyldesley, R. H. Spooner and Walter Brearley

Tyldesley's three careers; His feats at Edgbaston; A brilliant innings at Melbourne; R. H. Spooner's perfect style; The untiring Walter Brearley; His deeds against Yorkshire; A. H. Hornby's signal; A band of brilliant amateurs; Worsley, Billy Cook, Huddleston and Heap

WHEN THE FIRST World War broke out, Johnny Tyldesley was nearly forty. What should have been four fruitful summers were taken away from him, and his subsequent career was limited to one full season, so this is a convenient point to consider the three stages of his connection with Lancashire, even if we have to anticipate. There was his first grand career as one of the most brilliant batsmen in an age of brilliancy; when he had finished this and his Test match days were done, he settled down as the senior professional and continued to score fluently for the county; and then he became the coach at Old Trafford, a smallish, grey man, who stood behind the nets, bat in hand, offering advice and encouragement, and he mixed them in equal proportions. He was indescribably courteous and kind, just as he had been so modest in his great days, the perfect cricket professional.

So many men have scored so many runs since 1919 that it is perhaps necessary to emphasise how good a batsman he was. This can be best done, maybe, by saying that when he retired his aggregate of runs (over 37,000) had up to that time been exceeded only by W. G. Grace and Tom Hayward. A life average of over 40 runs an innings, 86 centuries, a method which won him admirers on both sides of the world, a splendid reputation as a fieldsman in the deep during an age when rival batsmen offered catches with lofty hits—a great cricketer in every way was John Thomas Tyldesley from Roe Green, Worsley.

He could defend, and often did defend, with a method that was basically correct; but his preference was for attack, an attack that was gallant and fascinating to watch. He had no real weakness, but his glory was on the offside where he drove and cut with a ferocity that came strangely from so very modest a man.

Slow leg-break bowlers were reduced to despair when he drew away towards square-leg and cut them, and he even did that to Warwick Armstrong, who could bowl as accurately as anyone. He came into cricket when it was adorned by amateur batsmen who, not having averages and a tour every winter to worry about, played with dash and polish that have left the game perhaps never to return; among them he held his own with something to spare.

He had a phenomenal record at Edgbaston, where he hit eleven centuries and began a tradition carried on by his younger brother Ernest and then by Cyril Washbrook. Yet above all else it was his greatness on bad wickets that so firmly established him as among the supreme batsmen of his time. The pitch at Old Trafford was variable, and playing so many of his innings in the north he had to find a way of mastering the conditions. He succeeded with his attacking strokes, and his skill on these pitches served him in good stead when he took his place in the English Test team at home and abroad.

Not even Victor Trumper could be claimed as his superior when the bowlers were having things almost all their own way, and fortunate indeed were the spectators who saw both at their best in the Test match at Melbourne in January 1904. Tyldesley made 97 in the first innings, Trumper followed with 74 on a bad wicket, and then as conditions became even worse Tyldesley played an innings that has become historic. The course of the ball after pitching was unpredictable—shooters alternated with deliveries that hit the shoulders—but the Lancashire man made 62 with the next score 10 and the total 103.

We can link one of his Test match feats with the next great figure, R. H. Spooner, the batsman whose style remains the example of perfection even after the game has gone round the world. At the Oval in 1905, six English wickets were down for 103 runs, and saving the game rested with Tyldesley and Spooner; they did it, not by 'saving' tactics but by hitting 158 in an hour and a half and enabling F. S. Jackson to declare.

It was said of Spooner's first appearance for Lancashire that he treated J. T. Hearne and Albert Trott just as he had been treating the schoolboy bowlers he had met at Marlborough, and it must be a cause of lasting regret that he was never able to spare the time to go to Australia. In 1920 he was offered the captaincy, but had to decline after first of all accepting it.

Like Tyldesley, he was a glorious offside hitter, making his strokes with what H. S. Altham described as a flashing flick of the wrist. No English amateur batsman, says Mr. Altham, has ever made his art appear at once more beautiful, effortless and electric. The older members at Old Trafford still speak with awe of his double century against Yorkshire in 1910 when, after a little luck early on, he settled down to play an innings which is a landmark in Lancashire history.

When he was named as one of the 'Five Cricketers of the Year' in 1905, *Wisden's* said of him that not even Palairet himself was better worth looking at, and mention was of course made of his outstanding worth at cover-point. Here he formed a link in a Lancashire tradition, never broken from A. N. Hornby to Washbrook.

If Tyldesley and Spooner were modest men, what shall be said of Walter Brearley, their companion in many a great game? This fast bowler came into the Lancashire eleven like a breath of fresh air; to the elegance of MacLaren and Spooner and the dash of Tyldesley he added a homespun quality that was none the worse for carrying with it an unmistakable Lancashire accent.

Almost every season he vowed that he would never play again, and yet there were never really deep roots to his quarrels. They sprang from Brearley's longing for a gallery; he bowled fast, and bowled all day, because he liked it—but at the end of it, someone had to play up to him. He simply had to be in the picture.

His athletic prowess was legendary. He thought nothing of leaping the pavilion gate on his way to bat, and as often as not his walk to the wicket was a run ... there and back, quite soon afterwards. It is said he could vault a full-sized billiards table.

His belief in himself was unshakable. When he was turned fifty he was bowling at the nets at Lord's with astonishing energy and declaring himself the fastest bowler in England, and he was unsparing in his coaching of public school cricketers, just as he had been unsparing with his efforts on the field.

It was because he was willing to bowl all day that Lancashire often embarked on matches with what appeared on paper an ill-balanced eleven. When Dean appeared the team had four bowlers in two men, two in Brearley because of his well-nigh inexhaustible energy and two in Dean because he could bowl in two styles.

With only a brief interval Brearley was successor to Mold in the Lancashire eleven, but except for the short, easy run and the great pace, there was no other resemblance. Brearley's action was beyond criticism, because it came from body-swing. He was astute at using the full width of the crease, and he bowled a genuine out-swinger. His length was usually on the full side, indeed one old county player said that he never saw him bowl short. With his amazing vitality, his bounding run to the wicket and his sturdy frame he hammered life out of any pitch—as for instance at Lord's in 1905 when on what seemed slow turf he took seven of the Players' wickets.

Brearley took delight in producing his best against certain picked opponents. In the great matches against Yorkshire he appeared fourteen times, taking 125 wickets at under 16 runs each. For the Gentlemen, too, he was a great success, taking 48 wickets in seven matches and figuring in the famous match of 1906 when he and Knox gained their side victory in the Centenary match. We may imagine him bounding with delight when, two years later, he clean bowled both Hobbs and Hayward. Another of his famous duels was against Victor Trumper whom he dismissed six times in 1905. Altogether he took 844 wickets in first-class cricket, almost 700 of them for Lancashire, a splendid record for anyone but all the more remarkable because he did not commence his first-class career until he was twenty-six. He had previously played for Bolton and Manchester.

Another Lancashire man who appeared for the Gentlemen was A. H. Hornby, captain 1908–14. He was a dashing batsman, a magnificent fieldsman close up to the wicket, and on the whole a good captain, though he perhaps lacked the instinctive touch that made his father famous. He was not at first successful, and the professionals, led by J. T. Tyldesley, saw the committee about some points of dissatisfaction; afterwards things went better. He expected obedience and close attention, and it must have been necessary because when he wished a member of the team to move a few yards, he would indicate by lifting the toe of his boot to point the direction: and woe betide the man who missed the surreptitious signal.

The younger Hornby's part in some of Lancashire's splendid batting performances has been mentioned in the preceding pages, and we need recall here only his partnership of 113 with W. Findlay, made in half an hour off the Somerset bowling at Old Trafford in 1905. He made 69 on an uncertain wicket against the Players, at Lord's in 1914 when the attack consisted of Barnes, Hitch, Tarrant, Kennedy, the younger Hearne, and Woolley.

Keeping wicket in that same match at Lord's was Harold Garnett, so soon to be killed in action. A brilliant left-hand batsman he fell naturally into the county eleven early in the century when the pattern was set by MacLaren, Tyldesley and Spooner. He dropped out after a time, business taking him to South America, and then he reappeared. By this time he was a first-rate wicket-keeper and when he stumped Hitch in the match mentioned above, it was said at the time that the feat would have been wonderful even if done by Blackham at his best.

Kenneth McLeod was another of the amateurs who appeared before the first war. A magnificent games player, he was of course a splendid fieldsman, perhaps the most perfect runner who has ever chased a ball over the Old Trafford turf.

Like Garnett, Alfred Hartley was a victim of the war, and he was another Lancashire player to appear for the Gentlemen. A patient rather than a brilliant batsman, he applied himself to the game so that his career was one of steady progress. He was described as a worthy successor to Albert Ward. His elder brother, Charles Hartley, also played for the county between 1897 and 1909, and among several fine innings was a century at Gloucester in 1901 which yielded a tenth-wicket stand of 101 with Mold.

William Worsley was something quite different, a rough-hewn league cricketer summoned to the Lancashire side at short notice and holding his place by wonderful courage and much native humour. He was never quite top-class, and he must have had his hands knocked about, and it could not have been much fun keeping to Brearley with his pace and Dean with his in-curve, but Worsley stuck it. There is a delightfully humorous account of his first appearance for the county in Neville Cardus's autobiography.

Billy Cook looked like being a good fast bowler when he joined the county team; he preferred the league game, however, and helped Burnley to three consecutive championships. There was Huddleston, an off-break bowler who was denied chances of greater fame because Lancashire had their four-bowlers-in-two, and because the committee thought he could only bowl on soft pitches. Even so, he took more than 600 wickets for Lancashire and on his good days evoked comparisons with J. T. Hearne. And there was Jimmy Heap, a left-arm bowler who, offered only limited opportunities, took 400 wickets and often batted well enough to be styled an all-rounder.

Richard Tyldesley's time was yet to come, but three of the Westhoughton family (no relation to the Roe Green Tyldesleys) came out before the war. First in 1908 was Billy, a left-hand batsman who made three centuries. He was killed in the last year of the war, aged thirty. Next in 1910 came Jimmy, a fast bowler who often looked like developing into a genuine successor to Crossland, Mold, and Brearley. But though he claimed over 300 wickets, he never quite took the step from usefulness to greatness. Doubtless he would have had a long career as an all-rounder, because he was quite an efficient batsman, but for his early death while undergoing a minor operation. A third brother, Harry, appeared a few times in 1914.

A cricketer who occasionally achieved startling successes was the medium-paced bowler Frank Harry, who came from Devonshire. Fifteen wickets for 70 runs against Warwick in 1906, five for 14 at Stourbridge in the following season, and six for 18 against Leicester at Old Trafford in 1908 were among his best feats. Twice he bowled eight maidens in succession. After leaving Lancashire he took various club engagements, and played for both Durham County and Worcestershire.

CHAPTER 14

Championship Matches

1919–22 Captain: M. N. Kenyon

*Two-day matches; Johnny Tyldesley's last big innings; A
victory in the rain; A dramatic finish to the championship, 1920; Cheers too soon; Lol Cook's fine
bowling; Hampshire beaten by one run at
Liverpool; Amateur batsmen in form,
1921; Richard Tyldesley's all-round
form; Parkin joins the staff*

WHEN CRICKET WAS resumed in 1919, Lancashire had the elements of a strong team, even if Cook was still in the Forces and
Parkin was able to play only occasionally. The championship
was played under entirely new conditions, matches being restricted to two days. The idea emanated from Lancashire and it
was ironic that the county team should have suffered so severely
from the arrangement, for twelve of their twenty-four games
were drawn. In 1920 the long-standing arrangement of allo-
cating three days to each county match was restored. Still, there
need be no cause for regret that the experiment was tried. One
can theorise about games in endless discussions, but in the end
only a trial can prove whether an idea is sound or not.

With most of their prominent players available, and with
their own idea adopted for the one season, Lancashire naturally
entered upon the new period of cricket with zest. They found
a new captain in Myles Kenyon, passionately devoted to the
game, a Lancastrian through and through, and a man of generous and warm-hearted outlook. He held the office for four
years and though he did not have the happy experience of leading the team to a championship success, he almost pulled it off
in 1920, and it was he who manfully shouldered the extra burdens that naturally fell to a captain after the long break.

His playing days over, Myles Kenyon maintained a close

connection with the club as a committee man whose instincts and background led him towards the side of those eager to maintain all the traditional features of Lancashire cricket. He was president 1936–7.

1919: CHAMPIONSHIP MATCHES:
Played 24, Won 8, Drawn 12, Lost 4

Lancashire finished fifth in the table and they were probably a little disappointed at the record. One cause of the lack of match-winning powers was the ineffectiveness of Dean, whose 51 wickets cost almost 30 runs each. Cook bowled well late in the season when he was demobilised, and Heap, with so much extra responsibility, did well with 62 wickets at moderate cost. James Tyldesley actually took most wickets (71) and if they cost him 27 runs each, there was promise from his good physique and splendid action that he might become the fast bowler the side needed.

The batting was at an entirely different level. Ernest Tyldesley topped the county averages for the first time in his career, just in front of Makepeace, and then came Johnny Tyldesley, now in his forty-sixth year but on his good days capable of playing as well as ever, as an innings of 272 at Chesterfield showed. There was Hallows, too, second only to Sutcliffe among England's new men.

Besides his big innings against Derbyshire, J. T. Tyldesley also hit brilliantly in making 170 against Gloucester at Old Trafford, when his chief hits were 7 sixes and 17 fours. Seldom had he played a more punishing innings even in his palmy days as Test match cricketer, and with Ernest as his partner, 218 runs were obtained in under two hours.

There was a spirited match with Sussex at Old Trafford, played out to a finish in the most sporting fashion. The visiting eleven were all out for 205 against good bowling by James Tyldesley and Cook, and Lancashire were able to gain a lead of 53 thanks to Hallows's 70 and Ernest Tyldesley's 66. Sussex rallied well, Maurice Tate hitting away with gusto to reach his first century in big cricket, so that Lancashire were set to score 273 to win. They had to contend with the clock, bad light, and rain, but they were helped by their rivals who played on in heavy rain during the last twenty minutes when the batting side rushed to victory. Hallows followed Tate in hitting his first century, Makepeace made 65, and Lancashire won by three wickets.

There was a curious incident in the return game at Hastings. A. H. H. Gilligan played forward to, and missed, a ball from Harry Dean which turned enough to beat the bat and pass just over the wicket. In doing so, he dragged his back foot and R. A. Boddington knocked off the bails in an attempt to stump him. On looking round and seeing the bails off Gilligan walked away under the impression that he was bowled, whilst the Lancashire players thought he had been given out 'stumped', and the scorers so entered the dismissal. At the close of the innings, however, the square-leg umpire—rather belatedly, it seems—stated that Gilligan had not been stumped, so that as a matter of fact the batsman was not really out at all! As it happened, Sussex did not suffer for the curious error, gaining splendid compensation for their sporting play at Manchester with a win by six wickets.

Victor Norbury, an all-rounder of three counties, scored his only first-class century at the Oval, and another cricketer who played only briefly for Lancashire, C. S. Marriott, had a good day at Trent Bridge where on a perfect pitch he sent down 37 overs for 98 runs and eight wickets. James Tyldesley had an analysis of seven for 53 at Gravesend, and Heap bowled unchanged at Bristol to take seven wickets in each innings for 81 runs.

Almost at the end of the season, Spooner made his welcome reappearance in the side, which he led against Surrey in the absence of Kenyon, and though he did little there was compensation for the crowd in centuries by Hobbs, Knight, and Makepeace, the latter saving his side with 152 made in five and a half hours after Lancashire had followed on.

1920: CHAMPIONSHIP MATCHES:
Played 28, *Won* 19, *Drawn* 4, *Lost* 5

This was the season of one of the most dramatic of all finishes to the county championship, with Middlesex winning the title and Lancashire taking second place. We must jump ahead to the last days of August to find Lancashire playing Worcester at Old Trafford, Middlesex meeting Surrey at Lord's. Lancashire's task was easy, and it was virtually certain that, given time by the weather, they would win their last fixture. So it proved; early on the third day it was all over, Lancashire had won by nine wickets and club members in the pavilion were jubilant.

They had good reason for thinking that Lancashire had won the title, and for congratulating Jack Sharp (acting captain in Kenyon's absence) and the other members of the side. They had seen the morning newspapers and they knew that at Lord's, after two days' play, Middlesex were 268 and 27—0, Surrey 341 for nine, declared. It is history now that Middlesex pulled the game round, set their rivals 244 to win in just over three hours, and got the last wicket down with ten minutes to spare to win by 55 runs.

It was a disappointing end to Lancashire's season, but what a season it had been! They played a long fixture list, won more matches than any of their opponents in the table, and had two of the outstanding bowlers of the year in Cook and Dean. After his relative failure of 1919, Dean struck form in his benefit season but even he was beaten for average and number of wickets by Lol Cook who, relying on the cardinal principles of length and a little spin, took 150 wickets in championship matches at under 15 runs each. James and Richard Tyldesley each did well, and Parkin of course was a wonderful acquisition on the few occasions he was able to leave his league club to help the county.

Strangely, the batting hardly seemed as strong as in 1919 and after Makepeace and Ernest Tyldesley there was a big gap in the averages. There was no Johnny Tyldesley, Hallows did not hit a century, Spooner played only rarely, and a band of talented amateurs—J. R. Barnes, F. W. Musson, G. O. Shelmerdine and A. W. Pewtress—all had averages in the middle twenties, as did Jack Sharp, captain for half the season after Kenyon had broken down.

Lancashire's two matches with Middlesex produced exciting cricket of a high standard. At Old Trafford the home side had all the better of the early play but they failed so badly in their attempt to score 107 to win in 100 minutes, that five wickets fell for 50 runs and Sharp and Richard Tyldesley had to defend with stubborn skill to save the game. Soon afterwards the two great rivals met at Lord's, and the home side won in emphatic fashion by an innings and 37 runs in spite of two capital innings by Hallows and some wonderfully steady bowling by Cook.

There is a long list indeed of Cook's admirable performances this summer: ten for 87 against Hants at Liverpool; ten for 64 against Kent in Dean's benefit; 12 for 117 at Trent Bridge; ten for 106 at Cheltenham; ten for 67 against Sussex at Old Trafford; and most remarkable of all, seven wickets for eight runs at Chesterfield when Derbyshire made only 41.

Parkin had two great matches. He took 13 Leicester wickets for 90 runs and in Dean's benefit match he had eight wickets for 89. Dean did little in his own match (over in two days but successful financially), his best feats being his nine wickets against Hampshire, and ten at Trent Bridge, where Makepeace made 152 without giving a chance.

Ernest Tyldesley scored 244 at Birmingham in Charlesworth's benefit match, and he and Makepeace scored 166 together in 100 minutes at Stourbridge.

An outstanding match was played at Liverpool when Hampshire were the visitors. After rain, the start of the game was held up on the first day until early afternoon, when a fresh pitch was cut in order to get things going. Seven thousand people were waiting to see the game, and once the gates were opened they invaded the playing area, the enclosure, and the pavilion too, but although some material damage was inevitable, tempers were generally amiable and the game went on. Lancashire scored 182 thanks to a patient and skilful innings of 65 by Makepeace, and Hampshire were all out for 174. With Kennedy (nine for 33) in devastating form, Lancashire were all out for 57 in their second innings, so that Hampshire required only 66 to win, and half a dozen runs were obtained on the second evening by the night watchmen, Newman and Evans.

On the third day, after more rain, there was brilliant sunshine, and Harry Dean, realising the possibilities of a sticky wicket later on, and the advantage of keeping the tailenders in whilst it remained easy, was heard to say to Cook as they went on to the field, 'Don't bowl them out, Lol.' And so for an hour or more they were content to bowl a perfect length without attempting to do any damage, with the result that Evans made 21 and at one time Hampshire were 54 for five wickets. Then Dean, finding that the wicket was beginning to bite, spoke again to Cook as they crossed between the overs: 'Now then, Lol.' And so they launched their attack, the last five wickets fell for 10 runs and Lancashire gained a memorable victory by one run. It was one of the most thrilling episodes of a season packed with incident, and it goes to show what confidence these two great-hearted bowlers had in each other and what shrewd tacticians they were.

1921 : CHAMPIONSHIP MATCHES :
Played 28, Won 15, Drawn 9, Lost 4

Lancashire ought to have done better than finish fifth in the table this year. They were a powerful side on the many fast pitches met with in this gloriously fine summer, but they did not do themselves justice on at least three occasions. Defeat by Middlesex (champions again) was nothing to cause great concern, but there were failures against Notts, Leicester, and Warwick which were unexpected blemishes on their otherwise fine record.

The batting, sometimes suspect in 1920, was really powerful this year, with Ernest Tyldesley at the top, Hallows claiming the high place in English cricket that his form of 1919 and 1920 had promised, and the amateurs all improving their figures. G. O. Shelmerdine often forced the pace most effectively, J. R. Barnes was better all round, and nothing was more welcome than a steady flow of runs from the bat of the captain, Myles Kenyon, able to play regularly again. There was promising form from Frank Watson (a promise not belied by subsequent events) and Walker Ellis, son of the former county player, Jerry Ellis.

The bowling, even allowing for the hard pitches, was less satisfactory. Cook toiled with unfailing zeal; he bowled twice as many overs as anyone else, and took 143 wickets. But James Tyldesley was expensive, Dean often ineffective, Parkin still only an occasional member of the side, and after Cook the most successful bowler was Richard Tyldesley with 78 wickets in championship fixtures.

Again there were some splendid finishes and again one of them was against Hampshire, this time at Old Trafford. Lancashire were headed by 57 on the first innings, but when they batted again Ernest Tyldesley followed his first-innings 71 with a superb century, his 137 including 20 fours. So the home side were able to declare and set Hampshire the task of scoring 211 to win. They went boldly for the runs, and when Tennyson hit 21 in an over from Parkin, it was anyone's game. Parkin had the last word with eight second-innings wickets for 90 runs and a match return of 14 for 180, and Lancashire won by 27 runs on the stroke of seven o'clock. Amid all the splendid individual feats, none was better than Richard Tyldesley's fielding that brought him six catches in the last innings to equal a record, still unbeaten.

Two weeks later the teams met again at Southampton and they went at each other like terriers renewing an old feud. Tennyson took fearful toll of the bowling on the first day and Lancashire were outplayed up to the point of being set 322 to win. They had all day to accomplish the task, but in spite of a steady innings by Hallows they were in trouble until Richard Tyldesley and Kenyon added 105 for the seventh wicket. The captain was still there when victory was completed with three wickets in hand.

Ernest Tyldesley's special triumph was to score two separate hundreds at Leyton while Hallows twice accomplished the feat of carrying his bat through an innings, against Sussex and Leicester. Perhaps even finer was his double performance of 227 and 46 not out against Warwick at Manchester when Lancashire won by six wickets after fielding all through Saturday against a score of 365. A few days later the team were at the Oval where 1,004 runs were scored and only 20 wickets went down.

The season brought great disappointment to Jimmy Heap, out of the game for most of the time with lumbago, but his benefit match, with Middlesex as the attractive visitors, yielded him over £1,800.

These were great days for cricket. The Australians brought their powerful side, the weather was fine, the war was gradually fading from people's minds, and gates boomed everywhere. For Lancashire, there was a profit of almost £3,000 in spite of lavish expenditure on the ground, and membership stood at 4,661.

1922: CHAMPIONSHIP MATCHES:
Played 30, Won 15, Drawn 8, Lost 7

For the second season in succession, Lancashire finished fifth in the table, but in very different circumstances from 1921 when they never challenged for the title. This time they set off in such brilliant style that they won their first seven fixtures, and until well into July they were a grand match-winning combination. Afterwards they fell away and of their last thirteen games they lost five and won only three.

The big event this year was the arrival of Parkin as a member of the staff. Since his remarkable début at Liverpool before the war, he had turned out only occasionally but had performed so well that he had already achieved Test match recognition and no one had any doubts about his success. In championship matches he took 172 wickets for less than 17 runs each, and with Cook as steady as ever and Richard Tyldesley steadily improving, the attack was in some circumstances very powerful. With James Tyldesley falling off, however, more variety was required and the need for a left-hander to replace Dean was plain.

Ernest Tyldesley, Hallows, and Makepeace were again the outstanding batsmen, with Rupert Howard (afterwards secretary) showing good form on occasional appearances and J. R. Barnes playing in good style especially at Lord's where his method in a not-out century evoked memories of William Gunn.

Parkin had some wonderful days. He took 11 wickets against Glamorgan at Old Trafford and 11 again at Worcester, had eight for 47 in the first innings at Gloucester, and 14 wickets for 73 runs at Chesterfield. Cook was an admirable partner, and James Tyldesley, if generally failing, had a hat-trick against Worcester at Old Trafford. Worcester, indeed, felt the full force of Lancashire's prowess, for in the return match, apart from Parkin's 11 wickets as mentioned, Makepeace and Hallows scored 270 together for the first wicket and took only 200 minutes about it.

There were three thrilling finishes, one against Yorkshire described in full in the appropriate chapter. Three days later they met Hampshire, who seemed to bring excitement whenever they met Lancashire about this period; after Hants had tried to force a win with a declaration, the game was given up at seven o'clock with Lancashire wanting four runs to win and eight wickets in hand. They had tried to score 121 in 75 minutes, and at this distance of time it seems strange that having done so well, they should not have gained victory even if losing more wickets.

Earlier in the season Lancashire had won in a remarkable finish at Leicester. The home side required only 153 to win, and after some splendid bowling by Parkin and Richard Tyldesley and some rather reckless batting, the game reached a point at which eight men were out, eight runs still wanted. Benskin failed to score, and then Sidwell and Skelding got within three runs of victory before a hopeless muddle led to a run out and a Lancashire win.

Right at the end of the season came an unexpected defeat at Bournemouth from their keen rivals of Hampshire. Tennyson sent Lancashire in and his players answered the call so well that the visitors, out for 77 in their second innings, were beaten in two days. A great innings by Mead and clever bowling by Kennedy and Boyes were the chief factors in Hampshire's first-ever victory over Lancashire.

CHAPTER 15

Championship Matches

1923–5 Captain: John Sharp

*A unique career in cricket and football; McDonald
and Duckworth arrive; A great first day at Cardiff; Rain spoils sport; Parkin's season
of triumph and tragedy, 1924;
Exciting games with
Glamorgan; A fine
bowling side*

No ONE ELSE has ever had a career in sport quite like that of
Jack Sharp, the former professional cricketer and footballer
who now succeeded Myles Kenyon in the captaincy. As a
soccer player he achieved the greatest honours open to him: he
appeared in successive Cup Finals with Everton (he played at
outside-right), and had the happiness to be on the winning side
on one occasion in these great games at the Crystal Palace. He
was capped more than once for England, including an appearance against Scotland which was generally reckoned in those
days to be *the* international match that really counted. He
retained his connection with Everton when his playing days
were over, and ultimately became a director of the club which
boasts such a wonderful playing record and such a noble
ground. On the cricket field he was a fast bowler, a hard-
hitting batsman and splendid field at cover-point, and here, too,
he gained everything the game could offer. He was in the
championship side of 1904, played for England against Australia in 1909, and though chosen with the main purpose of
acting as the fast bowler, scored a century at the Oval that was
the only three-figure score hit for England in that series.

So much would have been more than sufficient for most men,
but this sturdy, thick-set sportsman from Hereford was no
ordinary mortal. After the First World War, he played cricket

as an amateur, and he led Lancashire from 1923 to 1925 when they boasted one of the strongest attacks in the country with E. A. McDonald qualifying by residence and joining hands with Parkin and Richard Tyldesley. In the second year of his leadership he capped everything by being elected to the Test Match Selection Committee with John Daniell and H. D. G. Leveson-Gower.

The records show that his bowling for Lancashire was a rather uneven affair so that though he played cricket for so long (he began in 1899) he took no more than 448 wickets in first-class matches, average about 26 runs each. He took 112 of them in 1901 when he also scored 883 runs. He was not fast in the sense that Richardson, Larwood, and McDonald were fast, and he was not a Walter Brearley, but when on the occasions the Old Trafford pitch was allowed to become fiery, he was able to make the most of the conditions with his break-back and natural capacity for making the ball lift.

His batting was of a different and finer quality. He scored more than 20,000 runs for Lancashire and nearly 23,000 in all first-class matches with an average of 32 runs an innings. He hit very well on the offside with drives and cuts and, like so many short batsmen, pulled with a power that was sometimes quite violent.

Sharp's bowling feats included taking nine wickets in an innings at Worcester, and five wickets for 14 runs at Derby. At Lord's in 1909 he took six Middlesex wickets in 26 balls, and had a return for the innings of seven for 25. His best innings was one of 211 against Leicestershire in 1912, and all told he hit thirty-eight centuries.

Such a man was bound to have the respect and admiration of the professionals who played under him, especially as added to his ability with bat and ball, and his reputation as a footballer, was a wonderful agility in the field. A buoyant, good-humoured games player, he can fairly be awarded a high place among cricketers of all the ages, and among Lancashire captains. Under him Lancashire finished third, fourth, and then third again in the table. In the last season in which he was captain they won nineteen of their thirty-two championship fixtures and they were such a good side during these three summers that they may perhaps be accounted a little unfortunate to have been overshadowed by the really exceptional Yorkshire eleven of the time.

The great events of this period were the completion of McDonald's residential qualification and the arrival of George Duckworth, whose success was immediate from the time of his début in 1923.

1923: CHAMPIONSHIP MATCHES:
Played 30, Won 15, Drawn 13, Lost 2

The new captain found himself under a handicap at the very commencement of his first year of office, the untimely death of James Tyldesley leaving the team virtually without a fast bowler. Some variety was added by the presence of Hickmott, a left-hander, and there was a successful trial for Stanley Ellis, brother of Walker Ellis and son of Jerry. But almost all the bowling had to be done by Parkin and Richard Tyldesley, for Cook's form was gradually falling off.

Another handicap for Sharp was his own attack of influenza, and a long absence through illness of Hallows. In the absence of the captain, Leonard Green or J. R. Barnes took charge, and on one memorable occasion Johnny Tyldesley reappeared to lead the team against Yorkshire.

Makepeace, so often behind Sharp in the Everton side on some of their greatest days, was a splendid lieutenant to his old football friend. He scored 1,976 runs in championship matches and in the extra games joined John and Ernest Tyldesley who up to this time had been the only Lancashire batsmen to total 2,000 runs in a season for the county. He carried his bat for 106 out of 208 in an admirable display at Trent Bridge when Richmond proved too good for all the others and he made 203 at Worcester and 200 not out against Northampton at Liverpool.

Hallows, too, had some wonderful days despite his illness, carrying his bat for 179 out of 393 at Southend and then scoring 41 not out when Lancashire went in to knock off the few runs required for victory. Ernest Tyldesley was not quite the dominating batsman of other seasons, but he rose to the occasion in great style when, after following on, Lancashire found themselves in trouble at the Oval. With a wonderful display of hooking and driving he hit 236 in five hours without giving a chance, and the game was saved. Sharp himself hit one brilliant century at Lord's.

Among the bowlers Richard Tyldesley took more than 100

wickets and did specially well when, taking 12 wickets for
100 runs at Northampton, he more than made up for Parkin's
absence. He also bowled well at Gloucester where Lancashire
won after being behind on the first innings. Leonard Green
here made the only century of his first-class career.

But despite all these feats, it was Parkin's season—176
wickets in the championship, and 209 in all games. In match
after match he proved too much for his opponents and there
were such returns as seven for 57 in Surrey's first innings at Old
Trafford, 15 for 95 against Glamorgan at Blackpool, 11 for 89
against Derbyshire at Old Trafford when the visitors were all
out for 37 in their second innings, 13 for 97 at Birmingham, ten
for 58 at Gravesend, and ten for 82 at Lord's. With the rise of
Maurice Tate and Macaulay it looked as though England had
found a Test match attack, and even at this distance of time
one feels the most acute disappointment that of the three men,
only one had the temperament to see him through the sternest
struggles.

When Parkin took his 14 wickets against Glamorgan, it was
the first county match at Blackpool since 1910, and it was
generally a successful occasion. Great crowds also watched
Cook's benefit match against Middlesex at Old Trafford, Lancashire getting home by six wickets just before seven o'clock
on the third day. Parkin was among the wickets again, but it
was consistent batting that really won the day, a first-innings
total of 385 being reached with a top individual score of 79 and
only one man failing to reach double figures.

Those who have so far followed the on-the-field events closely
will recall that in 1905 Lancashire dismissed Somerset for 65
and then scored 428 runs—all on the first day. Now, eighteen
years later, their successors did something comparable at Cardiff where on the opening day the visitors scored 332 all out,
with a specially fine century from Ernest Tyldesley, and then
got down nine Glamorgan wickets in an hour and a half for
88 runs.

Yet again Hampshire were concerned in a thrilling finish.
Lancashire scored 255, their visitors 259, and then the home
side, in attempting to force the pace, were all out for 177, leaving Hants 174 to get, two and a half hours available. No one
except Tennyson got many, but all scored a few, and at last
Hake, the last man, reached the wicket with seven runs wanted,

one minute to go. Hake took a single and at the end of the over stumps were pulled.

The county met Oxford University in a twelve-a-side game, and the South African A. E. Hall appeared, to take eight wickets, a performance he repeated against Cambridge University in the following fixture.

1924: CHAMPIONSHIP MATCHES:
Played 30, Won 11, Drawn 17, Lost 2

Lancashire had a fine side in their Diamond Jubilee year, with McDonald becoming available by residential qualification, and only circumstances beyond their control prevented them from making a closer bid for the championship. Every home fixture except one at Blackpool was interrupted by the abnormally bad weather, and even on this one more fortunate occasion, the start was put back because Essex were delayed on their journey. Of a dozen matches at Old Trafford, only two were finished.

The team went unbeaten until the middle of August, when they surprisingly went down against Glamorgan, and their other defeat was in the last fixture of all at Dover. It is not unreasonable to assume that if the middle of the season had given them finer weather, they would have finished higher than fourth and might even have toppled Yorkshire from their throne. As it was they had to be content with their great triumph at Leeds when they put their old rivals out for 33.

Parkin had a season of triumph and tragedy. He took 200 wickets again, finished third in the averages only a fraction behind Macaulay and Kilner, but put himself out of Test cricket by a glaring indiscretion. He, McDonald, and Richard Tyldesley captured between them 366 championship wickets at moderate cost, and each had a list of splendid feats. Parkin had eight for 20 in one innings against Derbyshire at Old Trafford, six for 6 and four for 30 against Glamorgan at Liverpool, 13 for 115 at Brighton, ten for 170 against Sussex at Old Trafford, ten for 142 against Essex at Blackpool, eight for 65 at Lord's, 12 for 71 at Dover, five for 6, and 11 for 63 at Chesterfield. Richard Tyldesley had his special triumph against Yorkshire, and also took seven cheap wickets against Glamorgan at Liverpool, 11 for 131 against Surrey at Old Trafford (where he also batted for an hour to save the game in company with

Leonard Green), 11 for 193 at Leyton, and a dozen wickets against the South Africans.

In two instances Richard Tyldesley even surpassed anything that Parkin did. Against Leicester at Old Trafford he took five wickets without conceding a run, a feat previously accomplished only by Pougher and George Cox, senior (and since equalled by Mills), and a month later at Liverpool he sent down 14 overs, 12 maidens, to capture seven Northampton wickets for six runs. He and Parkin bowled unchanged in both innings against Warwickshire, sharing the wickets equally.

McDonald captured six Kent wickets on his first appearance, shared in the haul against Northampton at Liverpool, and also had ten in the return. Naturally there was not much opportunity for any other bowlers, and Cook dropped right out. Hall appeared after some dispute about his qualification to play in championship matches, but did very little, and the next best bowler after the three great men was Watson, who added to his useful batting by taking 31 wickets at moderate cost.

Among the batsmen Ernest Tyldesley was first, Makepeace and Hallows both finding their averages affected by the wet pitches: Tyldesley batted beautifully on a difficult wicket against Kent at Old Trafford, making 57 and 148 not out. This was McDonald's first match, and also that of H. D. Davies, an amateur international footballer, later to become a member of the county committee, and a distinguished contributor to the sporting columns of the *Manchester Guardian*.

Hallows hit two not-out centuries at Ashby and shared in a partnership with Ernest Tyldesley of 185 runs in two hours. Hopwood hit his first century against the South African touring side.

The Yorkshire match at Leeds was of course the event of the year. Another game which produced more than its share of excitement was against Glamorgan at Liverpool where Lancashire, batting first, were all out for 49. It is said that telegrams of congratulation for Mercer, Spencer, Ryan, and their captain J. C. Clay began to arrive very quickly from their South Wales friends . . . but by the time they were delivered, Glamorgan in their turn had been routed by Parkin and Richard Tyldesley for 22. Makepeace and Hallows went in again, scored 107 together, and that won the match. It was in the return at

Swansea that Glamorgan won a completely unexpected triumph, Frank Ryan being carried shoulder high from the field by partisans who had at last seen the Welsh county justify their admission to the championship.

There was a tense finish to the game with Notts at Trent Bridge where the home side seemed set for victory at tea on the third day. Then Richard Tyldesley bowled so well that seven wickets went down in an hour, and when the extra half-hour was claimed it was Lancashire who thought they could sight victory. In the last quarter of an hour John Gunn and Matthews, the last pair, defended stubbornly and the game was left drawn with Notts still 15 runs short.

1925: CHAMPIONSHIP MATCHES:
Played 32, Won 19, Drawn 9, Lost 4

Bad weather had been against Lancashire in 1924 and now, in the following season, they set off with high hopes of the title. McDonald was fully available, there was the eager young Duckworth to keep for him, there was great batting talent— what could deny Lancashire the title? Only bad luck, and bad luck it was. Ernest Tyldesley was in great form, averaging 50 runs an innings, when he was taken ill, operated on for appendicitis, and put off the field for the rest of the season. It was a cruel blow to the side, and it is significant that three of the four defeats were incurred after he had dropped out. Not even the grand form of Watson could quite compensate for the loss of such a player.

The bowling was very strong. McDonald took 182 wickets in the championship, 205 in all games, and Parkin 121. Richard Tyldesley had 116 wickets and beat them both in the averages, Watson took 57, and there was a new name in Frank Sibbles, whose 43 wickets at 13 runs each actually put him on top of the county's bowling table.

McDonald took 20 wickets in the two games against Surrey and he had 11 for 144 against Leicester at Old Trafford and ten for 68 in the return, ten for 97 at Swansea, and ten for 68 (including the hat-trick) at Brighton. Parkin, a little more expensive this season, had 12 for 98 at Oxford, and Richard Tyldesley had eight for 40 at Chesterfield where Sibbles had five for 30 in the second innings and Derbyshire were put out for 67 and 79.

Twice Jack Sharp sent opponents in to bat without securing the result he hoped for. At Leyton, Essex made 293, and at Birmingham, Warwickshire scorned the supposed danger in the pitch by running up 414 for six wickets.

Somerset renewed fixtures with Lancashire after an interval of fourteen years, and their re-appearance at Old Trafford produced a one-day finish. The opening day was blank, and then on the second, Somerset were dismissed for 74. Lancashire fared little better until Richard Tyldesley and McDonald hit briskly to add 55. Somerset failed again for 73, only John Daniell showing fight with three drives for six off Parkin, and Lancashire won by nine wickets at seven o'clock. McDonald, Parkin and Richard Tyldesley all shared in the havoc.

Jack Sharp did not play regularly, and in his absence the side was led by J. R. Barnes or A. W. Pewtress. Barnes hit a magnificent century against Glamorgan at Old Trafford after the side had lost five wickets for 28 runs, and it was the prelude to victory. For Sharp it was a sad farewell to the game he had adorned for so long. In Parkin's benefit match he dropped H. W. Lee, of Middlesex, off the first ball sent down, and a partnership of 121 developed. The crowd treated the captain cruelly for this mistake and his first reaction was to give up the game immediately. Under pressure from the committee he relented, though it was no surprise when he resigned the captaincy and retired from the game at the end of the summer. In the last fixture of the season at Old Trafford he batted for two hours and a half to score 75, and on this occasion the big crowd made amends by showing their appreciation with a remarkable display of enthusiasm. It was in this match that Hammond (250) and Dipper (144) made 330 together, a record stand against Lancashire on their headquarters ground.

Great crowds attended Lancashire's home matches this season. There were 10,000 people at Liverpool to see the fixture with Sussex, and an equal number at Nelson, given a game as part of the agreement which released McDonald to the county. The fast bowler was among the wickets on his old league club ground, but the honours were taken by Hallows who carried his bat through a full innings for the second time in the season.

CHAPTER 16

Championship Matches

1926–8 Captain: Leonard Green

*Three years of triumph; Parkin leaves Lancashire; Ernest
Tyldesley's record run; A thrilling race with Yorkshire;
Slow batting criticised, 1927; Sibbles and Iddon make
progress; Hallows's two hours for seven runs; A
dramatic finish, 1927; No doubts this time,
1928; Hallows scores 1,000 runs in May;
Watson's Old Trafford record of
300; Duckworth's haul; Mc-
Donald the match-winner*

To FEW MEN has cricket brought such success as accompanied
Leonard Green's three years of leadership. By strength of
character, by a sense of leadership developed in a man who
regarded himself as a servant of the community, he welded a
group of great individualists into a champion team. In each
of his three seasons Lancashire finished at the head of the table
and if they possessed the finest bowler of the age in McDonald
and one of the cleverest right-arm slow bowlers in Richard
Tyldesley, if the batting was strong, and if there was a brilliant young wicket-keeper—it still required a captain to lead
the side to victory, and it required captaincy of a particular
brand.

Leonard Green's instincts and training led towards a sol-
dierly discipline but as a cricket captain he proved a kindly
commander, one whose own personal modesty inclined him
always to give others credit. A useful batsman, a courageous
fieldsman, he surmounted the difficulties provided by the dropping of Parkin in midsummer of 1926; he harnessed the somewhat emphatic personalities under his command, and after
two close finishes completed his hat-trick of championships
with a runaway win in 1928.

By 1951 Leonard Green had become Colonel L. Green, C.B., M.B.E., M.C., T.D., D.L., a devoted servant of the County Palatine, and election to the presidency of the cricket club with which he had been so long connected crowned his distinguished cricket career.

1926: CHAMPIONSHIP MATCHES:
Played 32, Won 17, Drawn 13, Lost 2

Lancashire became champions in 1926 for the first time since 1904, and if they won the title by a narrow margin, and if they lost twice whereas Yorkshire went through the summer unbeaten, the final leaders won seventeen matches, two more than any other county and three more than their nearest challengers, their old rivals from across the Pennines. Towards the end of the season, when the fight was really on, Lancashire won their matches whereas Yorkshire lost the finishing touch, and in this one respect at least the title went to the deserving side.

There was nothing at the outset to herald what was to come because the first four games were so badly affected by the weather that all were drawn and almost the only excitement in this period was at Gloucester, where Parker and Mills got down the first five Lancashire wickets for 19 runs. It was therefore mid-May before the first victories were registered; Derbyshire went down at Old Trafford before the brilliant bowling of Parkin, R. Tyldesley, and Sibbles, and a fine century by Hallows, and then Leicestershire were beaten in extra time at Liverpool, Parkin again being the destroyer-in-chief and Makepeace this time the century maker.

There followed a sharp reverse at Bradford and another weather-ruined match against Kent at Old Trafford, and then Lancashire gave a hint of their real power by beating Surrey after the visitors had set up a first-innings lead of 95. A long, uphill innings by E. Tyldesley began the recovery and splendid bowling by McDonald, R. Tyldesley, and Sibbles (who twice dismissed Hobbs) brought victory by 34 runs in what must have been in any event the last over. Going on to Northampton, R. Tyldesley had one of his best performances, eight wickets for 15 runs, though the side owed almost as much to two dogged innings by Makepeace. Notts, so far unbeaten, were overcome at Trent Bridge where Makepeace's steadiness was again a dominating factor. He carried his bat for 92 out of 159 in the first innings when Richmond was threatening to carry all before him, and then, after McDonald's seven for 78 had limited Notts' lead to 50, Makepeace and his captain led off the second innings with a stand of 105.

Another rain-spoiled game at Lord's was followed by the expected win over Gloucestershire at Old Trafford, Iddon coming forward with one of his earliest bowling feats in support of R. Tyldesley and Parkin, and then the team journeyed to Ashby-de-la-Zouch. The side touched something worse than mediocrity (though McDonald took 11 wickets) and they were beaten by 144 runs. Here was a turning point in Lancashire's cricket history because following this match Parkin, who had so signally failed to exploit the difficult pitch, was left out of the side, never to return. Although at this point of the season his 39 wickets had cost only 16 runs, the committee decided that his skill was declining, and his proffered resignation was accepted.

The team thenceforward, wrote Cardus, was new in temper and ability alike. Ernest Tyldesley went from triumph to triumph and to this day only Sir Donald Bradman can claim to have equalled his sequence of ten innings of fifty runs or more. An innings of 44 broke the run but he followed with two more big scores so that in 13 innings he totalled 1,477 runs.

John and Ernest had always been so successful at Edgbaston that it now seems but the natural turn of events that Tyldesley should have started his great run at Birmingham. With McDonald taking 13 wickets on a good pitch, Lancashire won inside two days and journeyed on to Dover, the fast bowler took a dozen more, with a hat-trick thrown in just when Kent seemed like making a fight of it on the last day.

Sussex and Somerset in turn escaped defeat with the connivance of the weather, and at the Oval the bat mastered the ball so that a finish never seemed likely. And at Nelson, of all places, McDonald was freely hit by the Essex batsman, so that Lancashire's progress received a sharp check, and up to this time, twenty championship fixtures had yielded only eight victories. But of the last twelve games, nine were won outright, first-innings points were taken from two, and only one was left without decision. The revival began at Taunton where G. F. Earle broke a pane of glass in the scorers' box and E. Tyldesley later drove the ball through the same window! At Chesterfield

Hallows and Watson made 188 together, and then R. Tyldesley achieved wonderful figures, five for 17 and five for 18, so that Derbyshire, all out for 46 in their second innings, were easily beaten. Makepeace batted for five hours for his 140 at Leyton, and McDonald was supreme in the later stages, though Essex carried the game into the extra half-hour.

Yorkshire limited Lancashire to a first-innings decision and there was no profit at all from the next fixture against Middlesex, best remembered for McDonald's hard-hit century, his only three-figure score in big cricket. This game yielded the last of Ernest Tyldesley's thirteen innings:

June 26, 28—144, v Warwick at Birmingham.
June 30, July 1 and 2—69 and 144 not out, v Kent at Dover.
July 3, 5, 6—226, v Sussex at Old Trafford.
July 10, 12, 13—51 and 131, v Surrey at the Oval.
July 14, 15, 16—131, for Players v Gentlemen at Lord's.
July 17, 19, 20—106, v Essex at Nelson.
July 21, 22, 23—126, v Somerset at Taunton.
July 24, 26, 27—81, v Australia at Old Trafford (Fourth Test).
July 28, 29, 30—44, v Essex at Leyton.
July 31, Aug. 2 and 3—139, v Yorkshire at Old Trafford.
Aug. 4, 5, 6—85, v Middlesex at Old Trafford.

An outstanding innings of 94 by Watson helped Lancashire to overcome Glamorgan at Blackpool where scoring was generally low, and fine all-round cricket won the match at Worcester where Iddon and M. L. Taylor of the younger players were seen to advantage. It was Iddon, too, who saved the situation at Bournemouth where Lancashire were put out for 89 by Newman and Boyes. Hallows and P. T. Eckersley led a recovery but even so Hampshire required only 147 to win. A thunderstorm followed by sunshine gave Lancashire their chance, seized by McDonald with four for 28 and Iddon, five for nine.

Now the struggle for the title came to a head. Yorkshire, champions in the four previous seasons, were in the lead, but while Iddon was bowling out Hampshire, the White Rose team were faltering and losing first-innings points against Surrey. Lancashire returned north to overwhelm Northants at Blackpool, almost everyone coming off with bat or ball, and they did not falter at the finish, settling the issue by defeating Notts with Old Trafford as the perfect setting. Notts made 292 and then

Lancashire forged ahead at a great pace, with a stand of 279 between Makepeace and E. Tyldesley as the big feature of a total of 454. McDonald, with a match record of 11 wickets for 173 runs, completed the job, and Lancashire were champions.

It was a brilliantly devastating finish to the season, and the disappointing turn of events when the Champions met the Rest of England at the Oval took but little of the gloss off their triumph. McDonald, Sibbles, and R. Tyldesley bowled out the Rest for 217, a magnificent feat against the identical eleven which a month earlier had won back the Ashes from Australia. However, Lancashire's batting in turn failed and then Woolley hit their bowling for 172 in 125 minutes. Larwood, Tate, Rhodes, and G. T. S. Stevens proved too strong a combination for the champions, who were in somewhat reckless mood towards the end, and the Rest won a remarkable match by 374 runs.

1927: CHAMPIONSHIP MATCHES:
Played 28, Won 10, Drawn 17, Lost 1

It had been a close fight in 1926, but 1927 brought an even harder tussle for the title. It was a miserably wet summer and of the 240 fixtures comprising the championship, only 110 were finished, and though Lancashire came in for frequent criticism for their slow rate of scoring, the few victories (ten) must be partly accountable to the weather. The record certainly looks poor in comparison with the seventeen victories of the previous year, but whereas they lost only once, both Notts and Yorkshire, their nearest challengers in the table, were each beaten three times.

Lancashire's slow batting lost them friends this year and during the following summers. It almost cost them the championship in 1927 because on some days, after the opposing bowling had been worn down, there was a disinclination to push on regardless of the fall of wickets. The slow rate of scoring arose from a variety of circumstances, one of which was the team's profound belief that, with their powerful bowling strength headed by McDonald, they could beat anyone else. The general policy was certainly to wear down rival bowling and then, in the late afternoon and evening, take toll of tired opposition, and that the policy was sometimes not carried out to its fullest expression must be blamed against the temperament of some of the team.

Watson, for instance, was not given by Nature the habit to play an adventurous type of cricket, and it so happened that in 1927 an injury to Ernest Tyldesley put an extra burden on Hallows, who held in check his instinctive leaning towards fluent stroke play. Makepeace, too, missed several matches, and in consequence something went from Hallows's batting that never returned, because defiance became second nature with him. Of his 44 innings, 13 were not outs, and of the men who played regularly in English cricket this season, he topped the averages with more than 75 runs an innings.

In one other respect the team fell short of the ideal, and that was in fielding, despite the encouragement and example of Duckworth behind the stumps. Yet if the batting, strong as it was, left itself open to criticism, and if there was occasional slowness to be observed in chasing the ball, there could be nothing but praise for the bowling. McDonald led the way, frequently reducing his great pace so that he could spin the ball on the many wet pitches encountered this year, and Richard Tyldesley remained a terror to all but the most quick-footed batsmen. Sibbles made a notable advance, and Iddon and Watson often bowled well enough to be classed as all-rounders.

It was Iddon, indeed, who struck the first stout blow in Lancashire's attempt to retain the title. After taking three cheap wickets in Warwickshire's first innings, he improved with six for 22 in the second innings and put them out for 64 when a draw seemed certain.

A draw in the return at Birmingham was followed by an easy win over Somerset, Hallows batting superbly and Sibbles taking 12 wickets for 74 runs. Then the team went to Ilkeston, were led on the first innings, and finally attempted to score 106 in an hour. Derbyshire's bowling on difficult turf was too good for the champions, however, and the game was left drawn with the scoreboard excitingly showing 68—7.

Now followed one of Old Trafford's historic innings, 187 at a run a minute by the young Hammond, whose batting against McDonald at his fastest remains a joyous memory for those who saw it. With this game drawn, Lancashire's record was so far rather drab, but five successive victories sent the team to the top of the table and, as events turned out, went far towards settling the championship. Hampshire were accounted for at Aigburth, Watson (125) and Hallows (233 not out) putting on

260 for the first wicket, and Glamorgan went down inside two days at Swansea. Worcestershire put up a sturdy fight at Dudley, Root's bowling troubling Lancashire as it did on other occasions, but McDonald rose to the occasion with some of his fiercest and finest bowling, and the visitors got home with four wickets to spare. The fourth victory in this sequence was at Bristol where E. Tyldesley and young P. T. Eckersley each hit a century, and Hammond, making 76 and 63, brought his aggregate for the two fixtures between the sides to 425 (he had scored 99 in the first innings of the Old Trafford fixture). So the team returned home for Whitsuntide, and their fifth victory was sweetest of all, at the expense of Yorkshire with McDonald taking 11 wickets for 135 runs.

For fourteen days the team had played cricket of genuine match-winning style, but now came frustration: fourteen successive matches yielded only one win and thirteen were left drawn. Immediately following the triumph over Yorkshire, Sussex administered a check by scoring 442 against Lancashire's 251, and it required an exceptional effort by Hallows to save the game. For almost five hours he held up Tate, Wensley, J. H. Parks, Cox, and Jim Langridge, and at the finish he was 118 and still undefeated. Whit week ended with some more tall scoring, D. R. Jardine hitting a century for Surrey and Iddon marking up his first hundred for his side in a total of 522 for nine. *Wisden's* summing-up of the match contained the remark that was unconscious prophecy: 'Jardine . . . faced the bumping bowling of McDonald with rare skill.'

Two other distinguished amateurs stood in the way in succeeding games, A. P. F. Chapman at Maidstone with 260 in little longer than three hours and H. J. Enthoven with a brilliant burst of hitting at Lord's after Hallows and Watson had made 164 together.

Successive games with Derbyshire and Essex were spoiled by a break in the weather, and then came a grim struggle at Old Trafford against Notts, now standing second in the table. Sibbles had five wickets in the dismissal of the visitors for 191 but on the second day Lancashire fared even worse—all out 141 of which E. Tyldesley made 87, making light of the soft pitch and the excellent bowling of Sam Staples, Larwood, and Voce. Notts were busy hammering home their advantage when rain put an end to the struggle.

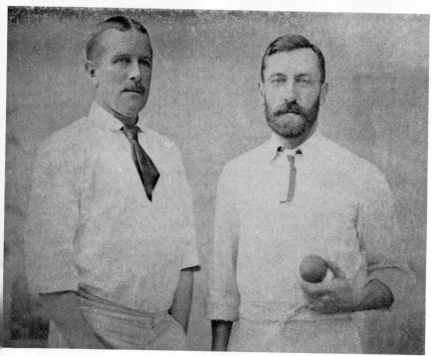

Above left: The first Lancastrian to score a century in the Roses match was Lt.-Col. Sir George M. Kemp, afterwards Lord Rochdale. *Above right*: Ernest Tyldesley scored his hundredth 100 in 1934. *Below*: 'O my Hornby and my Barlow...' The famous Lancashire opening pair, A. N. Hornby and R. G. Barlow.

Above: E. A. McDonald and Cyril Washbrook. *Centre*: C. H. Parkin and E. Paynter. *Below*: Harry Dean and J. L. Hopwood.

There was another rain-ruined match against Leicester and then the gloom was broken by victory at Southampton, the Hampshire batsmen lacking resolution against some excellent fast bowling by McDonald who, after a lean period, re-asserted himself with 11 wickets for 145 runs. Rain cut down the game at Taunton to a draw, and a dead pitch at the Oval was all against the bowlers. The bad weather persisted through three home matches against Northants at Old Trafford, Worcester at Nelson (where Root and McDonald were both in form) and Essex at Liverpool, and Lancashire were passed by Notts, who went to the top of the table as the competition entered its last testing month.

First-innings points were gained from Yorkshire, splendid all-round form won full points from Middlesex, and Lancashire were on top again. A strong position against Kent was nullified by rain, but the winning touch returned at Northampton with 12 wickets for McDonald and resolute batting by Watson and his captain. Then came a remarkable match at Trent Bridge with all the cricket world watching the tussle. Lancashire blundered in the field and, against a total of 420, they collapsed against Sam Staples for 148 and had to follow on. The rearguard action that followed not only saved the game but checked Lancashire's biggest rivals. No one was in sterner mood than Hallows who on the third day revived memories of Barlow by batting for more than two hours for seven runs before rain set in.

Defeat by Sussex was an unexpected set-back; it could not have come at a worse time, and Notts went into the lead again. The programme ended with a draw at Leicester, and the team journeyed home to await the outcome of the match between Notts and Glamorgan, apparently an easy task for the former because Glamorgan had so far laboured all season without a victory. A draw would have been sufficient to give Notts the championship but Mercer and Ryan put them out for 61 and the title stayed at Old Trafford. It was the most dramatic turn of fortune in the history of the championship.

This was the final position at the head of the table:

	P	W	L	1st inns W	1st inns L	No Result	Poss Pts	Pts Obt	%
Lancs	28	10	1	11	5	1	224	154	68.75
Notts	28	12	3	8	4	1	224	152	67.85

L

In addition to the matches reckoned in the table, Lancashire had four fixtures with less than four hours' play, and Notts two, not included in the championship.

The season ended with another rain-spoiled fixture, Champions v the Rest at the Oval, though there was just time for Hallows to hit his seventh hundred of the season.

1928: CHAMPIONSHIP MATCHES:
Played 30, Won 15, Drawn 15, Lost 0

If there had been doubts about Lancashire's right to the leadership in 1926 when they suffered two defeats, or in 1927 when they drew so many of their games, there were none in 1928. The third successive title was gained in the clearest fashion for they not only won fifteen of their fixtures—five more than in the previous summer—but went through the year unbeaten. True, they lost the lead in the table to Kent in midsummer, but towards the end of July Lancashire went ahead again and a brilliant finish to the season set the seal on their hat-trick of championships.

The year was a vintage season for batsmen all over the country, and Hallows, Watson, and Ernest Tyldesley shared in the revels, yet before paying tribute to them, the match-winning prowess of McDonald must be mentioned. Playing in every one of the thirty championship fixtures the Australian, though thirty-six years of age, kept up his form and his speed in a remarkable way. In championship games he took 178 wickets for 19 runs each and how much depended on him may be judged from the figures of the other bowlers: Richard Tyldesley 85 wickets for just under 21 runs each, Iddon 56 for 23 each, Hopwood 33 at 25 each, Booth 17 at 26, and Sibbles 32 at just under 30 runs each.

Outstanding among many batting feats was the triumph of Hallows in scoring 1,000 runs in May. He hit 100 against Northants, 101 and 51 not out against Glamorgan (all at Old Trafford), 123 and 101 not out against Warwick at Birmingham, 22 against Middlesex at Lord's, 74 and 104 against Warwick at Nelson, 58 and 34 not out against Yorkshire at Sheffield, and 232 against Sussex at Old Trafford. Following completion of his 1,000 runs, Hallows took his benefit against Surrey and though he himself made only 36, the match was made memorable by the success of other batsmen who so

dominated the fixture that only 13 wickets went down while
1,155 runs were scored. Before retiring with illness, Sandham
contributed 282 towards Surrey's total of 567, and then Lancashire scored 588 for four wickets, Watson's 300 not out surpassing J. T. Tyldesley's score of 295, an Old Trafford record
since 1902. Another record was set up by Watson's stand of
371 with E. Tyldesley (187), the highest Lancashire partnership for any wicket.

Another feature of this remarkable year was the success of
the first-wicket pair Watson and Hallows, who opened with a
three-figure stand on twelve occasions. They and E. Tyldesley
each totalled more than 2,000 runs in championship matches.
Tyldesley indeed had one of his best seasons; he played in the
Test matches against the West Indies (after scoring 160 not out
in a Test trial at Lord's), scored 112 for once out against the
Gentlemen at Lord's, and altogether aggregated 3,024 runs for
the season, average 79.57.

This season marked the return to first-class cricket of Hopwood, proving his value at once with 566 runs and 33 wickets
in 20 matches. Iddon, too, made a real advance, though not
unexpectedly Watson's value as a bowler declined. The all-
round excellence of the side was completed by Duckworth's
wicket-keeping; in this year he secured 107 wickets—77 caught
and 30 stumped—and only Ames's bag of 121 prevented the
Lancashire man from setting up a new record.

The team embarked on their championship programme
against Northampton at Old Trafford and after Watson (223),
Hallows (100), and E. Tyldesley (140 not out) had set the pattern for the season, R. Tyldesley won the match with 11
wickets for 91 runs. Having scored 200 together, the first-
wicket pair followed with 202 against Glamorgan and after
McDonald and R. Tyldesley had bowled skilfully, Hallows
and Watson knocked off the 107 required for victory. They
immediately followed with 118 together at Birmingham but
though Iddon had a remarkable first-innings analysis of eight
for 50, Warwick saved the game. A draw at Lord's, an easy
win at Nelson, a draw against Yorkshire, and then came Hallows's completion of his 1,000 runs against Sussex with
McDonald bowling finely. After the heavy-scoring match
against Surrey already mentioned the team were headed on the
first innings at Northampton and glad to get away unbeaten,

and when they failed to force a win at Swansea, Lancashire had completed ten championship matches and won only four of them. They won well at Cheltenham, where Iddon took five wickets in each innings, and then drew three more games with rain intervening each time.

Now McDonald roused himself, taking 11 wickets for 113 runs at Colchester so that only two runs were required for victory in the second innings. There was no extra-half-hour rule in those days, and Essex had to take the field on the third morning when two balls were bowled and Hodgson hit a boundary off the second.

Rain interfered with the home fixture against Worcester, so that now the record read sixteen played, only six won; but better things were to come, beginning with a comfortable win over Hampshire at Southampton where E. Tyldesley scored 115 and 80 not out and R. Tyldesley, after a rather lean spell, struck form again with six first-innings wickets for 41 runs. He bowled well again at Worcester, too, after Hallows and Watson had scored 230 together, though the home side saved the game with centuries by Gibbons and W. V. Fox.

Four splendid victories followed in succession. The first-wicket pair made 182 together against Hants and 142 and 56 (unbroken) against Essex and then at the Oval young Iddon, now a regular member of the side, played a six-hour innings of 184 before a blow over the heart compelled his retirement. At Maidstone, Watson and Hallows were in form again—200 together this time. In these four fixtures the chief batsmen of the side had performed great deeds, yet the true match-winner was McDonald who in a fortnight took 35 wickets for 526 runs, bowling with superb spirit though called upon for long spells.

Notts and Yorkshire checked the run of victories, then Middlesex were beaten thanks to E. Tyldesley's 168 and Hopwood's eight cheap wickets, and then as though to proclaim their right to the championship Lancashire scored one of the outstanding successes of the season, defeating Kent, their most powerful rivals, at Old Trafford in a match of dramatic surprises.

Kent went in first and, with Woolley at his best, the score stood at 262 for four. McDonald and Sibbles then bowled to such purpose that the last six wickets went down for 15 runs and the batsmen followed up this good work by making 478 for five. Watson and Hallows led off with 155 together, Hallows and E. Tyldesley went on with 207, and after an hour's batting on the third day Lancashire declared. The rest of the match belonged to McDonald who, bowling unchanged, put Kent out for 113, and built up a match record of 15 wickets for 154 runs.

At Leicester, E. Tyldesley hit 242—one of his most brilliant innings—and with Iddon (113) put on 300, and though rain prevented a finish, Lancashire were in no mood to falter. A partnership of 306 by Watson and E. Tyldesley and effective bowling by McDonald brought victory at Brighton and by 24 August the championship was safely achieved.

A friendly match at Blackpool with Wales as opponents might have been expected to give some relief from the strain of searching for points but the veteran Sydney Barnes, fifty-five years of age, took six wickets and Lancashire owed almost everything to Hallows's century in a total of exactly 200. Victory was gained in the end, though the game ran almost the full three days.

The championship programme ended at Burton where Lancashire won easily. Then only one task remained, to face the full might of the Rest of England at the Oval, and when Hallows and Makepeace (Watson was unable to play) opened with a stand of 134 there must have been high hopes that there would be revenge for the disastrous experience of two years earlier. It was not to be, because Lancashire were all out for 296 and then Hobbs, Sutcliffe, and Hendren hit so brilliantly that 603 runs were amassed in 345 minutes. The attack of Larwood, Tate, Freeman, and Hammond was too much for the champions and though E. Tyldesley hit 63 in an hour, Lancashire were beaten by an innings and 91 runs.

CHAPTER 17

Championship Matches

1929–35 Captain: P. T. Eckersley

*Two more championship triumphs; Should only Lancashire-
born cricketers play for the county?; Flying to a match; G. O.
Allen and Freeman each take all ten Lancashire wickets;
Makepeace retires, 1929; Ernest Tyldesley's highest
score; A determined finish, 1930; Paynter makes
his mark, 1931; The Eastbourne incident;
Washbrook, Phillipson and Pollard appear,
1933; All-round work succeeds, 1934;
Historic match with Notts, and an
unfortunate sequel; Farrimond
gets his chance*

AFTER THE THREE great seasons of 1926–7–8 the committee had
to face up to the knowledge that McDonald's bowling and
Makepeace's batting would soon become less valuable. As
events turned out, two further blows befell the team because
Hallows quite unexpectedly lost his form and his place, and
R. Tyldesley, differing with the club over a question of guaranteed salary, dropped out of first-class cricket when still at the
height of his powers. These were grievous losses yet the steady
reshaping of the team was so skilfully managed, and the extra
burdens so manfully borne by veterans and youngsters alike,
that during the new captain's seven seasons, the championship
was won on two occasions. A special cause of satisfaction was
the development of cricketers from within the county.

The policy of qualifying players from overseas had brought
results but equally had attracted criticism; it may be said here
that the Lancashire committee were not always the prime
movers, as for instance when approaches were made to the club
in 1930 on behalf of three outstanding overseas cricketers.

The rank-and-file members had always been divided on the

question, if only for the chaff they had to bear from Yorkshire-men on Bank Holidays, and at the annual meeting of 1935 an attempt was made to carry a proposal that the team be confined to those possessing birth qualification. This was opposed by the committee and the members instead agreed to the following expression of opinion:

> Whilst the committee should as far as possible only include Lancashire-born men in the county team it is undesirable that men who have settled and whose interests are in the county should be excluded from county cricket.

While this did not tie the hands of the committee it was a fairly strong indication of the wishes of the members, though three years later Mr. T. A. Higson (then hon. treasurer) was to declare that 'Boggling who was to play for Lancashire among those qualified by the rules of cricket, would land them in financial difficulties before long'.

During the period under review in this chapter much native talent was developed and discovered. Makepeace followed J. T. Tyldesley as coach and extra assistance was obtained by en-gaging for brief periods S. F. Barnes and Cecil Parkin. In this way losses were generally made good though, as will be seen, a marked trend set in that led to the replacement of great specialists by all-rounders.

P. T. Eckersley himself was not an outstanding cricketer; indeed, one sometimes had the impression that he found it hard work. He brought to his task, however, a belief in the mission of wealthy Lancashire amateurs to play their part in cricket and this sense of duty kept him going through many a long and test-ing day in the field. He had a natural gift for leadership ex-pressed not by giving orders or making rules but by example and genial personality, and he possessed the rare gift of attract-ing affectionate friendship. As a batsman he had a good eye but inadequate footwork and this defect let him in for occasional hard knocks, borne with fortitude. He was a keen amateur pilot and when war broke out in 1939 he was among the first to serve, though as a Member of Parliament he could have claimed exemption. He was killed less than a year later.

His period of leadership was noteworthy in other respects than that of merely winning matches. In his first year the com-mittee, possibly anxious to assist a new and young captain, imposed a ban on their professionals writing for the Press. Instructional articles were not intended to be affected, but the club did not wish to run the risk of any further ill-feeling such as had been engendered by Parkin's outburst some years earlier.

It was a tribute to the work of the team, the popularity of the captain, wise leadership from the committee-room, and the amenities of Old Trafford, that about this time the membership reached a new record of 4,055 plus 1,387 ladies, 173 juniors, and 121 popular-side season-ticket holders. These figures were not surpassed until after the Second World War.

Another event during Eckersley's period of captaincy was that the team became the first to fly to a championship fixture. This was following the game at Cardiff in 1935; the captain arranged for two aircraft to be made available and the side flew to Southampton in fifty minutes.

1929: CHAMPIONSHIP MATCHES:
Played 28, *Won* 12, *Drawn* 13, *Lost* 3

The season of 1929 saw the introduction of larger stumps, while the championship was contested under a system which, giving each county an equal number of fixtures, avoided percentages. Nottinghamshire won the title and though Lancashire tied with Yorkshire for second place this was due to a successful second half of the season and they never really looked quite capable of topping the table.

In Whit week bright batting by almost all the Sussex team and in particular a brilliant innings by K. S. Duleepsinhji sent Lancashire toppling to their first defeat since August 1927—by Sussex at Eastbourne.

Subsequent matches brought some splendid performances, as for instance when Watson (207) and E. Tyldesley (187) engaged in a partnership of 336 at Worcester. A remarkable victory was secured at Swansea after Glamorgan gained a first-innings lead of 72, spirited hitting by E. Tyldesley and Iddon bringing victory a quarter of an hour from time. Most remarkable of all however were two performances not for the team, but against them. At Lord's G. O. Allen took all ten wickets and Freeman emulated the feat at Maidstone where, however, Lancashire ran out winners by 189 runs.

When Makepeace returned to the side the batting was immediately stiffened and much was due to him for avoiding a second defeat by Sussex. He finished the season, and virtually his own career, at the top of the county averages. The weakness of the side was shown in the bowling figures—McDonald 140 wickets, R. Tyldesley 136, and no one else more than 44.

1930: CHAMPIONSHIP MATCHES:
Played 28, Won 10, Drawn 18, Lost 0

Alone of all the counties Lancashire went through 1930 undefeated and the championship was regained after a close struggle. There was slightly better support for the two chief bowlers, Hopwood taking 63 wickets and Sibbles 49. Yet it was the batting strength that was most impressive, with as many as ten members of the team showing an average of more than 20 runs an innings. E. Tyldesley, now forty-one years of age, had a wonderful season, playing in every match and heading the averages with nearly 55 runs an innings. Watson, the next man, was 11 runs lower, but then close up came so many heavy run-getters that the falling-off in the form of Hallows was hardly felt.

The team had the benefit of a bright start. Enterprising batting and clever slow-bowling accounted for Northants at Old Trafford and successive games against Gloucestershire yielded a win and then first-innings points from opponents who were to prove eventual runners-up in the championship. A break was made for a meeting with the Australians at Liverpool (where McDonald, to his unbounded delight, clean-bowled Bradman), and then came a magnificent match at Northampton where after A. L. Cox had caused a brief flutter by taking four wickets in five balls, Lancashire got home in extra time by two wickets. A tiring journey to Cardiff did not affect the match-winning powers of the team for E. Tyldesley hit two separate hundreds and then R. Tyldesley finished off the match by taking Glamorgan's last six wickets for 20 runs. A check by the weather at Lord's was succeeded by the complete overthrow of Leicester at Nelson where McDonald, R. Tyldesley, and Duckworth were all seen to advantage, and this brought the record to five wins in seven championship games. This was the limit of victories for some time, however, draws against Notts, Yorkshire, Sussex, Surrey and Worcester allowing Kent and Notts in turn to overtake them in the table.

An unusual feature of the Surrey fixture at Old Trafford was that R. Tyldesley was unable to play in his own benefit match as he was a member of the England team against Australia at Trent Bridge. A. P. F. Chapman and the remainder of the Test eleven issued an appeal to the Lancashire public not to allow the great bowler's absence to affect the financial outcome of the occasion, and the response was generous. Surrey played their part with consistent batting that won the long-drawn-out struggle for first-innings points.

At last, as June gave way to July, the winning touch was regained at the right time and against the right opponents. Kent were leading the championship table when they arrived at Old Trafford and Lancashire asserted themselves to such a degree that victory was won by an innings and 49 runs. Three telling factors were McDonald's fast bowling that earned him 11 wickets for 160 runs; centuries by Watson and E. Tyldesley who together scored 206 in three hours; and the wicket-keeping of Farrimond who, in Kent's second innings, equalled the record by dismissing seven batsmen. A hat-trick by McDonald was a feature of the next victory at Birmingham and in the return match, when Warwick narrowly escaped defeat, E. Tyldesley hit 256 not out, the highest score of his career.

This was the beginning of a run of eight drawn games, rain following the team wherever they travelled, and Yorkshire went to the head of the table for two weeks at the end of July. A close race for championship now developed, won by Eckersley's men as the result of three victories in their last five fixtures. Brilliant bowling by R. Tyldesley earned him 12 wickets for 64 runs and an easy win at Leicester, and splendid all-round work gained a second success over Kent at Dover. Two drawn games followed and then the side entered on their last engagement against Essex at Blackpool knowing that outright victory would give them the championship irrespective of what Gloucester or Yorkshire could accomplish. Consistent batting, led first by Watson and then by Paynter, was followed by keen fielding and steady bowling that well earned a winning margin of 174 runs quite early on the third day.

It was sheer anticlimax when the Champions, fielding and batting well below form, lost to the Rest of England at the Oval by ten wickets, though Booth gave a hint of his possibilities and Watson played an attractive second innings.

Lancashire did not play a prominent part in the struggle for honours during the next three seasons when they twice finished sixth and then fifth. The immediate causes were the decline and departure of McDonald, the dispute that closed the career of R. Tyldesley, and the illness of Watson. It was appreciated that McDonald could not go on for ever and whereas he captured 104 wickets in 1930, his falling-off was so sudden that in 1931 he took part in only fourteen matches and his 26 wickets cost about 39 runs each. His contract, with a further season to run, was cancelled by mutual consent and he returned to league cricket.

1931: CHAMPIONSHIP MATCHES:
Played 28, Won 7, Drawn 17, Lost 4

Watson's illness compelled him to miss twenty-one games and with Hallows failing to find his old form, the batting was a good deal weaker. In a wet summer the averages were generally lower, though Paynter made a big advance and Horrocks, a Warrington man who had played with success in Australia, hit one valuable century against Notts at Old Trafford.

With no hint as yet of impending separation, R. Tyldesley had a fine season with 116 wickets for under 16 runs apiece, and Sibbles, as though spurred on by the decline in McDonald's match-winning powers, increased his season's haul to 82 wickets at moderate cost.

The opening games of this season foretold the loss of the championship title. Sussex, for years doughty opponents of Lancashire's, won at Old Trafford thanks to Tate's excellent bowling; even more significantly the team were put out at Worcester for 75 and 85, Perks six for 44, and Root 12 for 50, giving the western county their first victory over Lancashire since their double success of 1913.

Once again Freeman took all ten wickets in a Lancashire innings, this time at Old Trafford. He ought not to have been credited with the record on this occasion as with nine men out McDonald gave an easy chance in the out-field and the fieldsman obligingly dropped it.

When Lancashire went to Eastbourne the professionals, recalling some ill-informed remarks made in the close season by the Mayor of the town, declined to attend an official lunch. Goodwill on both sides restored harmony on the following day and the incident was not allowed to interfere with the good relationship traditionally existing between the two counties.

1932: CHAMPIONSHIP MATCHES:
Played 28, Won 8, Drawn 14, Lost 6

If six defeats were suffered this season, the record was in some ways better. For one thing, the batting averages improved, with E. Tyldesley (now the only remaining playing member of the two families) the most successful; and a big jump forward by Paynter, who this season hit his historic century against Yorkshire at Bradford, confirmed the arrival of a great batsman not only for Lancashire but for England too. The big surprise was the advance of Iddon who, with 76 wickets in championship fixtures and 80 in all, joined the ranks of the leading all-rounders. Sibbles took 122 wickets, Hodgson 50, and if Hopwood's haul was rather smaller, the return of Booth with 52 wickets was a considerable event. Two new all-rounders were introduced in H. R. W. Butterworth and Parkinson, and the whole team strove pluckily to make good the loss of the great individualists.

Special emphasis was placed on keenness in the field, built round the happy leadership of P. T. Eckersley and the agile wicket-keeping of Duckworth.

An interesting occurrence at Worcester, where Lancashire scored 428 for two wickets and declared, was the prolongation of cricket to almost eight o'clock to secure a finish on the second day. Two or three counties were at this time experimenting with the hours of play in an attempt to attract a new public, but few people on either side of the boundary were really interested.

A county record was set up when Sussex came to Old Trafford, Iddon (200) and H. R. W. Butterworth (107) making 278 together for the sixth wicket, and the books of reference were turned again when Somerset, sent in to bat at Weston-super-Mare, defied the gesture and obtained their first victory over Lancashire since 1903.

1933: CHAMPIONSHIP MATCHES:
Played 28, Won 9, Drawn 18, Lost 1

The record improved again in 1933 in that, even if the victories numbered only nine, the defeats fell from four in 1931, and six in 1932, to a single reverse. With the big premium of

15 points now placed on each victory, immunity from defeat hardly carried its former distinction yet as Yorkshire, the champions, lost three times. Lancashire could feel that fifth place barely did them justice. Even the one defeat came about in unusual circumstances, dealt with in the chapter devoted to fixtures with Yorkshire.

Tribute has already been paid to the fashion in which the all-rounders had rallied to their task and now on the scene came Washbrook, Hawkwood, W. H. L. Lister, Phillipson and Pollard, first to give hints of their skill, and later to revitalise the whole team.

The summer was an exceptional one for batsmen, the weather being the finest since 1921. It was not surprising, therefore, that ten of the regular players came out with an average of 20 runs or more an innings. On the whole the bowling figures fell off a little.

The team started well enough, and in beating Middlesex at Lord's in their second game they effected a dramatic change in the fortunes of the match. At lunch-time on the third day a draw looked the only possible result but during the interval Walter Brearley took Frank Booth to the nets to illustrate his suggested use of the full width of the bowling crease. Whether it was the hint, or through some other entirely unconnected cause, Booth bowled magnificently in the afternoon, Middlesex were put out for 69, and from an unlikely situation a dazzling victory was fashioned. But once May was out, the hard pitches exposed the limitations of the attack, no matter how willing the spirit.

Phillipson and Washbrook made their début together at Old Trafford and the former made his mark at once—as a batsman. Nine wickets fell to the Sussex bowling for 209 before Phillipson and P. T. Eckersley put on 102 for the last wicket. Washbrook hit a few brisk fours in the second innings and then in the next match earned undying fame by taking 152 off the Surrey bowling. There were those present who saw in the eighteen-year-old professional a likeness to J. T. Tyldesley; did they know, one wonders, that he had likewise scored 152 in his second match in 1895? Washbrook's overall record for the season was modest enough but no one had any doubt about his ultimate success. At Leicester he had a distressing experience, a full swing of his bat striking Corrall on the head. The wicket-keeper was taken to hospital in a semi-conscious condition and did not play again all summer, and Washbrook's nerve too may have taken a little time to recover from such an accident.

W. H. L. Lister, who played for Cambridge University at Association football but did not gain his cricket Blue, also scored a century on his second appearance and showed immediate skill in shaping his style to the needs of the moment. Often he defended with resolution, yet he could hit finely as he showed at Worcester when he rattled up 96 out of 162 in an hour.

There were three glorious finishes this year. Set to score 131 at Buxton, seven men were out with 22 runs still needed before Iddon and Booth came together—the latter making the winning hit with a drive for six. It was even closer at Bournemouth where after E. Tyldesley and Mead had graced the occasion with centuries, Hampshire were finally asked to score 218 in 210 minutes. Seven men were out for 71 before Creese and Boyes changed the picture with a spell of brilliant hitting that added 134. It was Booth again who played the ace, this time coming back with the new ball to give Lancashire victory by 7 runs with seven minutes to spare. Later in the year Essex were beaten at Liverpool by 17 runs after the sides had tied on the first innings and once again it was Booth who struck the last blow.

1934: CHAMPIONSHIP MATCHES:
Played 30, *Won* 13, *Drawn* 14, *Lost* 3

This was the year of another championship triumph, and it is no disparagement of the players to say that their success came as a surprise to the cricket world in general. Yorkshire, head of the table for three successive summers, were weakened by claims of the Test matches against Australia, yet, having said that, one must direct attention to the many attributes of the Lancashire side. In the first instance, they were a young team; apart from Tyldesley, yet including such experienced cricketers at Iddon, Hopwood, Watson, Duckworth and Sibbles, the average age of the twelve players who made most appearances was only twenty-eight. The all-round fielding of the team was of a high standard, perhaps more effective than during the three great years, 1926–8, and the batting remained as strong as ever.

If the bowling lacked a McDonald or a Parkin, it contained something for almost every type of wicket, and six bowlers returned an average of something under 23 runs a wicket. It was, in fact, a team of all-rounders, and it broke a long championship tradition of emphasis on the importance of fast bowling. Of successive champions since 1919 Lancashire this season were the first to win the title without possessing any real pace. It has been said, indeed, that they were the first for many seasons to win without having recourse to the 'bumper'.

Nor, in spite of its youth, did the eleven lack staying power. From 22 May Sussex led the way and it was not until 14 August that Lancashire superseded them, but once they reached the top they held on with fine tenacity. One final cause of satisfaction was that their total of thirteen victories exceeded that of any other county and was more than Lancashire had won in any season since 1928.

The side gained much advantage from their captain's luck with the toss, batting first twenty-four times in their thirty championship fixtures. So often was a strong position obtained that there were eighteen declarations, and one's general impression is that a keen set of players, led with tact and understanding, thoroughly deserved their unexpected triumph. As the county also finished top of the second-class table it was a capital season in every way, rounded off by the discharge at long last of the liability on the ground purchase.

In the first seven championship fixtures, only one victory was gained—over Somerset at Old Trafford, thanks to a century by Watson and lively bowling by Sibbles and Booth. Leicester wriggled out of a tight corner and another disappointment came with a severe defeat by Yorkshire, followed by the loss of first-innings points to both Essex and Surrey. The last of the three Whitsuntide games was for Duckworth's benefit and the match was made memorable by Hobbs scoring 116—as things turned out, his last century.

At this point in the season the record was modest but when the team went on tour in June successive victories were gained at Bristol, Worcester, Southampton, and Nottingham. Against Gloucester, Hopwood and Tyldesley made 316 for the second wicket and Sibbles bowled with wonderful effect for a match return of nine wickets for 45 runs in 41 overs. Watson's all-round form—an innings of 148 and eight wickets—was the outstanding feature at Worcester and then Hopwood, Parkinson, and Iddon shone in turn against Hampshire so that in these three matches the full strength of the team had been nicely exhibited.

The side then moved on to Trent Bridge to play a match that has become historic. It was fought out at a level of skill fit for a Test match and it had a gripping finish with the last wicket falling to the third l.b.w. appeal in what must have been in any case the last over. Unfortunately that was not all; it was also fought out with an intensity of feeling that was to leave its mark on the relationship between the two counties.

It was known that Lancashire's official view was opposed to the methods still occasionally adopted by Voce and Larwood, central figures in the 1932–3 bodyline controversy, and there was a stormy scene in one of the dressing-rooms before the game started.

Roused by the background to the fixture, Larwood bowled at his fastest on the first morning; for most people on the ground it was the most brilliant exhibition of speed bowling they had ever seen and though he had five slip catches missed, his analysis at one time showed six wickets for one run. He followed this up with a capital display of hitting, his 80 made in 45 minutes including 6 sixes and 8 fours. Notts therefore scored 266 to Lancashire's 119 and if ever a match looked lost, this was it.

The recovery that followed forms one of the most glorious passages in the county's history. Against fast bowling frequently pitched short, Watson made 63, W. H. Lister 86, Parkinson 30, P. T. Eckersley 40, and above all Tyldesley hit a century which must count among the three finest pieces of batting even in his great career. He hooked Larwood and Voce with matchless courage and Eckersley was able to declare at 394 for seven.

The match was saved; could it be won? The answer came from the slow bowlers, of whom Hopwood was most successful with six wickets, though Iddon's accurate length played its part. When Hopwood and Duckworth appealed for the last time and the tenth Notts wicket fell at 146 to give Lancashire victory by 101 runs, the fielding side did not conceal their elation and at least one set of stumps was flung high in the air.

The sequel was less happy. The Lancashire batsmen had been knocked about and on their return to Manchester some of them told the committee that they would not care to play

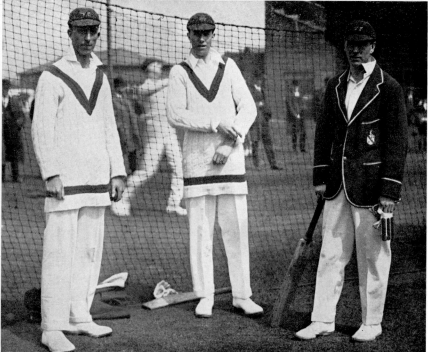

Above: A happy group of Lancashire players photographed during Hallows' benefit match (Lancs. v Surrey, June 1928). *Left to right*: E. Tyldesley, F. Watson, C. Hallows, R. Tyldesley and H. Makepeace. *Below*: At the nets early in the season. *Left to right*: J. Iddon, F. M. Sibbles and E. Tyldesley.

Old Trafford in the 1930s.

Left: Ernest Butler Rowley, who captained the team for half the season in 1896 and is now the last of the Rowleys who played for the county. *Right*: T. A. Higson, hon. treasurer 1924–32, chairman 1932–49, and a member of the committee for forty-nine years.

at Trent Bridge again in similar circumstances. Fixtures between the two counties were not made for 1935 and so a series of matches unbroken (save for the 1914–18 war years) since 1886 was at last interrupted. Fortunately it was found possible to resume the connection in 1936.

After these excitements there was a return to Old Trafford for a draw with Hampshire and defeat by Kent in two days on a rain-affected pitch. Victory over Glamorgan at Liverpool was largely secured by winning the toss, the Welsh county being sent in and Hopwood rising to the test first with seven wickets for 13 runs and then five for 55. A heavy-scoring game against Sussex was the occasion of Tyldesley's surpassing the county aggregate record of 32,267 held by his famous brother. A fifth consecutive home match took the team to Blackburn where almost everyone did something towards defeating Northants in two days and then the sides immediately played the return fixture at Peterborough where Sibbles bowled splendidly to thrust home the advantage gained early on by sound batting featured by Tyldesley's hundredth hundred.

Returning north to Blackpool the batting broke down badly against Worcester and a first-innings deficit of 108 threatened defeat, turned to victory by steady batting at the second attempt and superb bowling by Hopwood who had 15 wickets for 112 runs.

The batting failed again a week later at Lord's, and this time there was no recovery, Middlesex winning by ten wickets. This was, however, the last championship defeat of the season because the team, possibly a little tired and weakened by an injury to Sibbles, now had the reinforcement of Pollard's medium-fast bowling, which attracted attention when he skittled out Gloucester at Old Trafford and by steady work against Leicester at Liverpool.

Hopwood had another big haul of thirteen wickets against Derbyshire and almost everyone had something to say in the victory over Middlesex in which Duckworth did not concede a single bye while 465 runs were scored. When 167 runs were hit off in 130 minutes from the Middlesex bowling Lancashire went to the top of the table and they left Manchester for their southern tour with the knowledge that first-innings points in each match would give them the championship. They gained these by 12 runs against Essex, easily against Kent, and by 53

M

runs against Sussex. With this last challenge held off it only remained for first-innings points to be secured at the Oval and there was never any real doubt thanks to a century by the admirable Hopwood and sound support from Iddon, Tyldesley, Paynter, and Parkinson.

Defeat by the Rest of England at the Oval was largely due to the batting of Leyland, the wicket-keeping of Wood, and the bowling of Bowes and Verity, so Yorkshire, if they felt their championship chances had been prejudiced by the Test matches, had some slight compensation.

1935: CHAMPIONSHIP MATCHES:
Played 28, Won 12, Drawn 10, Lost 6

In 1935, though Lancashire won twelve of their twenty-eight fixtures, they lost six times and fell to fourth place in the table. The reason for their failures is not far to seek: Tyldesley and Iddon missed many matches through illness and injury and Watson lost his form to such a degree that he was for a time left out of the team. Three such batsmen were naturally much missed in spite of the progress of Washbrook and the arrival of a new and brilliant batsman in Oldfield. Sibbles and Booth were also prevented from appearing regularly though here the loss was less noticeable due to the advance of Pollard and Phillipson. More opportunities were given to Farrimond this season and besides keeping wicket skilfully he occasionally scored runs well in his highly individualistic style marked by vigorous sweeping strokes on the leg side.

The season opened with a low-scoring game at Lord's where in the final phase Middlesex needed 61 to win. Pollard gave events an exciting twist by dismissing the first five batsmen for 30 runs but this stout effort failed to ward off defeat. In the following fixture Washbrook foretold his successful season by carrying his bat for 49 through an innings of 124 and then taking a further 87 off the Worcester bowlers.

In Whit week Watson and Hopwood made 208 together against Kent, the first double-century partnership by a Lancashire opening pair since the halcyon days of 1928. Successive defeats by Essex (who sent them in to bat) and Derbyshire (who got home by seven runs with five minutes to spare) made it certain even before the end of June that the title would not be retained. At Kidderminster an unusual occurrence was that in the first Worcester innings Bull carried his bat for 57 out of 150 and Gibbons emulated his feat in the second with 83 out of 148.

One of the best performances was accomplished at Dover after Kent had secured a lead of 165. A. P. F. Chapman decided to go for quick runs in preference to enforcing the follow on but Pollard bowled so finely that the Kent declaration was long delayed till nine wickets were down. Faced with the task of scoring 396 runs in five hours, Watson and Hopwood led off with 103 in 90 minutes, Hopwood and Iddon made 149 in 105 minutes and with the help of Paynter and Tyldesley the runs were obtained with 18 minutes to spare.

Lancashire came in for criticism at Weston-super-Mare when Somerset after following on set them 102 to win with 75 minutes available. Against the fast bowling of Wellard and Andrews six wickets went down for 70 runs in 55 minutes and then to general surprise a tea-interval was taken. As afterwards only ten minutes remained stumps were pulled up before time.

In the last match of the season Wellard caused trouble again, this time with a display of hitting that equalled anything ever seen at Old Trafford. His 112, made out of 145 in an hour and a half, included five sixes and no one who saw a pull-drive that sent the ball crashing against one of the pavilion towers will ever forget the stroke.

CHAPTER 18

Championship Matches

1936–9 Captain: W. H. L. Lister

*Ernest Tyldesley, George Duckworth and Frank Sibbles
retire; Two splendid seasons for Wilkinson; Nutter's
all-round form; Paynter and Iddon scoring well;
A caution from the committee; Paynter's 322
at Hove, 1937; 972 runs without a bye;
A wet season 1939*

AT THE GENERAL election of November 1935, P. T. Eckersley
was returned to Parliament as Member for the Exchange Division of Manchester, and a new captain had to be sought. Eventually two principal candidates were considered by the committee—Lionel Lister, an amateur batsman who had already
shown his worth, notably in the strenuous Trent Bridge match
of 1934; and Ernest Tyldesley, one of England's most distinguished professionals, who, like his brother J. T., had
already led the side on odd occasions in the absence of the
elected captain. On a vote, Lister was elected, the committee
dividing 13—6 in his favour.

Lister led the side with cool assurance for four seasons.
During this time the eleven underwent various changes, the
first, and perhaps the most important, occurring almost at once
as Tyldesley, after a couple of games (as an amateur) decided
that the time had come to put into effect the retirement already
delayed beyond his personal wishes. His last innings for Lancashire were 12 not out against Yorkshire at Leeds, and 22
against Surrey in Jack Iddon's benefit match.

After Tyldesley's retirement, other problems presented themselves; the gradual falling off in Watson's skill, the retirement
of Sibbles through an arm injury at the end of 1937, the close
of Duckworth's brilliant career in 1938, the falling off in the
bowling of both Iddon and Hopwood, the disappointing careers

of Frank Booth and Leonard Parkinson—all these factors brought anxious times to the committee and to the young captain, and though several men were able to seize the chances thus presented, and a star of the first magnitude appeared when L. L. Wilkinson came out as a googly bowler, the overall record of the team for the period 1936–9 was only moderate. Eleventh in the table in 1936, the side improved to ninth in the following season, and to fourth in 1938, but dropped to sixth in 1939.

Wilkinson must have been near Test match selection in his first full season, and Nutter (like Iddon and Watson the son of a professional cricketer) only just missed the double event with 1,156 runs and 91 wickets in his first full summer. The loss of Duckworth meant the loss of an outstanding personality but so far as actual achievements were concerned, the gap was well filled by Farrimond, for so long an able and modest deputy to the great wicket-keeper.

1936: CHAMPIONSHIP MATCHES:
Played 30, Won 7, Drawn 17, Lost 6

Falling to eleventh place in the table, Lancashire had their worst record since 1914. It would have been even poorer but for a recovery effected during August, when they won five matches, with Paynter in such fine form that he hit three centuries in successive innings. He was far and away the best batsman on the side this season, though Iddon scored five centuries, one more than the famous left-hander. The pair were seen to great advantage when they scored 182 together in under two hours against Glamorgan at Old Trafford, a match in which Pollard had a first-innings return of eight wickets for 42 runs.

Lancashire beat Kent twice in exciting circumstances. At Liverpool they got home by two wickets, the winning run being obtained on an overthrow when an attempt was made to run out Phillipson. In the return at Canterbury, Lancashire made 241 in three hours in the fourth innings. They met with a reverse experience against Sussex, who, sent in to make 239 after a declaration, obtained the runs in 190 minutes.

The new captain had the modest batting average of 20 runs an innings, but he showed resolute hitting powers at Lord's when he made 104 not out in 110 minutes, thus playing a prominent part in one of the side's best victories.

Derbyshire were champions this season and curiously enough

two of Lancashire's outstanding bowling performances were against their neighbours. At Buxton, Booth had six wickets for 18 runs, and at Old Trafford Sibbles had seven for 36, but both fixtures were drawn, interrupted like so many others this season by the bad weather. Another bowling success was by Hopwood who, in the two Whit-holiday games against Sussex and Surrey, had 17 wickets.

New ground was broken by taking a match to Preston, and exciting cricket was seen. The opponents were Gloucester, who put Lancashire out for 45 in their first innings and went on to win by 175 runs, thanks to the fine bowling of Goddard and Sinfield.

1937 : CHAMPIONSHIP MATCHES :
Played 32, Won 9, Drawn 18, Lost 5

This was a season of erratic form, some brilliant individual achievements and—overall—of rather brighter cricket in the truer sense of that overworked term. It was brighter of necessity, because after a drab start to the summer, the committee issued an official reprimand against the policy of stone-walling. Players were made to understand that their positions in the team were not assured and that mere averages would be balanced alongside attractive cricket in the field. Dismissal for 54 at Portsmouth and defeat at Old Trafford in the Whitsuntide match against Yorkshire, prompted the lead given from the committee-room.

Victory over Warwickshire, in which Place showed the skill that had to wait until 1946 for its full development, represented the turn of fortunes and a brilliant victory over the New Zealand touring side, with 196 runs knocked off in two hours, showed the power still within the team's capacity. A week later there was an even finer performance at Lord's where Middlesex, after gaining a lead of 146, were beaten by 22 runs thanks to generally consistent batting in the second innings and lively bowling by Phillipson and Booth. In the following match at Old Trafford, Paynter scored 266 off the Essex bowlers without giving a chance, and his stand of 142 with Pollard set up a new eighth-wicket record for the county.

Washbrook, after being dropped, came back to the side to hit three centuries in four innings and after various experiments he and Paynter settled as the opening pair. Towards the end of July they scored 268 together at Hove. Washbrook (108) left first and then after Iddon had gone cheaply, Paynter and Oldfield (92) put on 271. Paynter was eventually leg-before when he had scored 322 in five hours, the highest innings ever played by a Lancashire professional and one of the most brilliantly sustained pieces of hard hitting in all cricket history. He gave only one chance, hit furiously on the off side, and altogether had 3 sixes and 39 fours in his memorable innings.

Lancashire were able to declare at 640 for eight, their highest total for twenty-six years, and after winning this match they journeyed north to Sheffield where Iddon's bowling won a famous victory over Yorkshire. Gloucester were next overcome at Old Trafford, though Lancashire had to contend with Hammond in his most masterful mood, and at Trent Bridge the winning form was maintained with Washbrook and Paynter achieving the rare feat of a hundred partnership at the opening of each innings. The fifth successive victory was over Kent, with Phillipson bowling to great effect, so that by the second week in August much of the disappointing form of the first part of the season was quite forgiven.

In all matches, a total of 100 wickets was achieved by Sibbles, Phillipson and Pollard, but there was a lack of variety about the attack and rather too much reliance on the new ball. Sibbles, whose benefit year it was, had an outstanding analysis of five for eight in the second innings of Essex at Old Trafford, and he actually obtained the last four wickets in seven balls.

1938: CHAMPIONSHIP MATCHES:
Played 32, Won 14, Drawn 12, Lost 6

Eleventh in 1936, ninth in the following season, Lancashire now made a big stride forward. They finished fourth, and it was a good fourth because for some time they headed the table. They won eight of their first twelve fixtures and up to the August Bank Holiday game they did splendidly. Then they lost to Yorkshire (it was the completion of the 'double' for the old rivals for the first time in twenty-eight years), and within the next three weeks they were also beaten by Kent, Somerset, and Gloucestershire. A change in the weather had something to do with the change of fortune; so long as the pitches were hard, Lancashire were a fine bowling side, but on soft pitches the lack of a slow left-hander was still felt.

The team were without Sibbles and Duckworth, the former suffering from an arm injury that ended his career while he was still only thirty-four years of age. Duckworth retired in his thirty-seventh year, so that the county lost two men who, in other circumstances, might have been expected to play on for some seasons.

With Phillipson out of the side for some weeks through injury, extra burdens fell on Pollard who worked heroically. Wilkinson made a big jump forward and there was fine all-round cricket from Nutter.

Among the batsmen, Paynter was pre-eminent. This was the season of his great score for England at Trent Bridge, and all through the summer he was in tremendous form. He came fourth in the national averages, and only Hammond scored more runs. Washbrook and Oldfield did well too, but Iddon fell away after beginning the year in grand form.

The season opened with a good win over Worcester at Old Trafford, with Pollard taking ten wickets and Iddon playing a vigorous innings of 185 towards Lancashire's total of 468 scored at 80 runs an hour. There were 972 runs scored in the match and Farrimond and Buller earned commendation for not allowing a single bye. At Ilford Lancashire kept their new resolutions by scoring 491 on the first day and it was forcing batsmanship that won a splendid victory over Kent at Old Trafford when, after being 83 behind on the first innings, Lancashire scored 266 for eight wickets to win with four minutes to go, the runs being obtained in 155 minutes. D. M. Matthews, an amateur who played occasionally this season, hit Woolley for three sixes during a brilliant partnership with Oldfield, paving the way to the exciting finish.

In the following match against Glamorgan the batting again asserted itself, centuries by Washbrook, Hopwood (the pair scored 188 together in two hours) and Oldfield swelling the total to 564 for nine wickets.

It was soon afterwards that Phillipson met with his unusual and serious mishap. Lancashire were at Worcester and Phillipson went rather lightheartedly for a short run off a shot from a no-ball. Jackson tried to throw down the wicket, the pair collided, and fell so violently that the Lancashire man dislocated a collar-bone and Jackson sprained his back.

The county's home matches were badly affected by the

weather and Hopwood was a special sufferer, the gate at his benefit match being no more than £140. There was more bad weather for the game against Somerset at Nelson where Buse and Andrews put Lancashire out for 79 on the first day and were then denied an opportunity of rubbing in their good work. There was a triumph for Washbrook at Bristol where Hammond, on winning the toss, sent Lancashire in to bat. The young batsman hit a score of 219 and carried his bat through an innings of 426 for nine, declared. As though to make up for his error of judgment, Hammond replied with a superb display that brought him 271 in a score of 561. Lancashire saved the game easily enough and Washbrook, scoring 51 not out, stayed on the field for the whole of the match. He followed with an innings of 135 at Hove, making 405 runs for once out. Wilkinson, too, distinguished himself here with a hat-trick, and also did well at Canterbury where, despite his 12 wickets for 125 runs, Lancashire were beaten.

Paynter had meantime been doing great things, beginning with an innings of 291 at Southampton where he and Oldfield scored 306 together and so beat the county third-wicket record which had stood for thirty-four years at 296, made by Spooner and Jimmy Hallows. Paynter hit seven sixes (six of them out of the ground) in an innings which was virtually flawless, and he was in comparable form later in the season when he hit a century in each innings at Birmingham, scoring 238 runs for once out.

After the disappointments of early August, the team contrived to finish with one of their most meritorious displays. At the Oval, Surrey led by 106 on the first innings, but then Wilkinson turned in one of his bowling feats, taking six wickets and putting Lancashire back in the game with a chance, for they required no more than 240 to win. Paynter and Washbrook rose to the occasion with centuries each and an opening stand of 198, and in the end Lancashire had eight wickets in hand.

1939: CHAMPIONSHIP MATCHES:
Played 31, Won 10, Drawn 14, Lost 6
(One Abandoned owing to war)

Lancashire did not maintain the improvement of 1938. They ran into one of the wettest seasons on record, and at one period

from 15 July to 4 August, six consecutive matches did not produce even a first innings decision. At the end of this dishearten-
ing run Warwick came to Old Trafford and in a desperate
effort to produce a result, a pitch was prepared on the practice
ground. It was not used, and this fixture, too, finished 'no
result'.

The side were handicapped in the falling off in form of two
men on whom so many hopes had been pinned. Nutter was
nothing like the player he had been the previous season, his
batting being less effective and his 40 wickets costing 37 runs
each, while Wilkinson came back from South Africa rather
tired after his efforts on the perfect pitches so often encountered
on the tour, and he too proved very expensive. Pollard and
Phillipson never flagged in their efforts, and Garlick showed
promise, but the high bowling averages and the long tail when
batting were the two obvious weaknesses.

Iddon had a grand season and was easily top of the county
batting averages, while Oldfield did well enough to gain his
first Test match honour. Washbrook failed to hit a century
yet totalled 1,547 runs in championship matches alone for an
average of almost 40, a strangely consistent record.

Besides Garlick, there was renewed promise in the batting of
Place, and two names appeared that were to be better known
in years to come—W. B. Roberts and J. T. Ikin. The captain
was often away through Territorial training and T. A. Higson
junior usually deputised. In late August, Lister was called
away from the Northampton match and Iddon took charge.

The season had a remarkable opening. Lister sent Gloucester
in to bat and at first the policy seemed to have gone astray for
Barnett hit a dashing innings of 120. Going in against 267,
Lancashire lost seven men for 157 but then Lister and Farrimond hit with spirit and a lead of 41 was gained. Then Phillipson (seven for 18) bowled splendidly, the home side were out for
79, and Lancashire won by ten wickets. There were high jinks
at Birmingham where Cranmer declared with his side still 74
behind. Lancashire in turn declared at 200 for two, and Warwick went in to score 277 for three wickets and to win with
20 minutes to spare. Strange happenings, too, at Leicester,
where Paynter and Washbrook scored 213 together for the first
wicket and then saw their good work go to waste when nine
catches were dropped in Leicester's first innings.

There were three splendid fourth-innings achievements this season. At Southampton, Hopwood and Iddon hit centuries when Lancashire made 385 for four wickets in four and a half hours to win the match. At Nottingham, after a first-innings deficit of 88, Lancashire struck back with some lively bowling by Phillipson and then obtained the 323 runs wanted with six wickets to spare, Paynter and Washbrook scoring 215 in the opening stand.

It was Lancashire's turn to lose to such a feat late in August at Dover, where Kent, 80 behind on the first innings, scored 382 for five wickets and won with an hour to spare.

Oldfield and Nutter set up a county fifth-wicket record of 235 against Notts at Old Trafford, and other batting feats included Paynter's 222 against Derbyshire, Iddon's 217 not out against Worcester, and a beautiful innings of 141 not out by Iddon against Hampshire—one of the best he ever played in point of style.

There was almost another fourth-innings feat when Surrey came north, Lancashire going boldly for the 320 wanted in four hours and losing by only 14 runs. In Farrimond's benefit match Jim Smith of Middlesex did the hat-trick, a feat equalled by Pollard against Glamorgan at Preston. The season ended when Surrey, whose ground was no longer available, visited Old Trafford for the second time. Pollard had time to take ten wickets and then on the third morning, the 1st of September, the game was given up as war engulfed Europe.

CHAPTER 19

The Second World War, 1939-45

Old Trafford requisitioned; Damage in the blitz;
Members' generous response to appeal; Games
for war charities; Cricket again, 1944;
The 'Victory' Test, 1945; Recon-
struction Fund brings in
£42,236

ON THE OUTBREAK of war, the ground at Old Trafford, including the buildings, was requisitioned by the Army. In due
course a unit of the Royal Engineers was established there, and
all thoughts of cricket were put aside. In the following months
many members of the playing, clerical, and groundsman's staff
joined the Forces and served in various theatres of war. They
included:

W. H. L. Lister, J. M. Brocklebank, R. Howard, P. Higson,
T. A. Higson junior, K. Cranston, F. M. Sibbles, A. J. Birtwell,
F. D. Beattie, W. S. Phillipson, C. Washbrook, R. Pollard,
W. B. Roberts, A. E. Nutter, L. L. Wilkinson, J. T. Ikin,
J. Bowes, J. Briggs, E. Price, J. Oldham, S. Banham, C. D.
Edge, and F. S. Booth.

Besides P. T. Eckersley, also killed on war service were J. M.
Barrell, a Liverpool cricketer who had appeared in the Second
XI; A. Kershaw, a brilliant games player from Rugby School
who also played with the Second XI; and H. Robinson, a young
professional wicket-keeper.

Following the Dunkirk evacuation Old Trafford became a
transit camp where weary troops were assembled before being
sent home or to new stations. The weather, providentially fine
for the great evacuation, still held up, so that the men were able
to sleep in the stands, under the stands, anywhere in fact where
they could lie down.

Towards the close of 1940, and again in the spring of 1941,
Manchester received the full force of the air raids, and Old

Trafford suffered serious damage. In one raid a sentry at the main gate was killed and on various occasions the top of the pavilion, the groundsman's residence, the splendid dining-room, and two of the stands were knocked about. Mr. Menzies, the Australian leader and an insatiable cricket enthusiast, was in this country, and he personally visited the ground to see what damage had been done.

Later on, the Army left Old Trafford and it was taken over by the Ministry of Supply. Where there had been men, there now appeared materials; huge packing cases, many of American origin, were dumped on the car parks and the practice ground. Bomb craters on the playing area were ugly scars, but capable of more speedy repair than the pavilion and stands.

Meantime a certain amount of administration had to be kept going, and a temporary office was opened in Manchester, for convenience near to Mr. T. A. Higson's own offices. The secretary (Major R. Howard) was later posted to Manchester and he was able, by sacrificing his leisure hours and his meal-times, to give a good deal of attention to the affairs of the club. Members were asked, as in the First World War, to continue their subscriptions on a half-rate basis, and again the response was generous.

Some clearing-up work was done at the ground. The valuable cutlery and catering equipment was salvaged as far as possible, and much of it placed in storage with a bank. Carpets were sent to North Wales for safe keeping 'for the duration'. Besides the chairman and the secretary, members of the committee who were available shared in the watch on the club's interests.

Though no cricket was possible on the ground from 1940 to 1943, several members of the committee were prominent in organising matches on other grounds in Lancashire and adjacent counties. These games had three purposes in view: to give entertainment to the sports-loving public; to raise money for war charities; and to give practice to such first-class players as were available. One fixture at Colwyn Bay—to quote just one example from many—was between a British Empire Eleven and a North Wales Eleven, and it raised more than £4,000 for the Red Cross Prisoner-of-War Fund. Dr. J. Bowling Holmes and Mr. George Cadman, of the county club, and Mr. Arthur

D. Proctor of the Welfare Section of the Ministry of Labour and National Service in Manchester, were among the most tireless organisers of these fixtures, many of which are reported in *Wisden's* for the war years.

In 1944 everyone connected with the club must have been heartened by the resumption of cricket on the famous ground, with three Services matches—Western Command v R.A.A.F. Unit XI in which Pollard, Jenkins, and Stocks all took cheap wickets; Western Command v R.A.F. North-Western XI in which Riddington of Leicestershire bowled well; and North of England v R.A.A.F. in which Washbrook made 133 in his most brilliant style, with Place and Constantine as his most useful partners. For the first of these games, the strip usually reserved for Test matches was used.

The committee gave consideration to post-war problems about this time and decided in principle that the damage to the ground ought not to prevent Lancashire's participation in the county championship whenever it should be resumed. Looking to rather more general problems, the club forwarded to the Advisory County Cricket Committee a plan for an annual knock-out competition—a reversal of club policy from the incident of 1873 recorded in an earlier chapter.

The sky was brighter in 1945. Services personnel and German prisoners-of-war (paid at the rate of three-farthings an hour) shared in the work of tidying the ground and buildings and at last, after five blank summers, a team labelled 'Lancashire' took the field again. Usually they were one-day matches, played in good lighthearted spirit, though there were two fixtures with Yorkshire played in more serious mood.

The first was at Old Trafford in July, a two-day match and therefore not included in the record of first-class games between the two counties. Batsmen generally had the worst of the argument against the medium-fast bowling of Pollard and Coxon and the slow left-arm spinners of Booth. Left to score 100 in as many minutes, Yorkshire finished 18 short with five wickets down. The three-day return at Bradford was played for the benefit of the widow and children of Hedley Verity, a Yorkshireman for whom Lancastrians felt affection and admiration second only to that of his own folk. Rain cut down play on the last day and the game was left drawn after the honours had been carried off by Washbrook (97 and 25), Rae (74),

Barber (88), and Nutter (five for 57). Receipts amounted to about £3,000, and the Memorial Fund totalled £8,233.

Later in the summer there was a 'Victory' Test match at Old Trafford and for three days players and spectators luxuriated in an atmosphere of peace-time cricket. England beat Australia by six wickets and happily two Lancashire players had much to do with this success, Phillipson and Pollard together capturing fifteen wickets. They often made the ball get up sharply from a good length, a significant pointer to a change in the character of the turf, and W. J. Edrich expressed the opinion that the conditions offered a fair balance as between bat and ball.

How keenly the public had waited for the return of first-class cricket was revealed by the attendance of 72,463, with receipts £11,627. After expenses had been met, the sum of £10,396. 4. 11. was forwarded to the Inter-Services Cricket Committee; a facsimile of the cheque hangs in the Long Room at Old Trafford to-day.

At one time the throng outside was far too much for the limited number of turnstiles which had been manned and for a little while there was a threat of chaos. Major Howard made a quick decision, gathered a few enthusiastic helpers, and dispensed with the orthodox method of admission. The waiting enthusiasts were instructed to have ready the exact admission money and they were then allowed in through the double gates, the secretary and his helpers taking the cash and stuffing it into leather bags. Were there, one wonders, any old-timers in the crowd who recalled that in the earliest days of Association football, this was the method generally adopted on big-match days?

The 'Victory' Test was the signal for preparations for the county championship of 1946. The committee were in no doubt about what they ought to do—raise a team virtually at all costs. While they cast around to see what playing resources were available, Williams and his staff laboured on the ground and stands and a public appeal was launched for a Ground Restoration Fund, with £100,000 as the aim. This figure was not reached, but when the fund, generally administered by Mr. A. W. Goodall, was closed, a sum of £42,236 had been collected.

Subscriptions came from all over the world. There was a

gift of £500 from H. Carter, the great Australian Yorkshire-born wicket-keeper, and by contrast there was a donation from four ladies of Glastonbury. Another cheque came from Vancouver. Some of those who sent money sent advice too. There were suggestions for brighter cricket, and for new and improved scoreboards.

As things turned out, the financial problems were not so serious as had at one time been feared. Members had so generously maintained their half-rate subscriptions during the war years that income had averaged more than £2,000 a year from this source. The great thing was to get the game going, and when, in May 1946, first-class cricket was resumed with a county championship, the visit of a touring side, and matches with the Universities, Lancashire took their customary place among the leading clubs.

CHAPTER 20

Championship Matches

1946 Captain: J. A. Fallows

*Finding a team; Players lured to league cricket; Death
of Jack Iddon; Washbrook's brilliant batting;
A bold bid for the championship; The
toss lost twelve times in succession;
Washbrook, Ikin and Pol-
lard selected to tour
Australia*

To DECIDE TO play in 1946 was one thing, to find a team at all
worthy of Lancashire's traditions was quite another. Of the
men who had formed the side in 1939, W. H. L. Lister (captain) was no longer available. Hopwood's career had been
closed by ill-health, Wilkinson's star had set as suddenly as it
had risen, Farrimond had no wish to pick up the threads again
at the age of forty-two, Oldfield and Nutter were lured away
to play league cricket, and Paynter, though urged to re-join the
side under the most generous financial inducement, thought it
more prudent at the age of forty-four to take up an opportunity
of going into business and to accept a sum in lieu of a benefit.
Pollard was still in the forces.

Almost on the eve of the season came a further blow. Jack
Iddon, who had hoped to play on for a year or two as an amateur, was killed in a road accident, and so the club lost the most
senior of their pre-war players.

It was hoped that T. A. Higson junior would become captain, but after election he found himself unable to take on the
post.

Jack Fallows, son of the hon. treasurer, and a cricketer who
had played a good deal with Manchester before the war, then
took over the captaincy though he knew full well his own limitations as a batsman. Added to the professional strength were

N

Phil King, a Yorkshireman who had played for Worcestershire; T. L. Brierley, a Glamorgan cricketer who was also a lacrosse player of distinction; and the brothers E. H. and G. A. Edrich from the family that had already produced a famous player in W. J. of Middlesex.

1946: CHAMPIONSHIP MATCHES:
Played 26, Won 15, Drawn 7, Lost 4

As things turned out, Pollard was able to secure leave to play quite often so that he was able to gain Test match recognition, Price came out as a first-class slow left-hand bowler, Garlick and Roberts made great progress, and Phillipson was a useful all-rounder if not quite up to his old standard. As Ikin also took some wickets, the attack was quite up to requirements with Price on top of the averages and Roberts with 110 taking most wickets in championship fixtures.

Brierley and E. H. Edrich shared the wicket-keeping, and among the batsmen there was encouraging form from Place, G. A. Edrich, Ikin, King, and Wharton, though all were overshadowed by Washbrook. The season of 1946 was, indeed, Washbrook's season. He was often away at representative matches but in twenty-six championship innings he scored 1,475 runs to average (with six not outs) almost 74 runs an innings. It was his method, rather than his mere figures, which drew crowds to watch him bat. The Old Trafford wicket had some life in it as a general rule, far more than in 1939, and the ball came through well for Washbrook's favourite hooks and cuts. It was he, with Place as partner and Fallows as an encouraging captain and splendid off-the-field co-ordinator of this experimental team, who gave the whole Lancashire eleven the inspiration to play bright, forceful cricket. For two months they topped the table, and but for two exceptional matches, they might have been champions instead of finishing third in the final chart.

The side got away to a good start with victory at Gloucester where King played a swashbuckling innings of 145 that included twenty-one fours and three sixes. Barnett and Hammond batted well too, but the England captain was absent with a damaged back in the second innings and without him the home side failed. There was a completely unexpected set-back in the shape of a three-wicket win for Glamorgan at Old

Trafford, manufactured by Matthews's fine bowling, but then came a splendid run of success. There was a particularly brilliant match against Middlesex in which Washbrook made 182, Pollard took 14 wickets, and Denis Compton scored a century in each innings, a feat hitherto accomplished at Old Trafford by only Johnny Tyldesley and P. Holmes. Lancashire got home by seven wickets, Ikin and Geoffrey Edrich hitting the last 50 runs in 25 minutes in a race against the clock.

An easy win over Worcester, with Price taking cheap wickets, was followed by a draw at the Oval and then the winning touch was regained at home against Warwickshire, Phillipson taking ten wickets. After a drawn Yorkshire match at Sheffield, the team returned to Old Trafford for the usual Whit-week games and great crowds saw Sussex and Surrey vanquished in turn. In the first of these fixtures, Place made 109 and 57 not out, his second innings being a hard-hit affair as with King and Wharton 127 runs were knocked off in 85 minutes to gain the day with only 25 minutes to spare. Three days later it was the bowlers who had to work against time, the last Surrey wicket going down with only 20 minutes in hand. Price had ten wickets for 64 runs in the two innings as a major share in the triumph.

Garlick, slowish off-breaks, now came into the picture with nine wickets for 48 runs against Leicestershire at Barwell (where Roberts had nine for 70), and ten for 46 in the following game at Buxton. Here, the slow bowlers did all the work so that Pollard and Phillipson never removed their sweaters, and though Derby were put out for 79 and 63, Place and King showed that rational batting was possible with a stand of 145. Washbrook, 137 and 51, not out each time, and Roberts with ten wickets, were the big men in victory over Notts with only eight minutes left.

An easy win at Colchester, where Washbrook and Place scored 237 together in less than three hours and Ikin and Roberts bowled skilfully, was succeeded by wins over Leicester at Blackpool, Pollard taking ten wickets, and Derbyshire at Old Trafford when Washbrook was seen at his very best with innings of 68 and 82 not out on a pitch that favoured all the pace bowlers and resulted in a good many cuts and bruises.

The date was mid-July, and it represented the peak of Lancashire's fortunes. Soon afterwards, without Pollard, they lost at Maidstone, and then came a critical match against Essex at Old Trafford. The home side set out to make 299 in 185 minutes and for a time they made wonderful progress on a difficult pitch, Washbrook and Place scoring 148 in 65 minutes. Afterwards Peter Smith, sometimes making the ball lift sharply as it turned, caused a collapse and Lancashire lost by 15 runs a quarter of an hour from time. Ten days later there was a similar challenge from Hampshire, the task this time being to get 212 runs in 150 minutes. Without Washbrook the side were beaten by 29 runs, eight minutes from time, and with these two defeats went the chance of the championship.

The part that fortune played can only be guessed, but the game with Hampshire represented the twelfth consecutive lost toss. Fallows won the spin of the coin at the thirteenth attempt against Somerset, and there was an easy win, with Price taking 11 wickets. Going south to end the season, Lancashire gained some slight revenge by beating Hampshire narrowly in the extra half-hour, and then drawing with Sussex when only rain prevented victory.

It had been a thrilling and eventful season, and the side had fared better than anyone had dared to hope. The future was bright for Lancashire as Washbrook, Pollard, and Ikin packed their bags for Australia.

CHAPTER 21

Championship Matches

1947–8 Captain: Kenneth Cranston

*A remarkable cricketer; Disappointments in the champion-
ship; Washbrook and Place make 350 together; A
great match at Buxton; A tie at Bournemouth;
The 1947 champions beaten; Tattersall's début; Pollard's 1,000th
wicket; Cranston's dra-
matic farewell*

WHEN KENNETH CRANSTON took the captaincy of Lancashire in
1947, he had all his way to make. The popular Jack Fallows,
known to all at Old Trafford either through his own association
with the club for many years, or through his father's even
longer connection, was succeeded by a man from Liverpool
who was hardly known to the public and whose probable election to the position was unhappily allowed to leak out prema-
turely. But within a week Cranston was 'all right' with members and the public. They knew a cricketer when they saw one,
and here was a player who wore his flannels with the grace of
a natural athlete, and of whom Dryden's words could be
echoed: 'Whate'er he did was done with so much ease, in him
alone 'twas natural to please.' In his first innings (at Oxford)
he made 79, then came to Old Trafford to take five Kentish
wickets and followed it with 47 runs.

There are various views about the excellence of Cranston's
cricket. When he had played only thirteen county games he
found himself in the England team, and in his second Test
match he won world-wide fame by taking four wickets in six
balls. He went to the West Indies as one of a weak team, and
at once achieved every cricketer's ambition by captaining England when G. O. Allen could not play in the first Test. Back
in England, he played against Australia, which was perhaps a

mistake, because Cranston never learned to play cricket the hard way required in a match of this sort. Talent needs to be harnessed in a peculiarly tight fashion to meet the green-capped enemy, specially when they are led by a Bradman.

At the end of his second season, Cranston dropped out of cricket to practise dentistry in Liverpool, where he went on playing club cricket in the summer and superb hockey in the winter. He played from mid-May 1947 to the first week in September 1948, and in that time he took 170-odd wickets with his medium-paced bowling, scored more than 2,000 runs, held nearly fifty catches, appeared in eight Test matches, averaged forty runs an innings for Lancashire, and did it all without any visible effort to application. The overall record stamps him as a remarkable cricketer, and it may be added that Harry Makepeace, who was not given to extravagant praise, thought that Cranston was the most gifted boy he ever coached.

The new captain took over a team that looked good enough to win the championship, but actually it was not, due to the falling off in the form of Phillipson who took only 25 championship wickets in 1947 and hardly appeared at all in the following season. Without the fast bowler, Lancashire were often unable to finish off opponents whom they had outplayed for a couple of days, and there was a rather embarrassing assortment of other bowling talents.

In 1947, Lancashire finished third in the table and in 1948 fifth. They lost only three times in the course of fifty-two fixtures in the two summers, as compared with nine defeats for Middlesex and eleven each for Yorkshire and Gloucestershire. That the team won only twenty-one times during this period was not through any reversion to the slow batting of the late '20s and early '30s, nor from any lack of spirit on the part of players or captain, but sheer inability to thrust home an advantage well won.

1947: CHAMPIONSHIP MATCHES:
Played 26, Won 13, Drawn 11, Tied 1, Lost 1

The feature of this season was the first-wicket association of Washbrook and Place. The former scored nine centuries, his partner ten, and each achieved a personal triumph in scoring two centuries in one match. They made 350 together against Sussex in an unbroken stand that was only 18 short of the county record set up 44 years earlier by MacLaren and Spooner. They made 233 in the return at Eastbourne, scored 183 together to win the game against Gloucester at Old Trafford, 190 against Essex and 177 against Cambridge University. With B. J. Howard hitting two centuries, the batting was very strong, for Ikin and G. A. Edrich maintained their form, Cranston was one of the country's leading all-rounders, and some of the tail-end batsmen were good for a few.

Pollard, out of the Services and not at all fatigued by an Australian tour, was the outstanding bowler with 131 wickets in championship matches. Roberts, Cranston, and Ikin lent him most support, for Price and Garlick were not given many chances and at the end of the season each left the county to look for wider opportunities. A tall, young, fast bowler with the imposing name of Bowes took 15 wickets but never looked quite the real thing, and there was greater satisfaction at the appearance of a new wicket-keeper in Barlow, not a Duck-worth certainly, but a reliable man who soon made his place secure.

The start to the season promised well, with Cranston's big part in a comfortable win over Kent, and after a draw with Yorkshire, there came the big performance of Washbrook and Place against Sussex in scoring 350 in under four hours. The stand, unbroken on the second night, was only ended by a dec-laration on the following morning when Cranston rightly decided that the prospect of victory was more important than a record.

Then came trouble in the shape of a huge first-innings deficit against Surrey, and it took a supreme effort by Washbrook, 251 not out in six and a half hours, to save the game. Presently came a wonderful match at Buxton, marked in its early stages by Gladwin's feat of taking all nine wickets that fell before Lancashire declared. Derbyshire made 273 in reply to their rivals' 350, but pulled the game back to level terms by dismiss-ing Lancashire for 75, Copson and Gladwin dividing the wickets. So Derbyshire needed no more than 153 to win and they got within six runs of victory with three wickets standing. Then Cranston bowled effectively and with the last pair to-gether Copson was run out so that Lancashire won by three runs.

Warwickshire sent the home side in to bat at Blackpool, and

the reply was 371, B. J. Howard and Geoffrey Edrich each hitting a maiden century in the championship. Pollard did the hat-trick, and Lancashire were well on the way to victory when rain came to finish the match. Soon Ikin followed his team-mates with a first championship century, and the season went on its way eventfully with skilful bowling by Price (six for 36) against Derbyshire at Old Trafford and Pollard (eight for 33) against Notts.

Then came the one defeat of the summer, by 36 runs at Frome when Washbrook and Cranston were playing for England and Place was acting as twelfth man. However, the side soon reasserted its power, for Gloucester were beaten after opening with 415. In their second innings Pollard and Cranston put them out for 106 and Washbrook and Place proceeded to score the 183 required for victory. Ikin took eleven wickets against Notts at Old Trafford, Place and Geoffrey Edrich scored 273 together at Clacton, and it seemed that the chapter of splendid personal achievements would never end when Washbrook and Place, going in with 233 wanted and only two hours to play against Sussex at Eastbourne, knocked off the runs with ten minutes to spare, the senior partner getting a hundred for the second time in the match.

Lancashire moved along the coast to Bournemouth to meet Hampshire. How often had these two sides wrestled with each other in the past, with a keen and level rivalry unconnected with their status in the championship! Now they enjoyed the best match of all, a tie after a game that was contested on level terms from the very start. Hampshire first made 363 by consistent batting with seven men reaching double figures. Lancashire's answer was 367 for nine, declared, a total arrived at thanks to Cranston's 155 not out, his first county century, and a few precious runs from Barlow and Roberts at the tail-end. When Hampshire went in again, there was less consistency about their batting but Jim Bailey followed his first-innings 95 with 63, Arnold and Rogers scored usefully, and the home side were able to declare with seven wickets down and ask their rivals to score 221 in two hours and a quarter.

The challenge was taken up at once, Washbrook and Place putting on 142 in the first ninety minutes. But there was not much support from the middle batsmen and Roberts was absent, in hospital with a broken hand. Ikin was held back as

W. Findlay   A. T. Kemble   R. A. Boddington

C. Smith   R. Pilling   G. Duckworth

Three amateur (*top*) and three professional wicket-keepers.

Four officers of the past. *Above left*: T. J. Matthews, secretary 1906–21. *Above right*: H. Rylance, secretary 1921–31. *Below left*: Major R. Howard, M.B.E., A.S.A.A., secretary 1932–48. *Below right*: S. H. Swire, hon. secretary 1869–1905.

Two Royal occasions. *Above*: H.R.H. the Prince of Wales visits Old Trafford on 7 July 1921 to see Lancashire play the Australians. *Below*: H.R.H. the Duke of Edinburgh shaking hands with members of the New Zealand team during the Third Test Match at Old Trafford in 1949.

Present officers of the club.

Left: Tom Stone, president. *Centre*: Dr. J. Bowling Holmes, chairman of committee. *Right*: C. G. Howard, secretary.

Bailey's bowling caused a collapse and so the sides came to the last over with Hill bowling, Ikin and Barlow together, the scores level. Off the fourth ball, with everything to play for, Barlow went for a short single, was run out, and the honours and the points were left honourably divided.

So to Lord's for the third match of the southern tour and with it the end of the season. Middlesex were already champions; their two great batsmen Edrich and Compton had scored thousands of runs, hardly knowing a failure; under the system of fixture-making now employed, they met Lancashire just this once, and it became a splendid battle, with Compton in his second innings overshadowing everybody and everything else by equalling Hobbs's record of sixteen centuries in a season (a figure he beat later on). The Lancashire bowlers gave him nothing and pegged him down in the nineties for half an hour.

Solid batting, steady bowling, and spirited fielding made Lancashire the better side and 60,000 people watched them over the three days gradually assume the upper hand. Even Compton could not shake off the grip and the champions were beaten by 64 runs. It was a brilliant finish to Lancashire's season of thrilling cricket.

1948 : CHAMPIONSHIP MATCHES :
Played 26, Won 8, Drawn 16, Lost 2

Lancashire were almost as hard to beat in 1948 as they were in the previous season, but they could not finish many of their matches. Ikin apart, the bowling was generally economical but lacking in penetrative power, too many overs being required for each wicket captured. So Lancashire dropped to fifth place in the table—a good fifth, twenty points behind Glamorgan the champions, whereas in 1947 they had been fifty points behind Middlesex when finishing third.

Once again it was Washbrook's season. He missed many county matches through the calls of the Tests and an injury late in the season, so that Lancashire had his services in only fourteen fixtures; in these he hit 1,391 runs, averaging more than 92 an innings, with a century every third innings or thereabouts, a display that was rewarded with the biggest benefit ever awarded a cricketer in any part of the world.

The batting all down was very impressive: Geoffrey Edrich, ninth in the table, averaged 28 runs an innings; Ikin was second to Washbrook, then came Cranston with 891 runs for the county, 1,063 in all games, to add to his 79 wickets. Nigel Howard was given extra chances and hit nearly 900 runs, Wharton maintained his promise, Place was a heavy scorer if not quite the machine of the previous summer, and Eric Edrich and Brierley, who generally shared the wicket-keeping to the exclusion of an inferior batsman in Barlow, were usually good for a few runs under varying conditions. There was a new all-rounder, too, in Greenwood, a useful soccer half-back who played for Chester in the Third Division of the Football League.

The season opened badly with a defeat at Gillingham by 36 runs at the hands of Kent, though there was satisfaction to be gained from the form of Greenwood with eight wickets in his first big game, and had Lancashire won the toss the result would almost certainly have gone the other way. A succession of drawn games followed, marked by a modest first appearance of Tattersall, and Washbrook's 200 against Hampshire when captain of an all-professional eleven. It was June before the first success was registered, an emphatic victory over Notts at Old Trafford when the visiting side were put out for 45 (Hilton five for 19, Roberts four for seven) and Lancashire were able to declare with only three wickets down thanks to another century by Washbrook. Notts failed again and Roberts brought his match record to nine for 46.

The second defeat of the season followed at the Oval, by the bare margin of one run. Surrey opened with 300, and Lancashire found themselves 124 behind when an innings each had been completed. Then Cranston bowled so well (seven for 43, and a match record of ten for 82) that parity was restored, and their fourth-innings task of 248 looked possible with Place getting a century and Wharton lending a hand. But the tail failed against Eric Bedser and when young Malcolm Hilton tried to settle the issue with one glorious drive, Fishlock ended the game with a beautiful catch at mid-off.

Better things soon followed. Cranston was among the wickets again at Horsham, where Place scored a century and Sussex were beaten in a single innings. A score of 395 for eight wickets was the reply when Worcester sent Lancashire in to bat at Old Trafford, though victory was unattainable in the limited time. Victory at Birmingham was largely founded on a sixth-wicket partnership of 260 between Cranston and Wharton. Meantime Pollard had been bowling in game after game in his large-hearted way and against Somerset, though overshadowed by Roberts, he had the satisfaction of taking his 1,000th wicket for the county.

There was a good last day at Cardiff where the visitors, wanting 291 in 200 minutes, had to be content with 266 for eight wickets and a drawn game. Place played a chanceless innings of 200 at Taunton where Roberts's six cheap wickets shared in the victory, and it was Place again, with 176, who was largely responsible for the harvesting of first-innings points against Essex at Old Trafford after the southern side had made 478 and declared with seven men out.

The younger men, Greenwood and Hilton, each had five cheap wickets in a drawn game at Wellingborough and then came another of those exciting finishes which were becoming such a feature of Lancashire's cricket. This time it was at Leicester, when the home side, requiring 124 in two hours, lost two men by run-outs and found the bowling of Pollard and Roberts razor-keen. Just as Hilton had done at the Oval, Leicester's last man Corrall went for a big hit and was caught in front of the sight screen by N. D. Howard, so that Lancashire won by four runs.

An old friend in Oldfield defied Lancashire by batting for four and three-quarter hours for 40 runs when Northants came to Manchester, a match in which the home side introduced an Army officer, J. H. G. Deighton, a useful pace bowler and an energetic batsman and field.

As the season closed, N. D. Howard made his first century against Derbyshire and then in the last fixture of all, Cranston took farewell of the team with a splendid personal performance. He sent Kent in to bat at Old Trafford, scored 82 to help Lancashire gain a first-innings lead of 83, and then made the winning hit when the required 133 runs were obtained for the loss of three wickets. And even as everyone regretted the parting with a handsome cricketer, there was a note for the future in the seven wickets taken by Tattersall.

CHAPTER 22

Championship Matches

1949–53 Captain: Nigel Howard

*Development of young bowlers; Fine catching; A share in the
championship, 1950; Change in the wickets at Old Trafford; Sussex beaten in one day; Washbrook's great
double century at Edgbaston, 1951; Sensational
collapse at Leicester; Marner becomes Lancashire's youngest cricketer; A tie with
Essex; A one-day benefit match at
Bath; All ten for Berry, and a
hat-trick for Tattersall*

WHEN KENNETH CRANSTON found it necessary to give up cricket,
the committee chose as his successor Nigel Howard, one of the
two cricketing sons of Major Rupert Howard, for sixteen years
secretary of the club and himself an amateur batsman of no
mean skill. Writing at the end of the 1953 season, it is too
close to Nigel Howard's period of captaincy to express a firm
opinion on his work, but it may be said that the county never
had a cricketer more keenly devoted to its cause. His batting
has, perhaps, scarcely fulfilled its early promise, though in 1950
he scored 1,105 runs in championship matches and averaged
nearly 40 runs an innings. He had the satisfaction of leading
the team to a share in the championship title in 1950 when
Lancashire and Surrey finished with an equal number of points,
and in 1951 he was honoured with the leadership of the M.C.C.
team to India and Pakistan, thus following in the steps of A. N.
Hornby and A. C. MacLaren in being England's captain in
Test matches.

The outstanding features of the five seasons 1949–53 were
the development of a number of bowlers all born within the
county, and the spectacular close fielding that gave them so
much support.

204

The Lancashire bowlers achieved so much success that four of them—Tattersall, Statham, Berry, and Hilton—all played for England in Test matches, and all went on tours. Berry was one of the original selections in F. R. Brown's Australian team of 1950–1, and he was later joined there by Tattersall and Statham, who were flown out to reinforce the party. Three of them went to India in the following winter under their own county captain and in two of the Tests, Tattersall, Hilton and Statham were all together in the England eleven. At Kanpur, when England won, Tattersall and Hilton between them took 17 of the 20 Indian wickets, and they combined to give V. S. Hazare, the great batsman, the only 'pair' of his distinguished career.

Curiously enough, while these four bowlers were all born within the county the three fieldsmen who gave them so much support at slip or in the leg trap all came from beyond the boundary—Ikin from Staffordshire, Edrich from Norfolk, and Grieves from New South Wales, Australia. It was a happy combination, giving the team's cricket a splendid attraction for watchers not blinded by the purely statistical side of the game.

1949: CHAMPIONSHIP MATCHES:
Played 26, Won 6, Drawn 13, Lost 7

The first season of Howard's captaincy brought a fall to eleventh place in the table, the lowest since 1936, and the seven defeats were as many as had been sustained in the three previous summers. The reasons for the falling off were not far to seek: a decline in Pollard's powers after many years of selfless toil, lack of a pace bowler to take advantage of the many hard wickets met with in this summer, and injuries to Washbrook and Place. With the recruitment of Grieves, there were seven bowlers available—all useful but none sufficiently destructive. Malcolm Hilton, hero in the previous year of his sensational double dismissal of Bradman, played in only three championship matches, and whereas nine men who played frequently averaged from 17 to 48 runs an innings with the bat, the bowlers were topped by Roberts whose 50 wickets cost almost 25 runs each.

With both Washbrook and Place injured at various times, extra responsibility fell on the other batsmen, but it was not until late in the season and on his promotion to open the innings that Ikin really made good the losses. Then he ran into a wonderful spell of run-getting and thoroughly restored his record. Wharton made a big advance and was beaten only by Washbrook in the averages. Wilson and Barlow shared the wicket-keeping duties.

The season began ominously, with a home defeat at the hands of Sussex for whom John Langridge scored a century in each innings. Wharton scored 124 in Lancashire's first innings, and Washbrook offered stern resistance on the last day, but Sussex got down the last home wicket eight minutes from time. Wharton hit another century at Peterborough, with 4 sixes and 19 fours testifying to the power of his strokes, and in the following fixture he and Howard played up well in a match-saving stand at Worcester.

Defeat by Gloucester in Whit week at Old Trafford was brought about by Goddard's 13 for 111, but the holiday ended on a happier note with victory over Kent though Washbrook and Wharton were both away playing for England. Grieves pulled out a splendid all-round performance with 79 runs and eight wickets, and there was a useful stand between Geoffrey Edrich (his brother E. H. had left the club) and Alderson, the latter scoring 55 on his first appearance. Place hit 226 not out on his favourite ground at Trent Bridge, and then came three successive defeats: at Birmingham, where Edrich made a big but unavailing effort to save the day; at Buxton in a low-scoring game; and at Old Trafford against Middlesex despite a century by Ikin. The bowling, though steady, began to look very thin as the summer wore on, and when Notts came to Old Trafford, Simpson (238) and Keeton (134) scored 318 together in five and a quarter hours.

Some exciting cricket decorated the second half of the season. At Llanelly, where Muncer took 14 wickets, 'time' was called with Lancashire's last pair together and four runs still needed for victory. The side moved on to Taunton for Hazell's benefit match in which Ikin did the hat-trick and Edrich scored a century. Gloucester completed the double at Bristol and then came some better things. Greenwood took ten wickets in the victory over Northants at Old Trafford, there was much splendid batting in Pollard's benefit match with Derbyshire, and he himself soon afterwards took his 1,000th championship wicket for Lancashire against Leicester at Blackpool, where J. H. G. Deighton batted with fine vigour. Victory over Surrey was won by clever bowling by Tattersall, Roberts, and Greenwood, and this was immediately followed by an easy win over Essex at Clacton, though here T. E. Bailey performed the splendid personal feat of taking ten wickets in an innings. The season finished with defeat at Folkstone in a match of much enterprising cricket.

1950: CHAMPIONSHIP MATCHES:
Played 28, Won 16, Drawn 10, Lost 2

Lancashire were this season joint champions with Surrey, and besides being a successful season, 1950 was a remarkable one at Old Trafford. Before the summer opened, Lancashire gave notice to the other counties that the heavy roller would be withdrawn from use, and watering was restricted in an attempt to restore the balance as between bat and ball. Naturally the spin bowlers appreciated the conditions though it must be emphasised that nine of the sixteen championship victories were secured on opponents' grounds.

The turning-point of the season was the decision to omit Pollard from the Yorkshire match at Whitsuntide. This particular match was won in most thrilling fashion, and the slower bowlers became the talk of the cricketing world. They were reinforced by the arrival on the scene of Brian Statham with his genuine pace, and eventually the problem was not whom to choose, but whom to leave out. Greenwood had to be dropped and the committee would have had further problems but that the Test selectors called on Berry and Hilton in turn.

Low scoring at Old Trafford reached its climax when Sussex were beaten in one day, and James Langridge, the visitors' captain, reported to the M.C.C. that the pitch was not fit for three-day cricket; he sportingly declared in public that Lancashire had the bowlers to exploit the conditions.

In such a season the bowlers earned praise in match after match, so that it is only fair to mention right away the performances of Washbrook who averaged almost 59 runs an innings and encouraged the other batsmen to score at sufficient speed to give the attack time to do its job.

The most destructive bowler was Roy Tattersall, who, after two years of modest promise, now made his mark as a great cricketer. Forsaking swerve and concentrating on spin, and never trying to do too much, he took 163 wickets for 12 runs each in championship matches, 193 in all first-class games, and topped the English averages. He was emphatically the man of the year—to everyone except the Test match selectors who contrived to lose three of the four Tests against the West Indies without calling on him.

Hilton, hitherto orthodox slow left-arm, was frequently used as an opening bowler and whether Lomax, Wharton or Statham was operating at the other end, he proved a fine contrast. Roberts, for all his accuracy, could not find a place in the side among such talent.

The first three championship games were all drawn, and then came a heartening win over Warwickshire, thanks to Place's second-innings feat of carrying his bat for 101 in a total of 244 and some splendid bowling by Hilton, Tattersall, and Grieves. Yorkshire were overthrown at Sheffield in a match described elsewhere, and then came an interesting drawn game against Surrey with Tattersall taking eight wickets in an innings for the first time and receiving his county cap. Victory in a low-scoring match at Gloucester saw Tattersall in form again, with twelve wickets for 68 runs. Defeat by Middlesex at Lord's was a set-back, and the team failed to force home their advantage over Gloucester at Old Trafford, so that by mid-June the record was modest enough. But all the bowlers found their form against Kent, beaten in an innings, and after a draw at Buxton, full points were won from the return with Kent at Tunbridge Wells (two days sufficed) and against Somerset at Bath where Statham took the first five wickets for five runs— his first important success for the county.

A low-scoring match at Old Trafford ended in defeat by Derbyshire, on 11 July, but this was the last set-back of the season. Next came the one-day game against Sussex in which the 20 wickets were shared by Greenwood and Hilton. Tattersall, the best bowler of the year, could not get on! On the difficult pitch there were two batting performances of real merit, John Langridge carrying his bat for 48 in the first Sussex innings of 101, and Edrich making 89 for Lancashire. Sussex were all out for 51 second time, Greenwood finishing with nine for 67 and Hilton, eleven for 50.

Next Essex were beaten by nine wickets, Tattersall taking twelve wickets and Washbrook making light of a soft pitch with an exceptional century. Another low-scoring game was at

Swansea, where Edrich's 50 was the highest individual score and Hilton and Tattersall each had a haul of cheap wickets.

Returning home, Lancashire beat Notts at Liverpool, Grieves and Edrich hitting hard in a stand of 125—a winning factor in a match of small scores. Middlesex were beaten at Old Trafford, Hilton's ten wickets costing only 74 runs, and the rich spell continued with a capital victory at Trent Bridge where the re-appearance of J. H. G. Deighton with his fast bowling proved a successful move. A seventh successive victory completed the double over Glamorgan at Blackpool, Ikin hitting a fine century and Hilton again bowling with deadly effect.

Yorkshire checked the winning sequence despite brilliant bowling by Statham; then full points were won from Worcester, Tattersall having twelve wickets for 94 runs. A struggle for first-innings points went against Lancashire at Northampton but the team, who had been at the top of the table since 18 July, still looked like finishing as champions. They were sent in at Bournemouth, scored 281, and then put out their over-bold opponents for 96 and 109.

However, Surrey had been winning matches in grand style—like their chief rivals, they had one run of seven successive victories—and it gradually dawned on the public that an exciting finish was in prospect with the chief protagonists due to meet at the Oval in the last week of August. The position was made all the more interesting because both counties had to meet Leicester.

Lancashire, after accounting for Hants, first met Leicester, and won easily in two days with good all-round form, Washbrook scoring 99, Howard 70, and all the bowlers meeting with success. Washbrook maintained his form with a flawless century against Warwickshire who, out for 80 in their first innings (Tattersall seven for 29), were saved from defeat by rain.

So the season came to its climax with the meeting of Lancashire and Surrey at the Oval; it was the visitors' last match, and they needed four points to make sure of the title outright. After a brilliant season of match-winning cricket, it must be confessed that they disappointed. Washbrook and Place failed, and thereafter Lancashire were rather more concerned about preventing Surrey from winning the full 12 points than with attempting victory on their own account. Surrey in turn hardly did themselves justice, dropping a good many catches, and

o

both Ikin and Howard were only able to reach their half-centuries with fortune on their side. Lancashire were all out for 221, and then Surrey made 287. Batting again, Lancashire scored 203 for four wickets, and all told the two crack teams of the season could do no better than to score these 711 runs in seventeen hours and a quarter. It was a disappointing match except from the standpoint of the Lancashire players, who, once they had set themselves to prevent a defeat, carried out their mission. It left Surrey with the task of defeating Leicester to draw level at the top of the table, and in this the southern side made no mistake.

1951 : CHAMPIONSHIP MATCHES :
Played 28, *Won* 8, *Drawn* 18, *Lost* 2

The county could not hold their place at the top of the table. They were placed third in 1951, and it will be seen that they won no more than eight matches. Some of the match-winning power went from the side, and it was not all due to the Test match calls on Tattersall, Statham, Hilton, and Ikin. There were better pitches at Old Trafford, and Tattersall undoubtedly felt the effects of his exertions of 1950 followed by his emergency trip to Australia and New Zealand. From taking 163 wickets for the county, his haul dropped to 74, and the difference was not made good even by Statham's good work in his first full season, Hilton's continued effectiveness, nor Wharton's splendid efforts to use the new ball. With Hilton bowling well, Berry's chances were fewer, and Grieves's value as a bowler was represented by no more than 20 wickets at high cost.

It would be an unusual season without compensations, and in 1951 one of the more pleasing aspects of Lancashire's work was in the consistency of the batting. Ikin, troubled by a back injury towards the end of the season, averaged 54 runs an innings, and he was followed by Place, Washbrook, and Edrich. Grieves, Wharton and Howard comprised the middle batting with averages of 31 to 26, and others, such as Greenwood and Lomax, though not being able to command regular places, were usually capable of scoring runs. Greenwood was often a useful member of the attack with his off-breaks, and he was such a good team-man that everyone was sorry that recurrent arm trouble eventually cut short his first-class career.

The season began, by a curious accident of fixture-making,

with a meeting at the Oval between the previous season's joint champions. The first day was blank, but afterwards the two teams played up with gusto and gave a far brighter entertainment than they had done eight months previously. Ikin carried his bat for 125 through Lancashire's first innings of 197, farming the bowling so successfully that he made 68 of the last 70. Statham bowled splendidly so that Surrey were 60 behind, but then Surridge and Alec Bedser in their turn were too good for Lancashire, who could manage only 76. Surrey were therefore left with 137 to make in 65 minutes and they went boldly for the runs only to find Tattersall in his most tantalising mood. In the end they were compelled to go on defence to avoid defeat, their score finally standing at 83 for seven.

After a drawn Yorkshire match there were three successive victories—Surrey beaten by nine wickets, with Statham taking nine wickets cheaply; Kent defeated at the end of Whit week with Greenwood scoring his first century and taking five wickets; and Middlesex overthrown at Lord's despite a hat-trick by Young. After two drawn games Lancashire beat Warwickshire, the eventual champions and already top of the table, and once again it was Statham who obtained the quick breakthrough in each innings.

Defeat at Portsmouth, where Hants made 175 for five wickets in 125 minutes and had only five minutes to spare, followed hard on the heels of this great win, but three more victories followed: first at Chesterfield, where on a difficult pitch the highest of the four innings was 194, yet Washbrook made a century, one of his most brilliant efforts in a great career. Hilton backed him up with 11 wickets, and Lancashire got home by 15 runs. Statham took nine wickets in the next victory at Tunbridge Wells with Tattersall unexpectedly playing his part as a batsman after being sent in as a night watchman. Third in the row was the win over Sussex at Old Trafford marked by centuries by Washbrook and Edrich who scored 271 together, Wharton's second-innings feat of taking seven wickets for 33 runs, and perhaps most memorably by Grieves's eight catches.

Edrich hit a fine century at Colchester and another against Hampshire at Liverpool. Lancashire won the latter game, but this, on 20 July, represented their last victory of the season, for of their last twelve fixtures they drew eleven and lost one. Still, the drawn games produced their measure of excitement and good cricket. There was, for instance, Washbrook's superb double century against Warwickshire at Edgbaston, which ground, newly enlarged and improved, housed a crowd of 25,000 on the first day. This was a truly great innings, with the batsman doing almost as he wished in scoring 209 out of 333 for nine. There was a century by Oldfield for Northampton against his old club, and in the same match Grieves scored his first championship hundred. Colin Smith, aged eighteen and a cricketer of rare all-round promise, hit a splendid 67 not out against Middlesex.

At Cardiff, after moderate scoring, Glamorgan tried to score 182 in 110 minutes, lost seven wickets, and were driven back on defence to save the game. It was Glamorgan who inflicted the second defeat of the season, winning by 34 runs at Old Trafford on a rain-affected pitch that aided the bowlers all through. Hilton and McConnon each took 11 wickets.

There was a partnership of 251 in 160 minutes by Edrich and Grieves against Notts, a fine innings of 163 by Place in the return at Trent Bridge, and two desperate finishes were seen at Eastbourne and Leicester. In the first instance, the fun began with Sussex sent in and yet scoring 339 with centuries by Sheppard and Cox. Unabashed, Howard declared with eight wickets down while Lancashire were still 84 behind, and Sussex in their turn closed at 107 for eight, leaving their rivals 105 minutes to score 192. Lancashire went for the target, got so far, and then the last pair, Lomax and Wilson, found themselves struggling to save the game, which they did at 176 for nine.

The Leicester fixture produced one of the most remarkable collapses in Lancashire's long history, the last seven wickets in the second innings falling in fifty minutes while only two runs —and those leg-byes—were added to the score. The home side needed 29 to win in ten minutes, scored five of them from seven balls, and then torrential rain ended the game and the season for both clubs.

1952: CHAMPIONSHIP MATCHES:
Played 28, Won 12, Drawn 12, Tied 1, Lost 3

Lancashire were third again this year, behind Surrey with their quite exceptional record, and Yorkshire. In scoring 52 more points than in 1951, and recording six more victories,

Lancashire showed a much improved overall record, and by beating both Warwickshire, the 1951 champions, and Surrey, the new leaders, they gave ample proof of their powers, but it would be flattery to say that these powers were always fully expressed. They were beaten three times, and two of these defeats came from Nottingham (sixteenth in the table), and Sussex (thirteenth). The other loss was sustained against much-improved Leicester who played good cricket at Aigburth to record their first triumph in these fixtures between the two counties since the celebrated match at Ashby in 1926, and made the most of the opportunity presented by Statham's absence and Washbrook's injury.

Illness in India, followed by a minor operation, affected Howard's form, and for a time he stood out of the side at his own request, Washbrook taking over as captain. Statham, too, felt the effects of the tour to India, though Tattersall, with his different style, came through it unscathed and was more like the cricketer of 1950, taking 130 wickets in championship fixtures. The committee, still faced with the problem of deciding between the left-handers Hilton and Berry, gave chances to both so that Hilton bowled about 340 fewer overs than in the previous season and took 47 fewer wickets. More opportunities were given to Lomax, who often shared the new ball with Statham and took 43 wickets. As he scored nearly 600 runs his all-round value was considerable, and he was given his county cap for these figures.

Washbrook had one of his leanest years, though an average of almost 36 runs an innings would be considered satisfactory for many batsmen. He was often troubled by injury, and would have stood out of many games but for Howard's inability to get going. The great batsman made his double century against Somerset virtually with one hand, and no one had any doubt that when fit again, he would be as good as ever.

Ikin topped the county averages for the second year in succession, followed by Grieves and Place, but in many respects Edrich, in fourth place, was the batsman of the year for Lancashire. He often had to go in after one of the opening pair had failed, and he thrived on difficult situations.

No one made greater progress than Frank Parr who, when Wilson was given a rest, kept wicket so well that he held his position in the side. He was sometimes untidy, but as against

that he frequently made a catch of the most spectacular character. Equally interesting was the appearance of Peter Marner,
who was included in the team in two matches towards the end
of the season and, at the age of sixteen years and four months,
superseded Johnny Briggs as the youngest cricketer ever to play
for Lancashire.

The season opened well enough with a victory over Kent in
which Tattersall played the biggest part with 13 wickets for 76
runs and at the beginning of June there were three successive
victories: over Derbyshire at Old Trafford when Hilton and
L. Jackson bowled superbly; Worcester at Old Trafford when
Ikin made 154 of the team's 471 for seven wickets scored at 80
runs an hour; and Warwickshire at Edgbaston in a game
between two all-professional sides of which the abiding
memory is Wharton's superb catch at short fine-leg when he
simply hurled himself at the fast-travelling ball in the manner
of a rugby player bringing off a tackle.

Washbrook's one-handed double century and grand fast
bowling by Statham failed to settle the Somerset match, and
then came the thrill of the season, a tied match with Essex at
Brentwood. It was a close thing all the way, with Lancashire
making 266 in their first innings and Essex 261. Lancashire
hit 226 in 200 minutes on the third day and declared with seven
men out to set their opponents the task of making 232 in 140
minutes. Essex cheerfully faced the prospect, made 100 in 50
minutes, 150 for five wickets in 80 minutes, and eventually
came to the last over of the day with nine runs more wanted,
and the last pair Trevor Bailey and Vigar together. Bailey
drove Hilton for six, took two more off the second ball, played
the third, and then went for the winning stroke. Howard at
mid-off made a fine catch and the game was tied, Lancashire
taking eight points and Essex four under the curious rule then
prevailing.

When Lancashire went to Trent Bridge, bowlers of all types
had a chance for once in a way, and both Statham and Tattersall had good figures, but Notts won by 47 runs. At Cardiff,
victory was secured with only three minutes to spare, and there
was another exciting climax at Burton-on-Trent where Lancashire, asked to score 112 in 45 minutes, finished with 105 for
seven. In Place's benefit match, with Middlesex the attractive
visitors, there was some high scoring, and Grieves and Statham,

hitting 149 for the eighth wicket, fell only one short of equalling the 1900 record of Albert Ward and C. R. Hartley.

Howard and Lomax made 193 together in two hours at Maidstone, and with Statham getting his quick break-through at the beginning of each innings, Kent were beaten. Washbrook was seen at his very best in a low-scoring match at Portsmouth with two innings of 45 and 60 on rain-affected turf. Here Hampshire were beaten by 25 runs after being set to score 192 in 155 minutes, Tattersall taking eight wickets for 71 with a match record of 13 for 121. A bowling feat of a different kind was Berry's against Gloucester, sending down 66 consecutive balls without conceding a run and having only 44 runs hit off 39 overs. Another fine innings by Washbrook under adverse conditions—93 in just under four hours—was seen at Weston-super-Mare, where Howard sent Somerset in and put them out for 141, thanks to Tattersall's seven for 32, but rain limited Lancashire's profit to first-innings points.

It was appropriate that Edrich, who had played so finely all season, should surpass his previous highest score, and this he accomplished with 162 at Northampton where Oldfield, not for the first time, did well against his old friends. When Northants came north for the return, there were three declarations and a wonderful finish, Lancashire winning by two wickets with the help of an overthrow off what would have been the last ball of the game in any event. Here again Edrich batted well, making 71 not out in the final task of scoring 176 in 110 minutes.

Lancashire's third defeat of the summer was at Hove, after a lead of 82 had been won on the first innings. It was here that Marner appeared for the first time and he was retained for the last game of the season at Lord's, where he attracted much praise in scoring 30 and also for the splendid catch near the end when his team were pressing on for victory. This was gained by nine wickets, thanks to good bowling by Statham, Berry, and Hilton and capital all-round work by Ikin.

1953: CHAMPIONSHIP MATCHES:
Played 28, *Won* 10, *Drawn* 14, *Lost* 4

There were hopes of the championship in 1953—hopes not borne out by events but bright enough to keep interest alive for most of the season, even when so much attention was focused on the Australians. Optimism was founded on the bowling strength of the team, plus the knowledge that Surrey would have to play ten matches at least without Alec Bedser. The Tests also called up Tattersall, Statham, Laker, and Lock at various times, and in the end Surrey gallantly overcame their more severe handicap and retained the title.

It was a season of exciting events and close finishes, foretold by the events of the opening fixture when Berry, last man in, defied Warwickshire's efforts to force a win at Old Trafford. After some fine cricket by Tattersall, Grieves, and Marner, the team came to the big match with Surrey, finishing on Coronation Day with the champions victorious.

The next great event was at Bath where H. T. F. Buse saw his benefit match finished not merely in one day but with 55 minutes to spare. Somerset were put out for 55 and 79, Tattersall taking 13 wickets for 79 runs, so that Lancashire's total of 158 was good enough for an innings win. Young Marner earned much praise for an innings of 44 in which he hit Buse for 6, 2, 4, and 6 in one over.

Successive victories over Hampshire (with 253 hit off in 160 minutes with five minutes to spare) and Glamorgan at Liverpool (with some really wonderful catching by both sides) provided spectacular cricket, and meantime Berry was showing signs of recovering his old skill. He turned promise into achievement by taking 13 wickets for 124 in a two-day win over Somerset, eight wickets in a lost game at Chesterfield (when the last man was out seven minutes from time), and then capping everything with 14 wickets against Worcester at Blackpool including the feat of capturing all ten in the second innings, Lancashire getting home with 18 runs and 20 minutes to spare.

The form of the team was variable about this time. They overthrew Notts at Trent Bridge with whirlwind bowling on the third day, and then lost to Northants in a desperate finish. A collapse on the second evening would have been even worse but for a stout effort by Edrich who, next day, was 81 not out, having gone in first wicket down, when the innings closed for 141. Northants, an improved team but without a win over Lancashire since 1914, had to make 128, and they got home by one wicket after losing five men for 45 runs.

All the bowlers next shared in an easy win at Cheltenham

and now the championship title seemed possible. But rain stopped the side at Swansea after they had scored 256 and dismissed their rivals for 88, and limited play in the following game against Kent to a couple of hours.

Notts were defeated for a second time, Tattersall taking 14 wickets and dismissing Hardstaff, Stocks, and Dooland for a very good hat-trick. Then came a blank first day at Lord's and in a desperate attempt to make good lost time, Howard declared when Lancashire had made 175 for three against the Middlesex 174. Victory was beyond grasp, however, and so Surrey were again champions. All that remained was the struggle for second place, directly between Lancashire and Sussex at Hove, and the home side took the points and the honours quite comfortably, Howard's men hardly doing themselves justice after he had won the toss.

When the final averages were made up Grieves was on top of the batsmen for the first time, a fraction of a run in front of Edrich and Washbrook. Statham headed the bowling, Tattersall had most wickets, and close up was Berry, whose recovery of form was one of the most important, and at the same time popular, events of the season.

Shortly before this book went to press, Nigel Howard announced that he would be unable to continue to play regularly, and so resigned the captaincy. In his place the committee elected Cyril Washbrook, who thus became Lancashire's first regular professional captain.

CHAPTER 23

Great Modern Players

Ernest Tyldesley's 102 centuries; The perfect team-man; Harry Makepeace as batsman and coach; Dean and Cook; The great triumvirate of Parkin, Dick Tyldesley and McDonald; Value of Sibbles, Phillipson and Pollard; The all-rounders, Iddon and Hopwood; Three heavy scorers, Hallows, Watson and Paynter; Wicket-keepers Duckworth and Farrimond

WE MUST NOW turn back the pages of our reference books to list some of the outstanding Lancashire players of more recent times, with special reference to those who linked the first decade of the century with the cricket following the first war and to those who lifted the team to such eminence in the mid-twenties. We cannot do better than begin with Ernest Tyldesley, not first in point of time, but winning a place all his own by reason of his 102 first-class centuries and his 38,000 runs, with an average of 45 runs an innings.

On figures alone Ernest is Lancashire's greatest batsman. It is hardly necessary to embark on a comparison of his play with that of his brother J. T., sixteen years his senior. If their batting was contrasted, they shared personal characteristics of modesty and wisdom; a gentle manner off the field gave little hint of their prowess on it—for if Johnny blazed forth an unsuspected ferocity with his square-cut, did not Ernest, too, with his celebrated hook?

Each brother topped the 1,000 runs nineteen times, each went past 2,000 in three or four years, and each had a 3,000 aggregate just once.

Ernest first played in 1909, and he did not put aside his bat until 1936. It was a long career, and even then he did not break his connection with the club. He became a member of the committee, one of the few first-class professionals so honoured

218

by the members of a great county; later on he was joined in the
council chamber by Frank Sibbles, for so long his team-mate.
Mere facts, however, do not tell of the vast amount of pleasure
Ernest Tyldesley gave to thousands of cricket-lovers with his
splendid batsmanship. His style was the essence of comfort at
the crease, and once he had got over his first two or three overs,
he looked as though he had been born bat in hand. It was not
the style of a Spooner or a Walters, but the style of a complete
craftsman, and when he gently pushed the ball wide of mid-on,
he was more than a craftsman, a veritable master. For so mild-
mannered a man, his hooking was astonishing. He himself
places his 178 against Yorkshire in 1922 as his finest innings, and
close to this must come his 109 against Notts in the great match
of 1934. He was then forty-five years of age, and to stand firm
against Larwood and Voce as he did that day, and to play the
innings that first of all saved the match and then won it, was
a wonderful performance and a striking tribute to physical
fitness as well as the perfection of his on-side play.

The legend that he could not play in the keen atmosphere of
Test match cricket has long since been demolished. The facts
are that he played twenty innings without ever being really
sure of another chance, scored 990 runs, made three centuries,
six times passed the fifty mark and averaged 55 runs an innings.
Even allowing that Hendren stood in his way, no one now can
have any doubt that the selectors barely did him justice or that
given additional chances he would have been a success. When
he went to South Africa in 1927–8, he was for the only time in
his life certain of a place in the Test team. He played better
than any other batsman had ever played on the matting wickets,
adjusting his defence in a fashion remarkable in a player who
had been so long in the game.

Ernest Tyldesley's value did not finish with his batting. No
captain had a more loyal friend or a better adviser, and there
was never a man who so often considered the other members of
the side. One example may be noted: if he played a long innings,
he was scrupulous about attempting to stay in over an interval
or to see a new ball off, in order that those who came after
might be able to take advantage of the work he had done.

Before Ernest Tyldesley came into the side, Harry Makepeace
had already scored a modest few hundred runs. He was already
a great footballer, and like his Everton team-mate Jack Sharp,

he won a Cup medal and played for England at both games. His development as a cricketer was slow, but it was like the man himself—safe and sure. He played from 1906 to 1930, scoring more than 25,000 runs, and for a time his first-wicket association with Hallows was one of the strongest in the country.

Makepeace was a canny player. He did not forget what he had seen and learned, and he did not give much away to the bowlers. It was he who was generally given the blame or the credit for the laboured Lancashire cricket of the years immediately following the first war, but as Neville Cardus has said, the county's batting told of the change in the economy and social life of Lancashire county at large. It is possible too that Makepeace had become convinced of the soundness of his ideas when, in Australia in 1920–1, he saw how it was possible to wear down an attack before tea, and flog it afterwards, and for some years this was a policy often deliberately adopted by his own county team. Frequently one batsman would be detailed to 'look after' one rival bowler, such as Maurice Tate, with a view to drawing the sting. This was a technical exercise requiring much skill, though sometimes it made for slow scoring until the middle of the afternoon.

After Johnny Tyldesley, Makepeace was chief coach, a post he held until shortly before his death in December 1952, so that his link with the county extended for forty-six years. When he gave up the coaching post, the club granted him a pension and elected him an honorary life member.

There have been few more beloved cricketers at Old Trafford than Harry Makepeace. If he taught the younger players the value of defence—well, that was his character; it must never be forgotten that he also taught them loyalty to their club and courage in face of the most critical adversity. In his last year at the ground he saw Ikin stand fast against McCarthy's bumpers, and it is Ikin's own statement that as he took the knocks that were inflicted on him, he was emboldened to play his part by recalling his mentor's words: 'Over your dead body.'

In 1906, the year of Makepeace's début, there also appeared Harry Dean and Lawrence ('Lol') Cook. The former was a left-hander of rare quality, a natural bowler with a splendid temperament. On hard wickets, he bowled in the Hirst or Voce fashion, swinging into the batsman and employing a leg-trap. On soft pitches he moderated his pace—though he was never really slow—and spun the ball. He was two bowlers in one, a wonderful asset to any team, and though his career was broken by the first war, he took more than 1,300 wickets in first-class cricket, with an average of about 18 runs a wicket. His great triumph for Lancashire was to take 17 wickets against Yorkshire at Liverpool in 1913, and for England, to take four wickets for 19 runs in the deciding Test match of the Triangular Tournament in 1912. He and Woolley carried all before them in the Australians' second innings, which was all over in two hours for 65.

Lol Cook must be accounted a remarkable cricketer because though he first played for the county in 1906, when he was twenty-one years of age, he did his best work from 1920 to 1923. In 1920 he took 156 wickets, in the following season 151 (and appeared for the Players at Lord's), in 1922 he had 142 wickets, and in 1923 he took 98. All told he captured more than 800 first-class wickets at about 21 runs each. His great virtues were length, a little spin, and courage. He was never as fast as Billy Cook, and it might be said rather disparagingly that he was never quite 'class', but he was a good Lancashire cricketer, and the Old Trafford crowd admired his never-say-die spirit. It was his misfortune always to be the second or supporting bowler, and he seemed destined always to bowl against the wind, which he did without complaint. At Chesterfield in 1920 he took seven wickets for eight runs, one of the deadliest pieces of bowling in Lancashire's history.

After Dean and Cook came the great triumvirate of McDonald, Parkin, and Richard Tyldesley. They had but one full season together, and it was left to McDonald and Tyldesley, with the aid of Sibbles, to ensure the championship successes of 1926–8, Parkin dropping out after eleven championship matches in the first of the three big seasons.

Parkin took more than a 1,000 wickets in his career, played for England many times, and earned undying fame for his skill and his jests, yet how much better he ought to have been is a subject of endless debate. He was a bowler of most original gifts; he could bowl very fast, he could bowl his off-breaks with a rasping spin that brought him countless successes on pitches that were in the slightest degree helpful. He had an endless variety of tricks, and he had the benefit, after the first war, of playing alongside some great cricketers in the Lancashire side.

Durham-born, Parkin played a few times for Yorkshire, returned to league cricket, made a sensational début for Lancashire in 1914 when he took 14 wickets, and reappeared after the war with an almost immediate success against Yorkshire. By this time he was thirty-three years of age, and herein perhaps lies the clue to his one weakness, the inability to stand up to reverses. He had never had the strict training which comes to most youngsters with the leading county teams, and he was essentially a cricketer of spasmodic energy and achievement.

His lean, angular figure, his trick of flicking the ball up with his foot, his pointed gestures—all these made him a figure of fun and Old Trafford's big post-war crowds welcomed him and his antics. Parkin readily responded and rightly or wrongly believed that he had a double job—to bowl and to entertain.

Parkin was always wonderfully effective against left-hand batsmen, and he was usually successful against players, right or left, who were meeting him for the first time. His surprise value rather fell off, and by 1925 his average was beginning to climb rather significantly. He had, unfortunately, already put himself out of Test-match cricket, after playing for England against Australia on tour in 1920–1 and again in the 1921 series. In 1924 the South Africans were here and Parkin, of course, was chosen for the first Test at Birmingham. Subsequently in a newspaper article he took exception to A. E. R. Gilligan's captaincy, alleging that he had not been given his proper share of bowling and that, of course, was the end of his career as an England cricketer. Whether Parkin saw the article before it was published or whether his journalistic 'ghost' let him down, is of little import; an international cricketer of mature years ought to have known his responsibilities when giving his name to features in a newspaper.

After the defeat at Ashby in 1926, when Parkin failed to make the most of the conditions, he was left out of the team for the following match at Birmingham, and, objecting to fulfilling the role of twelfth man, was allowed to return home. Almost immediately club and player parted company, a sad going-out for a cricketer who, whatever his failings, ranks as one of Lancashire's finest bowlers and a character who enlivened every match.

After Parkin's death in 1943 his ashes were scattered over the turf at Old Trafford, and three months later Richard Tyldesley, so often his partner in victory, passed away, the last surviving member of the Westhoughton brotherhood. He was the opposite of Parkin in every way, a bulky, heavy man, stolid and given only to occasional (though then devastating) bits of repartee; a slow bowler of rare artistry and perseverance; a man of curious dignity, as evidenced by the splendidly new flannels he invariably wore for a Yorkshire match.

There has perhaps never been a right-arm bowler with a more beautifully curving and alluring flight than Richard Tyldesley's. He spun a little from leg, often bowled a genuine top-spinner, and represented sudden death to tail-enders who played back to him. His accuracy of pitch, resulting from years of practice as a boy under the eyes of his father (a club professional), was remarkable, and he insisted on careful placing of his field.

He was naturally limited in his own fielding ability, being such a heavy man, but close in, or to his own bowling, he had a splendid pair of hands and was absolutely fearless in tackling the hardest hit. As he took 328 catches, and scored more than 6,000 runs, his usefulness was by no means limited to his bowling, and he is one of the few men who have taken six catches in an innings—against Hampshire at Liverpool in 1921.

Altogether in first-class cricket Dick Tyldesley took more than 1,500 wickets, 1,447 of them for Lancashire. He therefore ranks third to Briggs and Mold, and takes first place among those born within the county. For England he played in Test matches at home and abroad. He took five South African wickets in his first Test match, and was specially valuable for steady work at Nottingham in 1930 when, with Larwood ill, a weakened attack just got England home in face of a challenge by Bradman.

For match-winning quality under all conditions, both Parkin and Dick Tyldesley were surpassed by Ted McDonald, the Australian fast bowler who came to England with the 1921 side, joined Nelson as club professional, and so acquired residential qualification for the county. No one can say with authority that this man or that was the greatest fast bowler of all, but it is permissible to venture the opinion that under all conditions there has never been one finer than McDonald. The great pace of his early years, his superb run-up and delivery that made him capable of the longest spells and of going on until he was nearer forty than thirty years of age, the wonderful variety of his bowling, the ability to produce the extra quick one at will, the tremendous break-back and above all the whip from the pitch that rapped the batsman's knuckles even on the truest surfaces—these factors placed him among the greatest cricketers. He was the best Australian bowler in the 1921 Tests and when he qualified for Lancashire, though past thirty, he was the most effective fast bowler in the world.

There were many stars in the Lancashire team, but it was McDonald who was the principal factor in the three consecutive championship wins of 1926–7–8. His steely temper was a magnificent complement to his technical skill; the better the batsman, the better he bowled, and even when he was not taking wickets—and every bowler must be mastered at times—his duels with such men as Hobbs, Sutcliffe, Hammond and A. P. F. Chapman thrilled spectators to their very marrow.

McDonald's career began with Victoria in 1912, and ended with Lancashire in 1931 when, quite suddenly, the thirty-nine-year-old bowler found that the mainspring of his splendid mechanism had lost its power. He returned to league cricket and was killed in 1937 when, after a motor accident, he was involved in a second mishap.

In his best season of 1925 McDonald took 205 wickets, but just as creditable was his work in 1927 when, in a wet summer, he took 150; in the four seasons 1925–6–7–8 he totalled 720 wickets. He had three hat-tricks for the county, and three times took three wickets in four balls.

Though it is strictly beyond the scope of this book, McDonald's association with J. M. Gregory must be mentioned. They were only briefly team-mates for Australia, but in the course of a few months they established a reputation that will last as long as cricket. As an opening pair they can hardly ever have been surpassed; the bludgeon at one end, the rapier at the other, cut down the flower of English batsmanship.

Personally Ted McDonald was rather reserved, as though holding back his energies for the bowling effort to come. With his tall, athletic figure, and his sharp bronzed features, he was the very picture of what a fast bowler ought to be. His idol was

Victor Trumper, and he himself became a figure idolised by cricketers on both sides of the world.

After Parkin, Tyldesley and McDonald came a succession of bowlers who, though lacking the same qualities of genius, were reliable team-men and grand workers for the county. Linking the 1926–8 era with later seasons was Frank Sibbles, a medium-paced bowler with a high action whose record of 900-odd wickets at 22 runs each would have been even more impressive had his career not coincided with a period when the pitches at Old Trafford were prepared at a level of excellence never equalled before or since. He often had the inferior end, he was troubled by an arm injury, yet comes out ninth in the list of great Lancashire bowlers.

Just as Briggs jumped to the front when Crossland dropped out, and Hallows did his best work in the emergency caused by the departure of Barnes, so Sibbles forged ahead when an effort was most needed. In 1931 McDonald left, and when soon afterwards Richard Tyldesley went, Sibbles manfully shouldered the burden, added the off-break to his resources, and was for some seasons one of the best stock bowlers in the game. His great triumph was to take seven Yorkshire wickets for ten runs in a famous match at Bradford. Besides the easy pitches at Old Trafford, Sibbles's bowling was perhaps handicapped by his good nature. One sometimes felt, watching him at work, that he might have won wider fame had he been less well disposed to his fellow-men, for few cricketers have possessed a more serene temperament. Like Ernest Tyldesley, he was subsequently elected to the committee of the club.

Dick Pollard was generally known to the others in the team as 't'owd chain-horse', in appreciation of his capacity for work. As a boy he went to Old Trafford to watch Tate, and became fired with the ambition to bowl like him. On the quick side of medium-pace, doing just a little bit in the air or off the ground, Pollard was ideally built for the job, and he toiled away uncomplainingly on the hottest days. After Richard Tyldesley and Dean, he became the third Lancashire-born cricketer to take over 1,000 wickets for the county. He played in a Test trial as early as 1938, but had to wait until after the war to obtain Test match honours.

His partner in so many matches, Eddie Phillipson, never had the good fortune to play for England in a full Test, though he

P

was prominent in the 'Victory' games of 1945. Faster than
Pollard, and with much swerve and lift, Phillipson often touched
real greatness even if his swerve sometimes seemed beyond control. He was by no means negligible as a batsman, as his life
average of 25 runs an innings shows, and he could fairly be
classed as an all-rounder.

For such as Pollard and Phillipson, the war came cruelly.
They were bowlers with a strictly limited span of playing time,
they were both two or three years under thirty, and it can
hardly be doubted that both would have won the highest Test
match fame in other circumstances.

Bill Roberts too was a cricketer who was just making his
way in 1939. A slow left-hander with a rather low delivery, he
did not spin or flight the ball in the classic fashion, but he was
accurate and fielded with great zeal, especially to his own bowling. Like Phillipson, he played in the 1945 'Victory' Tests.

Len Wilkinson's work was all done in two or three seasons
before the second war. A googly bowler with a lovely action,
high and without any complications, he looked the real article
from his first appearance. Lancashire and English cricket lost
much from his inability to pick up the threads again in 1946.

During the period under review, Lancashire produced two
true all-rounders, Jack Iddon and Len Hopwood, both of
whom batted right and bowled left, and both of whom played
for England. Iddon was the son of a cricketer, a natural player
with superb drive which, if sometimes kept in check, often
flashed out to delight the crowd and destroy the slow bowler's
length and spin. For some years he was somewhat overshadowed by the great men in the team, but he steadily developed a strong and likeable personality of his own and no
one took a greater interest in the younger players as they were
drafted into the team.

An aggregate of almost 23,000 runs (over 21,000 of them for
the county), an average of over 36, and 46 centuries, placed
Iddon high in the list of Lancashire's batsmen; in addition he
was a good enough slow-bowler to capture over 500 wickets.
He was variable, it must be confessed; on his poorer days he
seemed disinclined to spin the ball and to prefer dropping it in
the rough patches, but on his good days he was very good indeed. To suit the needs of his side he often bowled under
orders, dropping the ball outside the leg stump to keep runs

down. When the pitch was helpful, though, he often seized his chance and bowled in the orthodox left-hander's fashion. He won a Yorkshire match with one sensational performance at Sheffield by accurately exploiting a worn patch.

It has been said that Iddon's father, knowing the value of a left-hander, tied his right hand behind his back and compelled him to use the 'wrong' arm; it is a good story—but unfortunately it is not true.

If Iddon, sadly killed in a motor accident just before the opening of the 1946 season, was a natural cricketer, his contemporary Leonard Hopwood owed more to patient study of the game and a great determination to succeed. He scored more than 15,000 runs, average almost 30, and took more than 600 wickets at a cost of 20 runs each. If his batting was somewhat utilitarian, and rather spoiled for style by a short backlift, there could not be such criticism of his bowling. His arm was high, he spun the ball, and he was accurate, and no one asks much more of a slow left-hander. He had an outstanding analysis of seven for 13 against Glamorgan at Liverpool in 1934, twice took nine wickets in an innings, and in 1934 and 1935 completed the double of 1,000 runs and 100 wickets, a feat previously accomplished only by Cuttell and Jimmy Hallows among the county's players.

Besides Ernest Tyldesley, Harry Makepeace, and Jack Iddon, the great run-getters between the wars were Charles Hallows, Eddie Paynter and Frank Watson. Hallows scored more than 20,000 runs, average 40 an innings, and hit 55 centuries, and is among the select band of cricketers who have totalled 1,000 runs before the end of May. For a few years his left-handed batsmanship was of the highest class, and there have been few better drivers. A nephew of Jimmy Hallows, he played a little before the first war, and immediately the game was resumed in 1919 jumped right into the front rank. After two years he was playing for England, and but for a decline in his fielding he would have appeared more often in Test matches. Naturally a forcing batsman, he schooled himself to more watchful methods and often came in for criticism for slow play. His career was relatively short, considering his great gifts.

Frank Watson was Hallows's partner in many great stands. In 1928 they shared in a dozen first-wicket partnerships of more than 100 runs and it was in the same season, during his partner's benefit match, that Frank Watson scored 300, the highest innings ever played at Old Trafford. If Hallows often went slowly because he chose to, or because he had deliberately set himself out to play a particular innings for a particular occasion, Watson scored slowly because that was his forte. He had many strokes—a late chop earned him many runs—and he played leg-break bowling with special skill.

Besides scoring almost 24,000 runs, he often bowled with success, at an easy slow-medium pace. A total of over 400 wickets would seem to place him in the all-rounder class, but they were spread over his full career of eighteen seasons and he was generally regarded as more useful at breaking a partnership than as a consistent member of the attack.

Fewer runs but greater fame came to Eddie Paynter, who, after a slow beginning to his career, became one of England's greatest Test match batsmen. He spent a long time on the ground staff and it is generally believed that but for the patience and encouragement of T. A. Higson, Paynter's services might have been dispensed with. At last his chance came as Hallows fell away, and in 1931 he hit two centuries. It was his great innings at Bradford in the following season that attracted wider attention, and, perhaps to his own surprise, he found himself a member of D. R. Jardine's team in Australia in the following winter. His innings of 77 at Adelaide turned the fortunes of the game, and then in the next Test match at Brisbane he left hospital to play an innings of 83 which, according to R. C. Robertson-Glasgow, 'varied from almost tottering survival to an heroic assumption of dominance'. It has gone into the history of matches between England and Australia, and it was right that he should, later in the match, make the hit (a swinging blow for six) that won the game and secured the rubber for his side.

He went to Australia a useful cricketer, and came home a great one. From then until the outbreak of war he was one of England's leading batsmen, though he had to endure the curious whims of selectors. He was left out of the 1936–7 team, then asserted himself in 1938 when he hit a wonderful double century at Nottingham. Going to South Africa he hit two centuries in one Test match, and finished the tour with a staggering average.

His feats for Lancashire were legion. He loved Yorkshire

matches, because he was a born fighter, and some of his slowest and best innings were played in these games. At other times he batted brightly and vigorously and when he made his 322 at Hove he made the first hundred before lunch and spent only five hours over the whole innings.

Captain of the Players at Lord's, holder of a Test match average only a fraction under 60 runs an innings, scorer of 20,000 runs at an average of about 42 runs an innings—and then only half the tale is told. For Paynter was a quaint character, a little man with a pointed sense of humour, and a batting style that owed very little to the long hours Johnny Tyldesley and Harry Makepeace spent with him. He appeared to make his best shots with both feet off the ground, and he feared no one. He was a wonderful runner between the wickets, too, and it must have been a delight for another batsman to be approaching fifty or a hundred with Paynter as his partner, because he could be sure that fieldsmen would be bustled and the score hustled.

Paynter was one of the best outfields or cover points of his time. He was quick, neat and splendidly balanced when running, and he had a tremendous throw. All told he was a remarkable cricketer, and one can see him now, running over the grass in front of the ladies' stand at Old Trafford, or sweeping the ball to leg with one of those mighty lunges, or perhaps missing, as he often did miss, with one of his 'fancy cuts'. Or it may be the picture is clearest for some of the Lancashire team, tired after a late finish and a long journey, hanging about Crewe station, as they frequently did after midnight waiting for the last connection to Manchester. And there would be Paynter (Eddie to the crowd, Teddy to his team-mates) turning cartwheels just to keep the party happy. Or perhaps he would be spinning a cricket tale and belittling his old enemy 'Tiger' O'Reilly, whose fast ball the left-hander was able to pick out 'because he shows his teeth'.

These were magnificent cricketers, and they were supported by two high-class wicket-keepers. In the years immediately following the war, the former Rugby cricketer R. A. Boddington (later hon. treasurer of the club) and the professionals Blomley and Parkinson kept wicket efficiently, and then there appeared on the scene George Duckworth, whose success was so immediate that the highest honours were at once forecast for him. He did not let down his well-wishers. By 1924 he was being given his first trial in a Test match, and by the end of 1928 he was recognised as England's first choice. Quick in his movements, Duckworth was even more remarkable for his quickness and breadth of perception. Alert and active, a student of the game and of his fellow-men, he played a match-winning game from a position not always associated with positive cricket.

He had a spell on the ground staff at Edgbaston before returning to his native county, and now it seems incredible that he could ever have thought of playing anywhere else, breathing the spirit of Lancashire as he does. Pigeons, Rugby League, politics—a wonderful conversationalist, and always it comes back to cricket.

Duckworth was not always the tidiest of wicket-keepers, but he was the most decisive. If he stumped a man, he did not flick a bail off with the elegance of Oldfield; he preferred to let the victim hear the death-rattle. If he caught a snick, the gloved hands and the ball were raised aloft and there was the great cry of 'Owzat?' that came to be imitated by crowds in many parts of the world. Sometimes they punned his name and aped his appeal by calling out 'Quack, quack', and yet it was all done in admiration for a foe worthy of respect and admiration.

For a long time William Farrimond stood in the shadows at Old Trafford, content to be Duckworth's reserve. When the latter went away to Test matches, Farrimond stepped into the team and the sunlight, a first-class cricketer despite lack of practice at taking high-class bowlers. In his rough-hewn way he was quite a batsman, with a leg-sweep that was the despair of bowlers. In the winter of 1930–1 England sent a team to South Africa and Duckworth and Farrimond were both chosen. When the former was taken ill with pneumonia, Farrimond moved into the Test team so that both of the Lancashire men played in this specialist position in the same series—surely a unique occurrence?

Some other cricketers who played for the county in modern times included J. R. Barnes, an amateur of great talent. He was nervous about his own batting, but proved an excellent captain when he took charge of the side in the absence of the regular leader. G. O. Shelmerdine and H. R. W. Butterworth were Cambridge Blues, the former a splendid forcing batsman and the other a leg-break bowler and a courageous batsman.

Among the professionals was Frank Booth, a medium-fast bowler who took more than 400 wickets and often looked on the verge of real greatness. He recently followed such great names as Emmett and Cuttell as coach at Rugby School. Leonard Parkinson, a slow leg-break bowler and a useful bat, also often looked like crossing the line between second- and top-class without quite taking the decisive step.

Two players who left the club—or declined to return, at any rate—after the war, were Norman Oldfield and Albert Nutter, the former a really beautiful batsman already recognised by the Test-match selectors, and the latter an all-rounder. Both dropped out of county cricket for a time and then played for Northampton with success.

Another player who showed great promise was Malcolm Taylor, a left-hand bat who believed in hitting the ball hard. There were too many other good batsmen for him to have many chances, and he went to Canford School where he has coached with ability. The fast bowler Gordon Hodgson, who came from South Africa, made a bigger name as a fine soccer forward with Liverpool, Aston Villa, and Leeds United.

It must be left to a later historian to pay full tribute to the worth of those players still actively engaged in Lancashire cricket at the time of the completion of this volume (1953). Here one can only briefly but warmly refer to the brilliant batting of Cyril Washbrook, whose life average is higher than that of any other Lancashire batsman; the lion-hearted courage of John Ikin; the solid worth of such men as Winston Place, Geoffrey Edrich, and Alan Wharton; the artistic bowling of Roy Tattersall; the spirited fast bowling of Brian Statham; the contrasted left-handed skill of Malcolm Hilton and Bob Berry; the hard-hitting batsmanship of Ken Grieves; the untiring wicket-keeping of Frank Parr and Alan Wilson; the devotion to Lancashire cricket of the captain, Nigel Howard; and above all to the really excellent fielding and dazzling close-in catching which from 1949 onwards made Lancashire one of the most successful as well as one of the most attractive sides in the championship.

CHAPTER 24

Administration, 1899-1953

*Members jib at the increased subscription; Bank Holiday fix-
tures with Yorkshire confirmed; Adverse report on the
ground staff, 1908; Administration overhauled, 1913;
Boom years after the First World War; Greyhound racing proposal for Old Trafford
rejected; The second eleven and club
matches; Prominent administrators
from John Stanning to T. A.
Higson*

IN 1899, AFTER the purchase of the ground, S. H. Swire felt he
could claim that the club was worked on more economical lines
than any in the kingdom. But more money was needed to pay
for the ground and to carry out ambitious schemes of improvement, and the committee asked members to approve an increased subscription of two guineas and an entrance fee of one
guinea. The resolution surprisingly failed to gain the requisite
two-thirds majority, and a special meeting was called to consider
setting up a sinking fund.

A second attempt to raise the subscription failed, and it was
not until December 1901, three years after Old Trafford had
been bought, that members at last agreed to pay an extra five
shillings a year, making the subscription 26s. During the debate
a member from Burnley told the meeting they ought to be
ashamed of themselves for carping at the increase: 'We have
weavers earning 22s. a week paying their guinea cheerfully to
see club cricket at Burnley,' he declared.

About this time an application from the British Mytascope
Company was refused—was this a first attempt to procure
moving pictures of a cricket match? The committee seem to
have given closer consideration to the problem of getting the
gate money safely to the bank. The minute says: 'That Mr.
Haworth's offer to count and bank the gate money for the sum

of £25 in addition to the amount of £18 paid to his clerk be accepted. Mr. Haworth to give satisfactory security for the sum of £1,000 and to be responsible for the money from the time it is taken from the turnstiles until put in the bank. But in case the money be taken by violence in transit to the bank, the Club would not hold Mr. Haworth liable.'

The increase in the size of crowds is doubly borne out: firstly by the Australians taking £1,854 from the 1899 Test match, and secondly by a note that there were many compensation claims. It was decided to resist those arising from incidents in the refreshment bar! And by 1902 the caterers were paying the club £700 annually for the privilege of serving refreshments. Reynolds was ground manager, S. H. Swire was still honorary secretary and over all still loomed the might of A. N. Hornby; was there ever such a mighty midget? We find a note in the minutes of a letter:

'Dear Mr. Hornby. The Match Committee, while holding the highest respect for the President's opinion and being desirous of giving him every privilege belonging to his position, respectfully ask that the team when once selected may not be arbitrarily interfered with.'

When S. M. Crosfield resigned from the position of coach (for which his temperament ideally suited him), A. C. MacLaren took over the duties, with the title of assistant secretary. But soon afterwards Arthur Paul was made coach, and instructed to make periodical visits to league matches in the hope of discovering promising players. It was about this time that S. F. Barnes came to the county, Burnley receiving £100 for releasing him. Not all the captures proved to be swans; there had been an earlier case of a Gloucester fast bowler being engaged, and then proving so erratic that he could not always bowl the ball within the bounds of the nets; and now came another duckling, a Bombay cricketer being brought over on an engagement, and then sent home again almost immediately.

Early in the century the Bank Holiday games with Yorkshire became the matter of a definite agreement. About this period Notts asked Lancashire to play a time-limit match, but the offer was declined, as was a suggestion from Somerset that home-and-home gate receipts should be pooled. County cricket was generally settling down to the game as we know it, and Lancashire were always in the forefront; it was from Old

Trafford that the idea emanated of a new ball every 200 runs.

In 1904 the county decided on simpler methods for preparing pitches at their headquarters ground. They won the championship in that year, going through the season unbeaten, and of the eleven matches at Old Trafford eight were won outright. There is an article in the *Wisden's* of the following year, written by A. C. MacLaren, on the then prevailing excellence of the pitches on some grounds, and it all reads very much like articles one has read thirty and forty years later. However, Lancashire did try to set an example; and they tried again in 1950, when they won the championship again and staged a Test match between England and West Indies which was finished in about nineteen hours of actual cricket.

In 1905 there was a record surplus of £3,440 and the money was badly needed. Not only was there the continual repayment of bonds on the ground purchase to be met, but the ground needed refurbishing. The Stretford surveyor complained of the condition of the stands, and men had to be set to work to make them safe for the Australian match. Two of the open stands on the railway side were condemned as unsafe, and an immediate decision was made to spend large sums of money, beginning with £12,250 for one new covered stand.

It was in this same year that Surrey asked Lancashire whether they had any objection to their qualifying a young man from Radcliffe, and the county raised none. The name: William Hitch!

In 1908 the committee considered a scheme for subsidising young players attached to clubs, rather than employing them on the ground staff. As a start, a cricketer named Valiant was allocated to Ormskirk, who were paid 10s. a week, but the idea seems to have died a natural death as it was bound to with such a vast organisation as the Old Trafford headquarters and the minor matches to be kept up.

For a time, indeed, it looked as though the club had taken on rather more than they could manage. In 1908 there was still a sum of £13,000 outstanding on the bonds, and the time limit was coming up. The sum of £5,000 was wanted immediately and two anonymous members (may we guess they were Rowleys?) promised to assume responsibility. But the position led to dissatisfaction with the government of the club and an 'Organisation Committee' was set up. Its report was drastic: the ground staff 'as a whole' was described as overpaid and inefficient.

Mention has been made from time to time of Fred Reynolds. First of all a professional bowler, he began to help with the general work of the club by collecting subscriptions, calling on members at their business addresses. He would tell a cricket story or two, a bottle would be produced, and sometimes his round ended at the second or third call. A somewhat pompous individual, he came to regard Old Trafford as 'my ground'— perhaps not surprisingly in one who had given virtually his whole working life to the club. He played for Cambridgeshire and for both the United and All-England elevens before settling at Old Trafford, where he spent forty-eight years. He retired in December 1908 with a pension of £100.

Barlow was appointed ground manager, a kindly-meant but unwise selection, and he soon gave it up. Three years earlier S. H. Swire had died and T. J. Matthews (formerly a journalist connected with the old *Manchester Courier*) had become Lancashire's first paid secretary; so gradually the division of responsibilities became more clearly defined. More work was undertaken by William Howard, whose first connection with the club had been as a boy begging for odd jobs and who had by now become established as a 'character', and Albert Ward took over the coaching.

Matthew Studholme became head groundsman, and we can here look many years ahead in anticipation, to record that he was followed by Arthur Widdowson, a Trent Bridge pupil of Walter Marshall's, and Old Trafford wickets (and the outfield too) attained an excellence that became a byword. When Widdowson returned to Nottingham, he was succeeded at Old Trafford by Harry Williams from Derbyshire.

We can break away from the talk of money and administration to refer to a Suggestions Book placed in the pavilion. It did not stay there long, because members declined to treat it seriously. Among the rather light-hearted proposals was one referring to the choice of daily newspapers, and in June 1912 some unknown member wrote:

'That the L.C.C. Committee suggest to the M.C.C. that umpires should be paid per hour for the time they have the teams playing and so save the fiascos that so often occur on this ground and especially during the Notts match June 27–8–9.'

Reference has been made elsewhere to Lancashire's lead in changing the long practice of beginning matches on Thursdays and Mondays. In 1908 the Yorkshire match was begun on the Saturday before August Bank Holiday. In 1913, another idea was tried—this time of beginning on a Friday, with Derbyshire as the opponents.[1]

There was a fresh crisis in 1913 when A. H. Hornby vigorously attacked the policy of the club. In a letter to the *Manchester Guardian* he criticised the intention of reducing the fixture list in 1914 besides raising other points, and a special committee was appointed. There can be little doubt that the control of the club had been restricted to too few people, and if the captain's strictures were rather severe, his letter was proved beneficial. The financial position was immediately improved, several prominent members (including Lord Derby, Lord Ellesmere, and Mr. Edward Hulton) promising increased subscriptions for three years. It was also decided to change the method of appointing a president, so that there would be a periodic change instead of one man's retaining the office as a privilege, season tickets for the ground side were instituted, and greater attention was promised to the second eleven and colts' matches. Closer relations were to be cultivated with the leagues, members were given permission to introduce friends to the pavilion, the county programme was not to be restricted, and all told an effective and welcome new broom swept over Old Trafford.

It should be mentioned here, in fairness to those who were members of the county committee at the time, that they had not been alone in desiring a narrower fixture list. The fact was that several counties had suffered severe financial losses and there was a general spirit of restlessness and a desire for a change. Northampton put up a proposal for two-day matches, thus anticipating the Lancashire-sponsored experiment of 1919, and amid all the discussion it leaked out that eleven of the leading counties had met in secret and were proposing to exclude some of the weaker teams. Both proposals were dropped, and the idea of cutting down the number of first-class counties —though sometimes argued in print—has never since been seriously put forward.

When the time came for the 1914 annual meeting to act on

[1] Saturday and Wednesday starts became general in 1920.

these decisions, members showed their affection for A. N. Hornby, the man who had been president since 1894, by electing him again under the new rule limiting his period of office to two years. A special appeal was launched and Lord Derby personally signed 3,000 copies of the appeal. The war affected the success of this effort, but £4,307 was raised at once in donations besides £1,323 from 84 life members who paid fifteen guineas each, and all told £7,137 was obtained.

After the Great War membership steadily climbed. In 1921 it stood at 3,642, plus 911 ladies, and in 1926 it was 4,151 plus 1,327 ladies. Even so the financial position still called for care. In 1925 a new committee-room and press-box cost almost £2,500 and further extensions to cost £18,000 were planned (including the great dining-room subsequently destroyed in the air raids of World War II). Steps were being taken to acquire the adjoining land owned by the Gun Club, and in 1927 new dressing-rooms and a ladies' pavilion cost £6,000. All told the club had a liability of about £25,000 at this time.

An interesting newspaper venture in 1923 was of considerable benefit to the county. The *Daily Dispatch* (with the approval of the club) sent Tom Lancaster, who had occasionally played for the county but was better known as a league professional, on a scouting mission. He was accompanied by Ivan Sharpe, the well-known journalist, and their special mission was to unearth a fast bowler and a wicket-keeper. Various young cricketers were sent to Old Trafford for trials and though the tour did not succeed in its primary mission of discovering the fast bowler so urgently required, it was directly from this effort that the club renewed interest in Paynter, Farrimond, Halliday, and Preston. All four duly played for Lancashire, and two of them for England.

There was a record surplus of over £10,000 in 1926 but even so another appeal had to be launched. Sir Edwin Stockton was president 1925–6 and with characteristic enthusiasm he set himself to raise the needed money. Over £2,000 was immediately obtained and it was largely owing to Sir Edwin's good offices that Lord Ashton contributed a further sum of £5,000.

An application for use of the ground for greyhound racing must have tempted the committee, but they resisted it, and with the success of the team on the field and the appeal fund, they were at last able in 1928 to pay off £8,000 of the original purchase mortgage bonds, the outstanding amount having remained at £12,000 for a good many years.

By 1930 the palmy days were over, and three years later there was so strong a call for economies that the players' wages were cut by ten per cent—fortunately soon restored.

The liability for the ground purchase was finally completely discharged in 1934. Subsequently the club entered another period of financial prosperity, despite the difficulties and damage of the second war. By 1951 the annual income from subscriptions alone was over £23,000, and with membership standing at about 10,000, a waiting-list had to be instituted.

Most of the material contained in this history relates to Lancashire's connection with first-class cricket, because that is the cricket which attracts most public attention. But all through the years there has been a big programme of Manchester matches, as many as seventy-nine in one year. At one time the programme included two-day games against the best nomadic teams, but the overall plan underwent a change when Lancashire entered their second eleven for the Minor Counties championship in 1906.

The first experience was not encouraging, only one match being won and five lost, of the eight fixtures, but they soon put matters right, winning the championship in the following season by defeating Glamorgan in a deciding fixture. After another season Lancashire dropped out of the competition until 1921. In 1922 Albert Rhodes (now a member of the committee) did wonderful things as a bowler and the next year, with J. T. Tyldesley as captain, men such as Duckworth, Ellis, and Hopwood came to the fore. Since then it has been proved that the second eleven provides splendid match practice for young professionals, and almost every Lancashire player of note has met with his first experience of high-class competitive cricket in this team.

In 1928 the second eleven finished second in the table and so won the right to challenge for the title, but they were beaten by Berkshire at Reading by 85 runs. If the 'double' of both teams topping their tables was, therefore, missed, it was only deferred until 1934. In that year the first eleven won the county championship, having more victories than any other county, and the second eleven topped their own table by going through the season unbeaten and then drawing the challenge match with Surrey. They won the second eleven title again in 1937, finishing second this time but taking premier place by defeating Surrey in the deciding match, Wilkinson taking 12 wickets. Second again in 1938, Lancashire were beaten by Buckinghamshire in the challenge match, though Kenneth Cranston, aged twenty, did enough to foreshadow his later successes. The team were second again in 1939, but owing to the outbreak of war they were unable to play off with Surrey who, therefore, took the title.

After the war, the county soon produced a crop of splendid young cricketers and in 1948 they comfortably headed the table and then gained an easy win over Bedfordshire, the challengers. The three future Test bowlers, M. Hilton, Tattersall, and Berry, all did well this season.

The title was retained in 1949, and this season M. Hilton had the outstanding record of 103 wickets at ten runs each. Oxfordshire were heavily defeated in the challenge match, Lomax, Highton, and Hilton all doing good work with the ball, and Barry Howard, captain and brother of the first-eleven captain, hitting a century.

Results, however, were less important than the training of young cricketers, and there was an inevitable decline in power in 1950 as the three chief bowlers moved up into the senior side. There was an outstanding batting performance by A. Booth who made 253 against Lincolnshire at Grimsby, the fourth highest score in the history of the competition.

There was a remarkable finish to the season in 1951, Lancashire challenging Kent and then trying to extract victory from a rain-ruined match by two bold moves. In the first innings B. J. Howard declared at 44 for two, 149 runs in arrears, and then when Kent in turn closed and set the task of scoring 231 in 90 minutes, the batsmen went for the runs. It was too big a task; six wickets went down for 45 runs, and the later batsmen went on defence in a successful effort to avoid defeat.

Another aspect which must be mentioned is the series of games with Oxford and Cambridge Universities. Lancashire first met Cambridge in 1881, and Oxford joined the fixture list two years later. Inasmuch as they are not competitive, these fixtures do not attract a great deal of public attention though they are an essential feature of the English cricket scene.

Shortly before the Second World War, the club undertook its own catering arrangements. Old Trafford had always been famous for its good food and its capacity to match the great occasion (did not the very first mention of the new ground in 1857 refer to creature comforts?), and its reputation was well maintained under the new system. Among the most energetic of the catering committee in keeping a watchful eye on food and drink at the ground was, and is, Mr. George Cadman, who has also for many years had the responsibility of looking after distinguished visitors to Old Trafford on the occasion of Test matches and other big games.

In 1951 there was another development. Winter coaching was begun on a large scale, with nets erected in the dining-room, and besides individuals, many clubs arranged to send their players for practice under the direction of Stanley Worthington (who succeeded Harry Makepeace as chief coach) and county professionals, notably Winston Place and Geoffrey Edrich. This was a long overdue addition to the ground's amenities, and it came almost thirty years after A. C. Mac-Laren's proposal to provide covered practice wickets at a cost of £840 had been turned down by the committee.

About the same time the M.C.C. spread their interests to coaching the youth of the country and again Lancashire quickly showed their interest in a new venture. Mr. T. E. Burrows was energetic in linking up the organisation of this scheme. It had long been the custom for Lancashire to throw open their nets each spring to the sons of members.

We have progressed a long way from the removal of the ground in 1857. Among those who were responsible for the splendidly secure position achieved were many officials and friends of the club. One of the most practical supporters of Lancashire cricket was John Stanning of Leyland. Generous in his gifts of money and advice to younger professionals, he may be best described perhaps as an early edition of T. A. Higson. If a cricketer was sufficiently skilful, then he was good enough for John Stanning; like T. A. Higson, he linked with this enthusiasm a keen regard for the financial prosperity of the club, of which he was at one time a trustee. He gave up this position when, on the purchase of the ground, he became a trustee for the bond-holders. His position as trustee of the club was taken by C. H. Benton, for many years chairman of the ground committee, a member of the M.C.C. committee, and earlier a player for both Lancashire and Cheshire.

James Horner followed James MacLaren as hon. treasurer, and after him came Talbot Fair (also prominent in arranging club matches). Then came Sir Edwin Stockton, ideally suited to the position because of his wide social circle. There followed T. A. Higson, Albert Stockton (Sir Edwin's younger brother), John Boddan, J. C. Fallows, and R. A. Boddington, present holder of the office. The secretaries after T. J. Matthews were Harry Rylance, Rupert Howard, and (from 1949) C. G. Howard. It can be said without fear of contradiction that with the appointment of Major Howard in 1932 the club entered on a new phase of businesslike conduct. He was twice honoured with the management of a M.C.C. team to Australia and when C. G. Howard (no relation) moved from the Oval to Old Trafford in 1949, another efficient and personable official joined the club. He too was selected to manage a touring team, the side that went to India in 1951 under the captaincy of N. D. Howard.

Among the several player-administrators who maintained a long connection with the club was Oswald Lancashire, a Manchester man who gained Blues for cricket and soccer at Cambridge and appeared for the county as early as 1878, played intermittently along with the giants of the next ten years, and meantime gained a place on the committee. He was chairman from 1910 to 1928, taking in the office of president in 1923-4, and so kept his close link with the club for more than half a century. He was president when Lancashire celebrated the Diamond Jubilee in 1924. His vice-chairman and hon. treasurer in that year was Sir Edwin Stockton, and T. A. Higson was deputy-chairman. The committee then consisted of John Boddan, J. C. Fallows, Dr. H. H. I. Hitchon, H. Worsley, J. W. Carmichael, Joseph Eccles, W. B. Stoddart, Sir Meyrick Hollins, Dr. J. B. Holmes, M. N. Kenyon, and C. H. Williams, with co-opted members in M. Y. Barlow, Arthur Ellis, W. Fenwick, T. Ainscough and V. Walker.

One name must not be dismissed without further mention—that of T. A. Higson, known to all at Old Trafford as 'Tommy', a cricketer who played for Oxford University (without getting a Blue), Derbyshire, Cheshire, and Lancashire. He was a member of the committee for forty-nine years, and held

Q

at various times positions of chairman of the match committee, hon. treasurer and chairman of the committee. He held strongly the same views as John Stanning; an instance was the prominent part he played in securing McDonald for the county. The Nelson club was paid £500 and given two first-class matches for releasing the great bowler, the Lancashire committee voting 6–3 on the proposal to engage him.

T. A. Higson divided his interests between his profession (he was a member of a well-known firm of Manchester solicitors), his home at Grange-over-Sands, and the cricket club, and only a genius for organising his own life could have found time for it all. His aim was always clear: a strong team and good balance sheets. It was in accordance with his desire to see big crowds flocking to the ground that he led the way in 1930 in urging artificial drying of pitches. And to find out what the paying public thought, he often wandered alone on the popular side, pausing just to listen to their comments.

He was a member of both the M.C.C. and Board of Control Test Selection Committees. He helped to choose the team of 1932–3, but he did not think it inconsistent with his position to condemn the fast bowling tactics employed in that series, and he was naturally closely bound up with Lancashire's decision to break the fixtures with Notts after the 1934 match at Trent Bridge already described

Though T. A. Higson had a knack of getting his own way in many things, he failed in one: he could never convince other counties that single-innings matches were a worth-while proposition. Personally, he was a distinctive character; he would engage in a long conversation and then break it abruptly, and he was given to spontaneous acts of generosity. In committee, he was persuasive to a degree. Both his sons, T. A. junior and Peter, played for the county and the latter became a member of the committee.

Other officials of the county who will long be remembered are Talbot Fair, for some years hon. treasurer and well-known in the world of golf for his work in promoting the ladies' championship; A. F. Pope, a chairman of the match committee and energetic in getting up teams for the less important fixtures; and Dr. H. H. I. Hitchon of Heywood.

In 1953, the last year with which this book deals, the full list of officers was:

PRESIDENT
T. Stone

VICE-PRESIDENTS

M. N. Kenyon	President 1936–7
Sir Thomas Robinson*	President 1939–40
Sir R. Noton Barclay	President 1943–4
R. H. Spooner	President 1945–6
W. Findlay*	President 1947–8
Sir Edward Rhodes	President 1949–50
Col. Leonard Green	President 1951–2

G. G. Altham
R. A. Boddington
Sir Thomas Brocklebank, bt.*
T. Crosby*
Col. Sir Henry Darlington
Rt. Hon. The Earl of Derby
W. J. Garnett
A. W. Goodall
T. Harry Hewlett
Dr. J. Bowling Holmes
Stanley Holt
F. P. Nathan

The Rt. Hon. The Earl Peel
E. B. Rowley
W. Proctor Smith
Vice-Chancellor Sir John
   Stopford
Lieut.-General Sir Ronald
   Weeks
Sir Frederick West
G. Harold White*
Rev. Canon F. Paton
   Williams
The Rt. Hon. Lord Woolton

HON. TREASURER
R. A. Boddington

COMMITTEE
Dr. J. Bowling Holmes (Chairman)

F. D. Beattie	Major R. Howard
T. E. Burrows	Col. W. H. B. R. Kennedy
G. S. Cadman	W. H. L. Lister
J. S. Cragg	A. Rhodes
C. R. Davies	W. E. Seddon
H. D. Davies	G. O. Shelmerdine
J. P. Dewhurst	F. M. Sibbles
P. Higson	E. Tyldesley

SECRETARY
C. G. Howard

Royal patronage was extended to the club by King George VI, and continued, on her accession, by Queen Elizabeth II.

* Died during the year under notice.

CHAPTER 25

Lancashire v Yorkshire

What Barlow said; Ulyett's great match, 1883; Lancashire's brilliant 'double', 1899; Briggs tempts Ulyett, 1893; A sensational benefit match; MacLaren and Briggs, 1899; Walter Brearley's 125 wickets; Hirst's great deeds; A double century by Spooner; Seventeen wickets for Dean at Liverpool; Parkin makes his mark; A great innings by Ernest Tyldesley; The classic finish of 1922; Yorkshire out for 33, 1924; Record gates, 1925–6; Leyland sets up a record, 1930; Paynter and Sibbles at Bradford, 1932; Macaulay's hat-trick at Old Trafford, 1933; Nine wickets for Iddon, 1937; Lancashire's narrow win at Sheffield, 1950; Washbrook twice saves the day

THE BANK HOLIDAY Battle of the Roses provides, according to D. R. Jardine, the nearest approach to the atmosphere of Sydney or Melbourne—when the crowds are orderly. But there is more than tenseness to a match between Lancashire and Yorkshire; there is a rough good humour behind the partisanship to remind one that it is, after all, holiday time, and the sharp antagonism of the teams and the arguments among the crowd have never allowed any ill-feeling to persist. An Old Trafford crowd might shout at George Macaulay as, face black as thunder, he vainly appealed for leg-before; or all Bramall-lane might deride Frank Watson for his dead-bat play; but all was forgiven in the evening, and admiration was never far from condemnation.

'Something is bound to happen when these Yorkshire chaps come here' is a paraphrase (and probably a polite one) of what Barlow said about these great matches.

Outside the two counties, an opinion is widely held that

these matches are slow, uneventful affairs; but within Lancashire and Yorkshire it is appreciated that the meetings have produced much fine cricket, many historic feats—and even when the scoring has been slow, it has frequently been slow not because of inefficiency, but because it happened to fit the whole pattern of a particular match.

Reference has already been made to the Sheffield and Manchester matches of 1849 and to a third fixture in 1851, but the roots of the rivalry between the two counties lie even deeper. In 1844 there was a match between Manchester and All Yorkshire, on the former's ground, and after a blank first day, cricket was commenced at ten o'clock on the morning of the second day. Yorkshire scored 77, Manchester 80, and then the visiting side were put out for 39. Manchester knocked off the runs to win by five wickets, and a contemporary account of the game states that it was not finished 'till after 8 o'clock last evening'.

The Sheffield match of 1849 ended in victory for Yorkshire by five wickets, and they also won the return in August, this time by an innings. The 1851 match was played late in August and Lancashire, though having the assistance of Caesar, Sherman, and R. C. Tinley, were beaten again, though the visitors lost five wickets in scoring the 44 they required to win.

It was in 1867 that the two counties commenced what may be termed their official fixtures; there was a break in 1869 and 1870, but since then they have met regularly except when wars have put a stop to first-class cricket. It would be idle to deny that Yorkshire have established an advantage in these matches; they won all three games in 1867, and they have kept their lead through the succeeding years.

When the two sides met at Whalley in June 1867, Yorkshire's victory was overwhelming; they scored 188 and then Freeman and Greenwood, bowling unchanged, put Lancashire out for 57 and 75.

At Old Trafford Emmett and Cuttell (father of the all-rounder who later played for Lancashire) took most of the wickets and their side won by 165 runs, and then late in the year at Middlesbrough it was Emmett and Freeman who did the damage in another innings victory. Only one match was played the following season (at Holbeck) and it was something of a freak, because Lancashire were dismissed for 30 and 34, and 17 of their 64 runs were extras. Freeman had 12 wickets for 23 runs, Emmett seven for 24, and between them they hit the stumps 17 times. They did most of the work again in 1871 when Yorkshire won at Old Trafford, but a few weeks later Lancashire gained their first success with a ten-wicket margin at Sheffield. Appleby made 99 of the total of 343 and then took five for 87 and three for 54, with Hickton, Reynolds, and Barlow also among the wickets.

Old Trafford and Sheffield now became the grounds in general use for these big games, though Bradford had a fixture in 1874 and Huddersfield those of 1877 and 1878. For some years bowlers dominated the scene—Appleby, McIntyre, Watson, and Steel for Lancashire, Emmett, Allen Hill, Ulyett, and Clayton for their rivals. But there was a splendid partnership of 148 by Barlow and Hornby in 1875, and three years later they made 89 together, of which Barlow's share was nine! In 1879 William Bates hit the first century of the series at Sheffield. A year later the illustrious Peate had a haul of 14 wickets for 80 runs at Old Trafford, though this did not win the match, which was left drawn.

The first of the close finishes came in 1882 when Lancashire got home by 16 runs at Old Trafford thanks to fine batting by Barlow. In 1883 there was one of the first recorded instances of a big gate, 19,000 paying at the gates in two days at Bramall-lane. It was emphatically Ulyett's match; he scored 16 and 61, and did the hat-trick, and his innings of 61, made when the game was prolonged on the second evening to ensure a finish, was a dazzling bit of hitting. The game was also noteworthy for some splendid fielding, with Hunter standing up to the Yorkshire bowlers without a long stop.

Allen Hill took the Roses fixture as his benefit in the following season, and though it finished in two days, he had a good gate on the first day. This was Barlow's game, 13 wickets for 66 runs, with Yorkshire's score showing 15 for five at one time in their second innings.

In 1885 came Lancashire's first individual century, 109 by G. M. Kemp at Huddersfield, though he was on the losing side. Dewsbury was allocated the Yorkshire home fixture in 1885, and Lancashire, all out 53 (Bates six for 19, Emmett four for 10), got away with a draw.

In the following season it was very different cricket at Bradford,

1,210 runs being scored for 28 wickets—the first four-figure aggregate in which Lancashire had been concerned. Late in the season (it was actually the last fixture for both counties) the return at Old Trafford was won by the visitors, who thereby ensured the championship for Surrey.

At Old Trafford in 1888 the first day saw 25 wickets go down and the game finished with Yorkshire winning by two wickets, Peel, Briggs, and Watson all bagging cheap wickets. It was this same year that J. R. Napier took his four wickets for no runs at Sheffield.

It was even closer at Huddersfield in 1889, where the two teams played a match that must rank as one of the finest of all. Peel and Ulyett put their rivals out for 81, and then Yorkshire made 160, and in this phase the chief honours went to the fast bowlers Ulyett and Mold, making the most of the bumpy pitch. Among many batting failures, Lord Hawke made 52 not out.

With four men out in their second innings, Lancashire were still 57 behind; then Ward was dropped by Wainwright in the slips, and that was the turning-point. Somehow or other Ward kept his end up though repeatedly beaten, and Briggs hit away in his most brilliant manner. The tail-enders took heart, and Yorkshire were asked to score 75 to win. Mold opened in his most intimidating style, and had four men out with only nine runs scored and though Peel made a stand, he was dismissed in a fashion that was recalled by those who knew their cricket history when Close was out in 1950; he slipped on the treacherous turf and was run out. Though Wainwright carried on with the bold hitting no one else could do anything and Lancashire got home by three runs. While Briggs kept a length Mold bowled superbly to finish with a match record of 13 wickets for 111 runs. A few days later the 'double' was completed, Briggs capturing ten wickets.

Mold had a magnificent record the following year when he took nine for 40 in a drawn game at Manchester, and 13 for 76 in a big Lancashire victory at Huddersfield.

One of the outstanding all-round feats in these games was accomplished by Briggs at Old Trafford when in 1892 he took 13 wickets and played an innings of 115. In making 180 in the same match, Albert Ward hit the highest score so far then recorded for either side.

From 1889 to 1893 Lancashire achieved a clear-cut supremacy, winning eight of the ten games and losing only one. In the last year of this sequence they won by five runs at Old Trafford, the game starting on the Bank Holiday Monday with a crowd of 25,000 in the afternoon, a record for Old Trafford up to this time. Peel, Briggs, and Mold carried all before them in a match in which only 223 runs were scored for 40 wickets, and the finish has been described over and over again: Yorkshire wanted six to win, Briggs was bowling to Ulyett the famed hitter, and with that instinct which springs from a genius for games, the slow bowler tossed him one up. The ball was struck truly, and sailed through the air, only to hang and then drop just inside the rails where Albert Ward took the catch.

This, however, was one of the few matches that led to some feeling between the players. Jackson had been run out while apparently querying an umpire's decision, and Ernest Smith was given out to a catch at cover-point which was for ever afterwards disputed by the Yorkshire team. So while thousands of delighted spectators invaded the pitch and demonstrated their glee in front of the pavilion, in the dressing-room hard things were being said.

With ten wickets for 39 runs, Peel could be accounted desperately unlucky to be on the losing side, but for Briggs, with 11 for 60, it was the rounding off of a great double event, because earlier in the season he had taken 12 for 75 at Leeds where MacLaren's 54 on a poor pitch was also a magnificent feat.

The two great left-handers took their benefits in the following season, and they were given the two big matches of the year. That for Briggs came first, starting on Whit Monday (it fell as early as 14 May) and Lancashire covered the wicket in their desire to do their best for a cricketer who, though only thirty-two, had already served them for fifteen years. Lord Hawke made a brief inspection of the batsmen's paradise under the oil-sheets used in those days as a covering, returned to the pavilion, and said: 'I'm very sorry for Briggs, but I have come here to play county cricket, and not for a benefit match.'

So Mold was denied the chance of bowling on a fast wicket, and Briggs's match was finished inside two days—and a sensational match it was. Lancashire lost four Test-match batsmen —A. N. Hornby, MacLaren, Ward, and Sugg—before a run was scored, and seven wickets were down for 17 runs before a brief partnership between George Baker and A. T. Kemble enabled the side to muster 50. It was soon Briggs's turn, and Yorkshire, with seven men out, led by only 26—and one of the victims was Lord Hawke: bowled Briggs o, to the unconcealed delight of the crowd. But Yorkshire recovered, totalled 152, and won before lunch on the second day when Hirst brought his match record to ten wickets for 56 runs.

As things turned out, Briggs took £1,000 from the benefit, and when the return was played in August at Bradford, Peel did even better with a £2,000 reward which was a record at the time. Yorkshire won again, though Briggs took eleven wickets. Ernest Smith scored two fine half-centuries in a game of modest totals.

After two successful Bank Holiday games, Lancashire were keen to continue the arrangement, but a dispute arose and Kent were for a time the holiday opponents. One sequel was that in 1896 the sides met as early as the first week in May at Old Trafford, and there was a tremendous finish. Sugg made 74 at a run a minute, Moorhouse batted well for the opposition, and at the end Yorkshire had to make 167 to win. Against Mold and Briggs wickets fell at regular intervals until the close of the second day when the players and the crowd went home with the game in this position: 18 wanted, two wickets to go! Mounsey and Hirst got them next morning.

Three successive benefit matches followed for Hunter, Baker, and Wainwright, and then in 1899 came another wonderful match in this colourful series. It was at Sheffield, and Mac-Laren was in his most majestic mood, hitting 126 out of 203, with the next best score 18. On the last day rain cut into Lancashire's bid for victory, but at last they got the tenth Yorkshire wicket down, to win by 59 runs and with only half an hour on their side. Again it was Briggs who did most of the bowling, with ten for 124. When the sides met at Old Trafford in August (a week before Bank Holiday), MacLaren became the first man to hit a century in both games in the one season and John Tyldesley, after many failures, at last showed Yorkshire what he could do with an innings of 65. David Denton made a very good hundred in saving the game on the third day.

Meantime a new name had been coming up, that of Wilfred Rhodes, and in 1900 he took eight wickets for 43 runs when Lancashire were fortunate to escape defeat, rain coming on when they needed 199 on a difficult pitch. A curiosity here was that Cuttell junior bowled 52.2 overs unchanged in an innings of 230, finishing with five wickets for 115. At home this season Lancashire had rather the better of the play but Wainwright played a grand innings on the third afternoon and the home county were denied success.

In 1901 the clubs met at Bank Holiday again; at Old Trafford on Whit Monday there were 25,000 people inside the ground and they saw some remarkable play on a fiery pitch. Lancashire made 133, their rivals 134, and as though that keen fight were not enough, the spectators on the next day saw Lancashire bowled out for 44, Hirst having seven wickets for 23 and a match record of 12 for 77. The great Yorkshireman also scored 40, highest individual innings of the game, and his side won by nine wickets.

The return was very different, nearly 31,000 people on the first day being treated to a magnificent innings of 106 by Frank Mitchell in a score of 319. The size of the crowd took everyone by surprise, and they encroached so badly that in the afternoon play could not start again after lunch until half-past three, and even then with short boundaries. Lancashire replied with 413, MacLaren and Ward hitting hundreds, and not unexpectedly the game was left drawn. This was J. T. Brown's benefit, and again new record figures were set up.

Dismissed for 72 and 54 at Sheffield in 1903 (F. S. Jackson three for 5 and then five for 8) Lancashire were severely beaten in spite of Barnes's six for 39, and their bowling was hammered to the tune of 499 for five in the return at Manchester, played for Albert Ward's benefit.

Another new name appeared in 1903—Walter Brearley, who was destined in the course of fourteen matches to capture 125 Yorkshire wickets. He made his mark at once with six second-innings wickets at Old Trafford in a drawn game, but he missed the return at Bradford (Tunnicliffe's benefit) and Lancashire were beaten by five wickets, Hirst and Rhodes seeing the thing out in a partnership of 53, after Barnes had looked like winning the match.

Lancashire were champions in 1904, with Yorkshire second in the table, and fittingly enough the sides engaged in two eventful struggles, both drawn. At Old Trafford at Whitsuntide Yorkshire made 293, of which 162 were scored by Rhodes and Haigh in a ninth-wicket partnership after Walter Brearley had bowled at his best and eight wickets had gone down for 126. On a pitch affected by rain, Lancashire failed by 20 to reach their opponents' total, Spooner contributing 126. The third day was washed out.

In order to accommodate Hirst's benefit, the two clubs had agreed to switch the fixtures, and when Lancashire appeared at Bramall-lane in August MacLaren sent his opponents in with dire results. The bowlers failed to use the soft pitch, catches were missed, and in seven hours Yorkshire made 403 with Ernest Smith (dropped as soon as he went in) top scorer with 98. Lancashire fared badly, MacLaren, Spooner and Tyldesley going for four runs; but in the follow-on Tyldesley hit a magnificent century and the side wriggled out of a tight corner.

Lancashire won the Whit match of 1905 with Spooner and Tyldesley putting on 253 together but they lost the Sheffield game, though Brearley took 13 wickets for 157.

It was Hirst's year in 1906. At Bradford he hit the only half-century in a low-scoring game and took six wickets for 20 runs in Lancashire's first innings of 67. Haigh also did well with four for 30 and five for 35 and once again poor Brearley—nine for 83—had great personal success to no avail. In the return (John Tyldesley's benefit) the home side had all the worst of the wicket and were beaten for the second time this season. Hirst had a match record of seven for 96, and played a grand fighting innings of 85 in the second innings when Dean, Kermode, and Harry were doing well. A storm on the second night ruined Lancashire's chance of winning.

It was Rhodes and Hirst the following season, when Yorkshire won at Leeds and drew at Manchester, and then in 1908 came two extraordinary feats by Brearley, who took 25 wickets and yet was on the losing side in both games! At Sheffield, Hirst took eleven wickets and Yorkshire won by 193 runs, and at Old Trafford it was Hirst, Newstead, and Rhodes who shared the wickets.

Poor Brearley went on doing great things without getting his full reward. At Old Trafford in the following season he took nine wickets for 80 runs in Yorkshire's first innings, bowling 35 overs unchanged, and Huddleston had eight in the second innings for 24 runs, but the home side were dismissed for 89 and 57 and beaten by 65 runs, Hirst having a match record of nine for 57 and Haigh nine for 36 (including the hat-trick). In the return game at Bradford (Haigh's benefit) Rhodes had 13 wickets, Haigh himself six, and though Heap (11 for 95) bowled splendidly for Lancashire, another double defeat was recorded against them.

Another of Hirst's tremendous performances—four for 55, and nine for 23—marked a draw at Leeds in 1910, and then at Old Trafford in Jack Sharp's benefit, the tide at last turned. Brearley bowled up to form after a long absence through injury, Dean gave him admirable support, and over-topping everything else was Spooner's 200 not out, the great batsman surviving two early chances and then giving a display still talked about by those who saw it. Lancashire got home by an innings and 11 runs after an anxious wait through rain for their first win since 1905.

Rhodes had been playing in these fixtures ever since Wainwright's benefit in 1898, but it was 1912 before he hit his first century, a superb 107 on a difficult wicket at Bradford. Hirst, Drake, and Haigh followed up with effective bowling. At Old Trafford this year Spooner and Makepeace made 181 for the first wicket, and with Dean and Huddleston bowling well, Yorkshire only just saved the game.

In 1913 there were three games, the extra fixture at Aigburth being staged to mark the visit to Liverpool of King George V. Lancashire won this extra game by three wickets, after Dean had pulled out his best-ever bowling performance. On the first day so much rain had fallen that no play before lunch was considered possible, but the ground dried out so well that an earlier start than had been planned was agreed to. Dean was not on the ground when the game began but once he arrived he made his presence felt with nine wickets for 62 runs and then eight for 29.

Of the two championship matches, each side won once. At Old Trafford, Dean and Heap (11 for 39) were almost unplayable, and at Leeds there was a wonderful finish, Yorkshire getting home by three wickets, eight minutes from time. They had to make 217 in under two hours and a half, and Haigh (playing in his last Roses game) and B. B. Wilson were the heroes with 108 in fifty minutes.

In 1914 there were three fixtures again, championship games at Sheffield and Manchester, and an extra one at Hull. In a drawn game at Bramall-lane, Huddleston and James Tyldesley made 141 for the ninth wicket, and the return game was lost to some fine bowling by Drake, Rhodes, and Hirst. In the extra game, Whitehead for the first time in his career took eight wickets in an innings, and Rhodes hit a century. This game was badly hit by the weather, and left drawn.

As soon as the threads were picked up again in 1919, the two sides resumed their old rivalry in characteristic fashion. Their two-day match at Old Trafford in June was fairly described as the event of the season, and with Parkin available the home side won by 140 runs. But they were hard pressed for time, the last Yorkshire wicket going down only seven minutes from time, when Parkin shattered the stumps to bring his record to 14 wickets for 140 runs. The great bowler was at the top of his form, and his surprising variations were altogether too much for his rivals, not accustomed to his unique style. Nor should the part played by Makepeace be overlooked—105 and 78, with only one chance in the two innings.

Batsmen took the honours in the return at Sheffield, left drawn after Lancashire had fought a stout uphill battle. There were centuries by Holmes and Sutcliffe (who scored 235 together) and then by Hallows, who had splendid support from Ernest Tyldesley in saving the game.

The fixture continued to produce dazzling individual performances, as in 1920 at Bradford when Emmott Robinson took nine second-innings wickets for 36 runs to neutralise Dean's eleven for 113 and so give Yorkshire victory by 22 runs. The losers at one time needed only 52 with six men still to be dismissed but, playing over-cautiously, they completely lost their grip on the game. Holmes, with two separate hundreds, and Spooner with two characteristic sixties, shone in the August match when 58,000 people paid for admission at Old Trafford.

Spooner captained his team in the following season in the Whit week game, when Rhodes took seven wickets for 80 runs in a drawn game. At Leeds there was a huge crowd of 29,000 on the Bank Holiday, and they saw the curious record set up (though since surpassed) of only four Lancashire bowlers, James Tyldesley, Cook, Marriott, and Richard Tyldesley, taking the whole burden of an innings of 489 runs. They sent down more than 140 overs, Cook bowling 53 of them and taking six wickets for 145 runs.

It was about this time that rivalry developed to a point at which defeat became an almost intolerable prospect; partisanship ran high, and the rate of scoring began to fall away. For some years this slow scoring persisted though no one who has seen matches in more recent years can deny that the games have been played in good heart and with much entertainment for the public. Legends linger, however, and there is still an impression in many parts of England that Roses matches begin with 'How do you do?' and are then merely carried on by the single conversational phrase 'How's that?'

Particular criticism attached to the 1922 game at Bramalllane, though one player certainly had no reason to forget his own performance, for Ernest Tyldesley played the innings of his life against the formidable attack of Emmott Robinson, Waddington, Roy Kilner, Macaulay, and Rhodes, making 178 out of 307 when Hallows (66) alone of the other batsmen could do anything. Lancashire led by one run on the first innings, but failed on going in again and were beaten by six wickets, Sutcliffe and Roy Kilner batting finely at a critical time.

The spirit of 'We must not lose' was carried to its limit in the return at Old Trafford this season. On a dead pitch the batsmen plodded along at their own rate, scores were on a modest scale, and it was a big-hitting innings of 55 not out by James Tyldesley that topped the individual totals. Thanks to him Yorkshire wanted 132 to win, and under dismal conditions they set about their task. Parkin and Norbury took three wickets each, Oldroyd and Waddington were run out, Geoffrey Wilson was unable to bat (he had been seized with appendicitis) and as the match ran to its course in almost total darkness, Rhodes and E. R. Wilson were at once the hopes of their side and final obstacles against a Lancashire victory. For half an hour they stood firm, declining to take any risk, and only three runs came from the last five overs. In the very last over Rhodes declined to chance all on one big hit, and the game was left drawn when Yorkshire were three short of winning. Nonsense, perhaps, to an outsider; pure logic to those engaged in the struggle. It was the classic climax or anti-climax—have it your own way—to one of these matches.

In the following year there was the noteworthy reappearance of John Tyldesley as captain of his side and then in 1924 came another of those matches, one of the several in this series, that have become part of cricket's undying story. The scene was Headingley, and Lancashire's dreary batting—113 in 225 minutes—gave no hint of what was in store. Yorkshire gained a lead of 17 runs, and then on the second afternoon Lancashire failed so badly against Macaulay, Kilner, and Rhodes, that they were all out for 74, and Yorkshire's last task was to score no more than 57. But on the third morning Parkin and Richard Tyldesley pulled off the performance of their lives, getting their rivals out for 33. Parkin had a match record of eight wickets for 61, and his partner, who had six for 18 in the second innings, finished with ten for 87.

There were huge crowds for a rain-ruined return game, and though the watchers were robbed of anything like the excitement of Leeds, they saw a young man hit his first century in big cricket: Maurice Leyland, playing McDonald's most fearsome bowling with that sturdy batsmanship soon to gain him world-wide renown.

Old Trafford about this period was the scene of unprecedented interest in cricket and in 1925 the Roses match drew 60,000 people; the two following games against Kent and Surrey were watched by about 60,000, both totals being exclusive of members. Even these figures were passed in the following year when 75,000 saw the August match and the attendance of 46,000 on the Bank Holiday Monday (38,906 paid) remains to this day a record for any cricket match played in England. The great crowd revelled in Lancashire's total of 509 for nine wickets, the best they have put up against their keenest rivals, with centuries by Makepeace and Ernest Tyldesley and 92 by Watson. Yorkshire saved the game with ease, Holmes (143) and Sutcliffe (89) scoring 199 together. The last day was marred by a mishap to Oldroyd, struck on the head by McDonald.

Lancashire won at Old Trafford in 1927, McDonald taking 11 wickets, though they did not make the winning hit until nearly six o'clock on the last day, and after this there were nine consecutive drawn games, and it is not surprising to find, on looking at the scores, that batsmen generally took the honours if mere figures mean anything. Sutcliffe was a tremendous barrier in these years, making 95 and 135 at Leeds in 1927, and in the following year taking part in century stands with Holmes in both fixtures. In 1929 Hallows carried his bat for

152 through an innings of 305, and a year later Leyland set up an individual record with 211 not out at Leeds, a wonderful innings of terrific driving and vigorous pulls. At Bramall-lane in 1931 Holmes and Sutcliffe batted for almost all the first day, scoring 323 together. But there was a new star rising on the west side of the Pennines, one Eddie Paynter, and he saved this match first by scoring 45 not out and then, keeping his pads on and going in first in the follow-on, standing fast for 87 not out. The following Whitsuntide Yorkshire saw him in another mood when, at Bradford on a soft pitch, he launched an assault on the bowling that earned him 152 runs, including five sixes, four of them hit into the football stand off Verity who, despite this punishment, took eight wickets for 107 runs. This was startling enough, but on the Monday there were even more remarkable events. After the pitch had been artificially dried Sibbles bowled his off-breaks with such skill that Yorkshire were put out for 46. He had seven for 10, Hopwood three for 34, and in the follow-on the former had five for 58. Sutcliffe battled along for a time, and Leyland hit hard, but Yorkshire were beaten by an innings and 50.

So the long run of drawn games was broken, and Yorkshire immediately gained a verdict too, by an innings at Old Trafford with the help of a century by Sutcliffe. They won again in 1933 too, a match of controversy following a long, patient century by Mitchell and then an utter collapse by Lancashire on the Bank Holiday Monday when Macaulay did the hat-trick and took 12 wickets for 49 runs. The top of the pitch went and the South African fast bowler Gordon Hodgson was blamed—perhaps over-harshly at the time—for running on it and cutting it up. At Leeds this year Hopwood and Hawkwood made centuries, the latter overcoming lameness that compelled him to employ a runner.

This was a period of marked Yorkshire supremacy; beginning with 1932, they won nine, and lost only one, of fifteen consecutive Bank Holiday fixtures. They did so through the efforts of Mitchell and Verity at Sheffield in 1934, Bowes with twelve wickets at Bradford in the following season, Verity again at Old Trafford in 1937, and Verity home and away in 1938 when Lancashire were beaten twice for the first time in twenty-eight years. Yorkshire repeated this feat the following summer, Ellis Robinson and Bowes bowling well. At Leeds, the

Some of the county's famous bowlers in action. *Above left*: R. Tyldesley. *Above right*: R. Pollard. *Bottom left*: R. Tattersall. *Bottom right*: M. J. Hilton in the match with the Australians in 1948, when he bowled Don Bradman.

Above: Lancashire, county champions 1926. *Left to right*: *Standing*: G. Duckworth, J. Iddon, F. M. Sibbles, F. Watson, R. Tyldesley, C. Hallows. *Seated*: C. H. Parkin, H. Makepeace, Maj. L. Green (capt.), E. Tyldesley, E. A. McDonald.

Below: Lancashire, county champions 1927. *Left to right*: *Standing*: E. Paynter, G. Duckworth, F. M. Sibbles, J. Iddon, Webster, M. L. Taylor. *Seated*: C. Hallows, P. T. Eckersley, Maj. Green (capt.), E. Tyldesley, F. Watson, R. Tyldesley.

winning hit was a chance put down, and as soon as the players went off, the ground was flooded by a violent storm.

We must retrace our steps to record some Lancashire feats during this sequence of set-backs. There was Iddon's fine century on his own ground in 1934, there was an unorthodox, death-or-glory 141 by Watson at Bradford a year later, and there was above all Iddon's triumph in 1937 at Sheffield. This remarkable match began with a Sutcliffe century (the eighth of the nine he hit in these fixtures), then accurate bowling by Pollard limited the total to 246. Steady batting all down the list gave Lancashire a score of 324, though no one made more than 51, and then on the last day Iddon, bowling over the wicket, took nine wickets for 42 runs. His team had 91 to get and though Verity took three wickets at moderate cost, he could not duplicate Iddon's feat and the runs were obtained for five wickets.

Under the leadership of F. E. Greenwood and Brian Sellars, the Yorkshire team won the championship seven times in nine seasons, only Lancashire and Derbyshire breaking the sequence, and tribute must be paid here to the splendid match-winning cricket, the brilliant fielding, and the clever tactics of the side. Lancashire hated losing, but they recognised and honoured a great team when they saw one.

In 1945 a game was played at Bradford for the Verity Memorial Fund; Washbrook and Nutter took the honours in a drawn match, though Bowes, who had been a prisoner-of-war, took three wickets before pulling a muscle.

Championship matches were resumed in 1946 and there was some rather artificial excitement at Sheffield when, after rain, Sellars and Fallows agreed to split the remaining time. By those who dislike the idea of an arranged finish the further rain was, for once in a way, welcomed.

The two teams were running neck-and-neck for the title in August, and so great were the crowds at Old Trafford that the gates had to be closed. Place and the Yorkshire-born King made centuries in their different styles, Roberts, Pollard, and Phillipson bowled well, and on the last day a home win seemed certain. Five men were out for 120 and Yorkshire were still 96 behind, but Leyland and Sellars played a magnificent rearguard action, the captain revealing unsuspected powers in such a situation.

R

Hutton and Watson (W.) broke new ground for a Roses match by scoring a hundred together for the first wicket in each innings at Old Trafford in 1947, and it was this season that Smithson, a young left-hander, hit his remarkable 98 at Bramall-lane, an innings of rare brilliance and containing a promise that was unfortunately never quite borne out.

There was a crowd of 33,000 on the Whit Monday at Headingley in 1948. The match was one of big scores, Washbrook getting 170 (his first century in these fixtures), Edrich 121, and Hutton 100. In the return both Washbrook and Hutton reached three figures again but were overshadowed by Lester who hit two centuries to equal Holmes's feat of 1920. He hit his second hundred in 110 minutes.

Some remarkable cricket at Old Trafford in 1949 saw Hutton score 210 and 91 (he also captured five wickets) and Grieves played an astonishing innings of 69 when saving the game on the last day, getting his runs after being dropped four times in his first few minutes at the wicket.

The sequence of drawn games was broken in 1950 when Lancashire won at Sheffield. Wharton made 93 of their 257, and then Yorkshire fared so indifferently that Yardley decided to declare at 193 for eight. Lancashire were put out for 117, Close taking six wickets cheaply, and thanks to Hutton and Yardley, the home side almost got the 182 wanted for victory. Once Hutton was out, however, the captain stood almost alone though Close, who hit a six, looked like winning the match on his own. Poorly shod, he fell while taking a single after making 17 and was run out, and finally Berry had Yardley caught close up from an impossible ball, and Lancashire won by 14 runs.

A beautiful innings by Yardley also marked the return game, the captain saving his side after Statham had bowled with great effect on his first appearance in one of these matches.

There were two exciting finishes in 1952, and on each occasion Lancashire were hard pressed to avoid defeat. At Leeds three declarations showed that both sides possessed the will to make a real match of it and in the fourth innings Lancashire, after being set the task of scoring 233 in 150 minutes, first of all obtained 100 in 77 minutes but then collapsed. Washbrook was injured and had not intended to bat again, but he went in at No. 10 and he and Wilson played out the extra half-hour, the closing score being 148 for eight.

Trueman and Burgin bowled Lancashire out for 65 in the return, and on the third day the home side, 298 behind, owed a good deal to defence and defiance by Parr for saving the day at 166 for nine, the wicket-keeper being undefeated after an hour's resistance. Three of the Lancashire players each bagged a pair.

Still a third and successive rescue act was required at Old Trafford in the Whit match of 1953. On the last afternoon the home county were 99 for five, only 23 runs to the good; at this point Washbrook, who had been hit on the jaw by Trueman and compelled to retire, returned to the crease to play one of his best and most imaginative innings. A year earlier mere survival had been sufficient; this time runs were required and so well did the great batsman meet the occasion that when stumps were pulled, he had made 65, Lancashire were 186 for seven, and the game was saved.

At Bramall-lane in August Lancashire batted steadily for 373 (Trueman six for 109) and then Statham and Tattersall bowled so well that Yorkshire were all out for 177. Howard declined to enforce the follow-on and so began a controversy that will last as long as the counties meet. The reason for the decision was a doubt about Statham's fitness and the captain was not anxious to take the field again so soon without a fast bowler. Yorkshire eventually required to score 356 at 74 an hour and for a time the game was kept at an even balance by the splendid hitting of Wilson and the occasional fall of a wicket to a rash stroke. Wilson was denied his century by two runs and then, at 200 for six, heavy rain washed out the proceedings, with two hours still left for play. But for the break in the weather, Howard's decision on the second afternoon would have brought victory: but can any captain afford to ignore the weather in England?

If the unofficial games in the middle of the nineteenth century are ignored, Yorkshire have now won 52 of the 153 matches played, Lancashire's victories numbering 35 and the draws 66. These figures include the extra matches of 1913 and 1914, and the Verity Memorial fixture. Yorkshire prefer to include the 1849 and 1851 games, and by their reckoning the centenary was therefore reached in 1949. A dinner was held in Sheffield to mark the occasion with Sir William Worsley in the chair. Fifty-two Yorkshire and forty-one Lancashire players attended, including the oldest—Mr. E. B. Rowley, then seventy-nine, and David Denton, then seventy-five. A flag, beautifully decorated with the emblems of the two clubs, was presented by the Yorkshire club, and it is now flown whenever the teams renew their rivalry.

CHAPTER 26

Touring Teams

*The Australians arrive; George Giffen's feats; Trumper's bril-
liant batting; Tall scoring at Blackpool; Two Lancashire
victories, 1912; McDonald on two sides; Hilton twice
beats Bradman; South Africa join in; Dean and
Huddleston put them out for 44; A double
win in 1929; Valentine takes his chance
for the West Indies; V. M. Merchant's great batting; Ikin
shocks the New Zealanders*

THE AUSTRALIANS OF 1878, whose visit revolutionised cricket,
played at Old Trafford in August, and so great was public
interest that two stands were specially erected for the match.
Spofforth took nine wickets in the county's first innings, and
the tourists would almost certainly have won but for rain.

Playing various matches against odds they beat XVIII of
Stockport and District, drew with XVIII of Oldham and
Werneth, drew at Longsight, Oldham, Stockport, Liverpool,
Rochdale, Burnley, Buxton and Crewe, and were beaten by a
Longsight XVI (which included Fred Grace) by two wickets
in a low-scoring match.

The Philadelphians arrived in 1897, followed by the West
Indians in 1900, the South Africans in 1901, All-India in 1911,
and New Zealand in 1927.

The First Test match at Old Trafford was in 1884—the third
England v Australia match played in England. Since that time
Manchester has been an accepted Test-match centre and though
the weather has so often been unkind that a certain notoriety
has become attached to the ground, and there was even talk
recently of moving fixtures in an attempt to avoid what a Cor-
poration official called the 'monsoon season', there has been
time for much exciting cricket.

In the early years, Australian visits were more frequent than

they are nowadays, when the tours have to be spaced out to
meet a carefully-arranged programme of world-wide fixtures,
so that there were twelve visits between 1878 and 1905. Lancashire did not meet the 1880 team (which lost to XVIII of
Stockport), but they played a great match with the 1882 side
which the tourists only won by four wickets after the county
had followed on. The hero of the game was Barlow, who
carried his bat for 66 in a second innings of 269, a feat rewarded
with a collection of £15 in the pavilion.

In 1884 George Giffen met with great personal success,
accomplishing the hat-trick in dismissing Taylor, Robinson,
and D. Q. Steel, and then scoring a century, though it must be
added that he gave four chances. The Australians were beaten
by the North of England at Old Trafford this season, Hornby
hitting a spirited if lucky 94. They went on to Liverpool and
played what was styled a Liverpool and District XI but which
could well have been called a county team, as three Steel brothers, Briggs, Barlow, Crossland, and Watson were there.
Palmer, Boyle, and Crossland (11 for 70) all bowled in top
form, A. G. Steel scored 72 and 29, and in a tremendous finish
the touring side got home by one wicket, the winning run being
a leg-bye.

There was a real curiosity when the 1886 side came to Manchester to play the North of England. Ten thousand people
saw the first day's play when 31 wickets fell for 137 runs,
Australia making 45 and 43, Peate and Watson taking the
wickets unchanged, and the North scoring 34 and 15 for one,
Spofforth and Palmer doing all the damage. Two days' rain
prevented the chance of a finish to this extraordinary game.
When it came to Lancashire's turn to meet the touring side,
they gave a wretched display of batting and were severely
beaten, Giffen taking 16 wickets for 65 runs. A Liverpool XI
(this time really local, though it included some good cricketers)
did well in a two-days match, E. C. Hornby and A. G. Steel
batting well.

Two years later Lancashire beat the tourists, who had started
the season with some devastating form in their first five fixtures. On a fiery wicket bowlers generally held the upper
hand, but on the third day A. G. Steel, Joseph Eccles, and the
Rev. J. R. Napier batted pluckily and Australia had to make
90 to win. Briggs bowled in his best form—he had a match

record of nine for 49—Napier backed him up with his fast bowling, and the county won by 23 runs. A little later in the season the Australians beat the North of England at Old Trafford thanks to some superb hitting by P. S. M'Donnell, who, when his side went in to get 101, made 82 out of 86, so that Australia were able to get home with five wickets and ten minutes in hand. The usual fixture against the Liverpool side was won comfortably.

There was a match this season at Old Trafford in which Shrewsbury's team met the touring side, and Briggs not only made top score with 37 but took ten wickets for 80 runs in the two innings, his team winning easily.

In 1890, C. T. B. Turner's bowling was too much for Lancashire, who were badly beaten. The North put up a better show in a drawn match, and very late in the season there was an extra fixture to make up for the washed-out Test. An England XI included a majority of Test men, but the attendance proved disappointing—perhaps because the game was played as late as 18 September. The tourists had rather the better of a drawn game, J. E. Barrett scoring 170 for once out and Turner and Ferris bowling effectively.

Their old enemy Giffen was too much for the county again in 1893, though Albert Ward carried his bat for 45 in a total of 97 in the first innings, and later in the season Ward again showed fine form for the North. He made 93 and with MacLaren (66) put on 121 for the first wicket. There was some level scoring all through the match which ended with Australia getting their last 102 runs in 75 minutes to win by three wickets. The fixture against Liverpool and District was resumed this season, with the home men badly beaten. There was also a game at Blackpool against a XVI, not taken very seriously.

'Enormous crowds' were reported in May 1896, for the visit of G. H. S. Trott's side. Up to a point the county men fared well, Briggs and Mold bowling well, but the batting failed in the fourth innings and Australia won by 154 runs. The same pair did well for the North a month or so later, on a difficult Old Trafford pitch, but again the tourists came out on top, this time by 42 runs. A second game between Lancashire and the Australians was this season allocated to Liverpool, and it produced one of the most remarkable bowling feats of all time—13 for 38 runs by McKibbin. He bowled unchanged with

Trumble and 'got an almost incredible amount of break on the ball'. The present writer met McKibbin long years after this performance and remarked 'They say you used to throw?', and the old Australian, completely unabashed, replied: 'I daresay if I'd seen myself, I would have said so, too.' Lancashire, put out for 62 and 28, were beaten by 217 runs.

There was another bad beating, this time at Old Trafford three years later, though J. T. Tyldesley, hitting 56 and 42 on a bad wicket, rivalled the brilliance of Trumper, who made 82. In the second match at Aigburth the young Spooner foreshadowed what was to come in later years with 46 and 31 not out in a rain-ruined fixture, and I'Anson took seven cheap wickets. It was Trumper's year in the deplorably wet summer of 1902, and he did not disappoint when the team came to Old Trafford in the first week in June, hitting 70 out of 109 in 70 minutes without a mistake, though S. F. Barnes was in the county team. This match was left drawn through bad weather, but the second fixture at Liverpool was a very different affair. Lancashire included Kermode in their side and he and Littlewood bowled so successfully that the Australians made only 138. Trumble and Saunders in turn took advantage of turf affected by rain and sun, and the county were 18 behind on the first innings. Littlewood bowled to even greater effect on the second afternoon and with seven for 49 brought his match record to 12 for 98. Lancashire required 124 to win, but the bowling was just too good for them and they lost by 18—just their deficit on the first innings.

McLeod and Laver were too much for the county in 1905, though Brearley toiled with typical optimism and took seven first-innings wickets. In the second fixture at Liverpool, Billy Cook had one devastating spell when he hit the sticks five times, only for Lancashire's batting to break down against Armstrong (12 for 92) and Laver.

In 1909, Lancashire saw a lot of visitors. There was one ordinary fixture, allocated to Liverpool, when the tourists won handsomely after being bowled out for 87 on the first day, Dean having a match record of ten for 79. An England XI drew with the Australians at Blackpool in a match of 1,283 runs for the loss of 27 wickets, the pattern being set on the first day when J. W. H. T. Douglas and A. E. Knight scored 284 together, the biggest opening stand against an Australian side in this country.

In two other games, Lancashire and Yorkshire combined to meet Noble's men but unfortunately both occasions were ruined by the weather. One cannot imagine a present-day Australian side agreeing to such a fixture—they would probably complain that it approximated to a sixth Test match—but for all that it would be a magnificent attraction if staged at Old Trafford or Leeds or Sheffield. In 1909 the first of these experiments were put on at Manchester when, after two blank days, Armstrong scored a rather fluky century. Later on the match at Hull was no more fortunate, the second and third days being washed out after the combined teams had made 261 for four wickets with attractive batting from Spooner, Denton, Rhodes, and Makepeace.

The Australian team in the Triangular Tournament season of 1912 was a weak one, but all the same Lancashire could be well pleased at beating them twice. The first victory was specially meritorious because, though Dean and Heap each took four wickets, there was a first-innings deficit of 31, Macartney having hit 80. Makepeace batted well for 52 at the second attempt and then F. R. R. Brooke and Whitehead hit 63 in 35 minutes. Australia wanted 158 to win, but Dean and Heap were too good for them again and Lancashire won by 24 runs.

Some of the pleasure was taken out of the victory by the public's refusal to pay the shilling charge for admission. The grumble developed into a boycott and only 300 people saw the two left-handers bowling out the Australians on the third day.

Three weeks later the teams met again at Liverpool and A. H. Hornby boldly sent his rivals in to bat. Blunders in the field were expensive, and though when the home side batted Sharp made 60, their last six wickets went down for six runs and the Australians led by 20. The tourists made only 94 in their second innings, Dean taking five wickets to bring his record for the two games to 18 for 201. The county needed 115 to win and Spooner and Makepeace proceeded to get 110 of them, the former finishing with 66 not out, made in his most flawless style.

H. L. Collins made a century and Lampard bowled effectively when the 1919 Imperial Forces side beat Lancashire at Old Trafford. Two years later Gregory, Hendry, and Mailey were altogether too much for the county team (weakened by injuries to Makepeace and Ernest Tyldesley) though Parkin and James Tyldesley each bowled well and limited their opponents' total to 284. In the second meeting at Liverpool, McDonald took eight for 62 and then two for 16 before rain saved Lancashire from defeat. McDonald here showed great skill, slowing up for the soft pitch, and his figures would have been even better but that Myles Kenyon hit him for a six and three fours in one over.

It was Macartney's match in the first meeting of 1926, the great batsman hitting 160 in his best form. Hallows made 85 and 46 for the county who were easily beaten, Mailey bowling well and Macartney capping his batting display with four cheap wickets. The side did better at Liverpool, though the Australians set off with a score of 468 for six wickets, McDonald taking five for 135 against his old friends. Makepeace and Hallows scored 114 for the first wicket in reply and though Lancashire had to follow on, the pair then scored 116—the first time such a double feat had been performed against Australia in this country. Mailey had nine first-innings wickets for 86, but did little bowling in the second innings and the home side saved the game. An England XI met the tourists at Blackpool, and Woodfull wound up the season by carrying his bat for 116 through an innings of 281.

Both of the 1930 matches were drawn. At Liverpool McDonald bowled Bradman for nine, and Hopwood did well with three wickets in one over but the later stages were not very serious. The second match at Old Trafford was a dull affair chiefly distinguished by a century from Kippax and an opening stand of 110 by Watson and Hallows.

A. D. Baxter, an amateur fast bowler, caused a brief stir at Old Trafford four years later before retiring with a strained tendon, and afterwards the bat mastered the ball, McCabe, Woodfull, Brown and Tyldesley making centuries. In 1938 there was fine bowling by Phillipson and, on the last afternoon, a superb century by Bradman.

As in 1934, there was only one county game against the tourists this year, but An England XI met them at Blackpool. Though Amar Singh bowled well, O'Reilly and Ward carried their team to an easy win.

Cranston sent the Australians in when they came to Old Trafford in 1948 and as they made only 204 he had no reason to regret the gamble. Malcolm Hilton, aged nineteen, first achieved distinction by bowling Bradman for 11, and then world-wide fame by having him stumped for 43 in the second innings. The second fixture was restored to the list this year, and big crowds attended Old Trafford to give Cyril Washbrook a record benefit, though he himself was injured during the game and kept out of the last Test match. Bradman, who contributed to the success of the occasion by declining to enforce the follow-on, made 133 in the second innings. That his bounty was not limitless was shown when, on Ikin's reaching 99 on the last afternoon, he called for the new ball— and Lindwall answered the call by at once bowling the left-hander.

Back again in 1953, the Australians were three times at Old Trafford, twice to play Lancashire and for the rain-ruined Test match. At the first meeting (after a blank first day) Lancashire bowled out the tourists for 298 and it took R. N. Harvey, in good form all summer, three hours and a quarter to score the century which made even this modest total possible. The county's reply was 232 for nine, Howard making 78 not out, against the full attack of Lindwall, Miller, Johnston and Archer.

The return match produced some magnificent cricket. On the Saturday, Australia lost seven wickets for 167 runs against some excellent bowling by Tattersall, before Davidson, Ring and Lindwall set about the attack to such purpose that a score of 372 was attained, and all in sufficient time to get Lancashire in before the close. Without Washbrook, and then reduced to ten men when Place was struck on the head by Miller, the county contrived to keep the game going into the third afternoon before being beaten by seven wickets.

The South Africans of 1894 did not play Lancashire, though they did appear at Aigburth where they beat a Liverpool District XI with some ease. They won a similar fixture in 1901 but lost to Lancashire at Old Trafford, Webb taking four wickets in each innings and E. E. Steel hitting well for 23 and 69. Again in 1904 the Springboks beat the Liverpool District side, and then drew a dull game with the county at Old Trafford. The famous South African team of 1907, with its array of spin bowlers, won easily at Manchester, only Spooner doing himself justice.

The double victory over the Australians of 1912 has been

mentioned; Lancashire added to that feat by winning one of their two games against South Africa, being the only county team to do so. The victory was at Liverpool and it was due to a century from Sharp and good bowling on a helpful pitch by Dean and Huddleston, specially effective when they dismissed the tourists for 44 on the last day. When the return was played at Old Trafford conditions were so bad after heavy rain that the captains agreed to use, if necessary, a new wicket for each innings, but the weather continued so broken that very little cricket was possible.

It was twelve years before these popular visitors came here again, and Lancashire again beat them, Richard Tyldesley (12 for 78) and Parkin bowling very well, and Watson hitting a sound century. In a second fixture at Liverpool, batsmen had things all their own way, Hallows, Hopwood, and Nourse getting centuries.

So often disappointing against Australia, Lancashire continued their good form against South Africa with a double win in 1929, by six wickets at Manchester and ten wickets at Liverpool, where Richard Tyldesley and Farrimond were seen to advantage. Six years later Hopwood carried his bat for 73 through the innings of 128 at Old Trafford, this game, like a rain-ruined fixture at Liverpool, being drawn.

In 1947 and again in 1951 there was only one meeting, ending each time in a draw.

Of the other touring sides, the Philadelphians call for next mention because they came here as long ago as 1897. The bowling of Briggs, Hallam, and Cuttell was too much for them and Lancashire won by seven wickets. Six years later they did very well, the famous swerve bowler King taking 14 wickets for 108 runs and enabling the touring team to win by nine wickets. King was unlucky not to take all ten wickets in the second innings, as he captured nine and the other man was run out.

The West Indies first came in 1900, when Lancashire beat them by 57 runs at Old Trafford, Briggs bowling well in a crisis. They drew with a Liverpool District XI at Aigburth. They did not come again until 1923 when Lancashire beat them by five wickets, Ernest Tyldesley hitting a hundred and Richard Tyldesley bowling well. There was a draw in 1928, and both of the 1933 matches were unfinished.

In 1950 there was sensational cricket. This was the season

of moderated preparation of pitches at Old Trafford, and the West Indian left-hander Valentine seized the opportunity to take 13 wickets; a few days later he took 11 wickets in the Test match on the same ground. He did well again at Liverpool, taking eight wickets, and with Pierre also bowling well, the West Indies recorded their second victory of the season over Lancashire.

A weak All-India team of 1911 did not offer stern opposition to Dean, Lol Cook and Huddleston, but there was tougher opposition in 1932. The Liverpool meeting was remarkable for some brilliant batting by the touring tail-enders, and Paynter reached three figures for the county. In the return Lancashire won well, with Ernest Tyldesley and Watson sharing in a stand of 327, and H. R. W. Butterworth bowling his leg-breaks with success.

In 1937 Oldfield and Washbrook made centuries in a tall-scoring game at headquarters and then a little later in the season All India had the satisfaction of defeating Lancashire at Liverpool, where the county had not lost a match since 1909. V. M. Merchant won great distinction by twice carrying his bat, a feat that has been recorded only four times in the history of cricket. They repeated this victory in 1946 when Merchant, on the last day, was again seen to special advantage with an innings of 93 not out. In the return at Old Trafford he surpassed himself by making 242 not out.

India came again in 1952 and though they fared disastrously in the Tests, they often showed good form in fixtures with the counties. One such occasion was against Lancashire when Umrigar hit a double century and then Divecha and Ramchand put the county out for 68, so that the tourists were able to win by ten wickets.

To the list of touring sides, New Zealand were added in 1927. A draw in that year and another in 1931 were followed by a double victory for the county in 1937. At Manchester 196 runs were hit off in two hours, Iddon making 94, and then at Preston the touring side were thoroughly outplayed.

In 1949 there was a grand partnership of 248 by Ikin and Grieves, and the latter made it an all-round performance by capturing five wickets and so compelling the New Zealanders to follow on, though they saved the game. Two capital innings by Washbrook in a second match at Liverpool led eventually to a declaration and the tourists set to score 153 in 75 minutes. They boldly went for the runs and got them with nine wickets and seven minutes in hand.

Two Royal visits have been paid to Old Trafford when touring sides have been engaged. In 1921, when the Australians were playing the county team, the Prince of Wales spent half an hour at the ground. The players were presented to him during the tea interval. In 1949 the Duke of Edinburgh watched some of the play during the Test match between England and New Zealand. During an interval, players and umpires lined up on the field and were presented to His Royal Highness.

CHAPTER 27

Wages and Benefits

*A bonus for an Australian match, 1882; Praise
for Lancashire professionals; Wages,
1953; What the benefits have
brought in*

THE INSTITUTION OF the county championship did much for cricket, and it did something for cricketers, too. Reading the old newspaper files, one is struck by the many reports of the difficulties of old players, some of them among the most famous, and the lot of the professional was certainly improved by the regular employment which resulted from the system of organised competitive matches. Lancashire's earliest relationship with their own professionals was, it seems, one of benevolent despotism, and it was probably the best thing for the staff. Their wages were not high but they came in for many gifts and the county was always quick to help in times of trouble. There was talent money, too, paid from the earliest times.

One of the earliest references to terms in the Lancashire minutes is of the £12 a man for the Australian match of 1882, with an extra £3 for a win. In this year Crossland was employed in the winter at 25s. a week, and when Pilling was first engaged he received £2 a week, later increased by 10s. These are typical rates for the '80s.

In 1890 Mr. A. B. Rowley stated at the annual meeting that while other counties were complaining of the way in which their professionals were treated to drink and the consequent effect on the players, Lancashire was happily not under that stigma. Their professionals, he said, compared favourably with any body of cricketers in the country.

In the same year Pilling was allowed £150 towards his fare to Australia when he went abroad in search of health; in acknowledging the gift, he thanked the club for the kindness 'always extended to me'. With a view to helping Briggs prepare for his benefit, an advance of £25 was made and though players in those days often received large sums at their benefit matches (at any rate in the north), this recollection leads one naturally to a comparison with the elaborate organisation which has grown up in recent years.

The changing scene is noted in other ways, too; in 1891 it was ruled 'any professional bowling for practice on county match days must wear white trousers'. Two years later the young John Tyldesley was offered his first engagement, and the rate was still around £2 a week. The top rate for established men was £3 a week, plus match pay and talent money. But repeatedly there are references in the club records to gifts made to old players who were in adverse circumstances. The scorer about this time was a man named Southworth, who received 30s. a week and was 'to be generally useful when not scoring'.

Winter pay was not uniform. For instance, both Ward and Cuttell, on making a new engagement, were told their winter pay would not continue once they had received their benefits. When Hallam was ill in 1899, he was given £100, and in the following year, when Briggs was so ill that he did not seem likely to return to the side, a special fund was raised for him and with the £740 thus collected, an annuity was purchased for his wife.

When, in 1901, some members were jibbing at the prospect of an increase in the subscription to meet the cost of the ground, John Stanning told the annual meeting: 'They could not engage a ground bowler for two months only; he had to be engaged for the season (*hear, hear*). Then again, it was not to be expected that they should alter the system of giving a good match to a professional's benefit—giving up the Yorkshire match for Sussex or some other.' (*Applause*.)

There could not be much wrong with employers who were animated by such sentiments, and we have earlier evidence of a generous outlook with regards to benefits for in 1897, when Sugg's match was spoiled by rain after a big first day, the club agreed to pay the expenses of the return match. In the same season, each member of the team was given a bonus of £10 to mark the championship success.

After the First World War Lancashire took the lead in urging a standard rate of pay by the counties and following their

Above: Lancashire, county champions 1928. *Left to right*: *Standing*: J. L. Hopwood, F. Watson, J. Iddon, R. Tyldesley, M. L. Taylor, G. Duckworth. *Seated*: E. A. McDonald, H. Makepeace, Maj. L. Green (capt.), E. Tyldesley, C. Hallows.

Below: Lancashire, county champions 1934. *Left to right*: *Standing*: C. Washbrook, J. L. Hopwood, J. Iddon, F. Booth, R. Pollard, L. Parkinson, N. Oldfield. *Seated*: E. Paynter, E. Tyldesley, P. T. Eckersley (capt.), W. H. L. Lister, G. Duckworth.

Lancashire, county champions (with Surrey) 1950. *Left to right: Standing:* K. Grieves, R. Tattersall, A. Barlow, R. Berry, M. Hilton, B. Statham. *Seated:* J. T. Ikin, C. Washbrook, N. D. Howard (capt.). W. Place, G. A. Edrich.

suggestion, the 'Big Six' met at Lord's and agreed to a maximum payment of £440 a year for twenty-eight matches, to include ground pay but not win- and talent-money. In 1924 steps were taken to protect the proceeds of benefits by advising players on investment, and by the appointment of trustees.

In 1945, when the county felt keenly that some of their players had been taken away from them by the blandishments of league cricket, it was deemed advisable to make public that capped players were given a guarantee that their total earnings would not fall below £416 for the season.

The rate of pay in 1953 for capped men was £262 a year plus £12 10s. match fee, home or away, plus £10 expenses for each away game. A capped man not included in the eleven received £6 10s. a match. The minimum pay for the leading players was therefore £463 and the maximum £650, to which must be added talent money, awarded on a basis of marks for skilful play and afterwards calculated against an amount of money allocated by the committee bearing in mind the overall financial results of the season.

Lancashire have been kind to other than their own players in the matter of benefits. They helped George Hirst by agreeing to switch dates for the 1904 Roses fixtures and the sequel was a then record of more than £3,700. And as long ago as 1884 the two great northern counties gave proof of their concern for the well-being of professionals by fielding a joint eleven for William Mycroft's match. They played a team labelled 'England' at Derby and though the combined counties looked by far the stronger side on paper, they were beaten by an innings and 19 runs.

It will be seen from the accompanying list that since Albert Ward's match in 1902, there have been twenty-six benefit matches in forty-two actual playing seasons, plus eight grants and testimonials of substantial amounts.

Since the Second World War, Lancashire players have been fortunate in having the cares of organising outside efforts taken off their shoulders. Old Trafford enthusiasts, notably Mr. Tommy Burrows, Mr. Ken Allison and Mr. W. E. Briggs, have worked hard to guarantee the success not only of the principal benefit match of the season at Old Trafford, but of those evening and Sunday games that have so notably increased the benefit funds. When Cyril Washbrook's benefit in 1948 totalled £14,000 it surpassed the previous record set up by W. E. Bowes of Yorkshire by almost £6,000. Though Washbrook's figure is hardly ever likely to be equalled in Lancashire, it can be said that so thorough is the organisation nowadays, all the county's professionals are—so far as can be humanly foretold—assured of substantial sums in their turn.

Still, if the organisation is now so remarkable, some of the older professionals certainly did very well and £1,101 for Watson represented a very large sum of money in 1885. The North and South teams which played at Old Trafford were:

NORTH: Shrewsbury, Barlow, W. Gunn, W. Barnes, Ulyett, Briggs, Bates, Flowers, A. N. Hornby, Peate, Pilling.

SOUTH: W. G. Grace, J. M. Read, T. C. O'Brien, W. W. Read, W. E. Roller, G. G. Hearne, Tester, F. T. Welman, Beaumont, Woof, and C. E. Horner.

The attendance for three days totalled 30,000 and most of the big names came off, Shrewsbury making a century, W. G. getting 69 in his first innings, and Johnny Briggs twice passing the 50 mark. At the close the South were still 259 behind with only two wickets to fall and one man unlikely to bat through injury.

In 1889 the teams for Pilling's benefit were just as powerful and again the North had much the better of the argument, going in a second time with 67 wanted and a little over an hour to play. The pitch was very slow, and they managed to score only 47 for the loss of four wickets—so apparently rivalry was keen even in a friendly fixture. Attewell and Lohmann were the bowling stars in the following elevens:

SOUTH: W. G. Grace, Abel, E. A. Nepean, T. C. O'Brien, K. J. Key, Quaife, Lockwood, Lohmann, F. Fielding, Beaumont, Martin.

NORTH: Ulyett, Ward, W. Gunn, W. Barnes, Sugg, Peel, Briggs, A. G. Steel, Attewell, A. N. Hornby, Sherwin.

Watson's reward was the first four-figure benefit on record, and it is believed that Pilling in turn set up a new record four years later. Some of the earlier benefits, however, were only approximately recorded because so many gifts were made direct to the players. It has not been possible to unearth figures for some of the old matches, one of them Frank Sugg's; his was a Bank Holiday fixture, like so many of the benefits of that period, and there were 22,000 people present on the first day, so he probably came out of it fairly well in spite of the rain that spoiled the rest of the match.

Benefits known to have been awarded include the following:

		Opposing Team	Amount
1870	F. R. Reynolds	Surrey	'Disappointing'
1878	C. Coward	Notts	Not known
1881	W. McIntyre	Gloucestershire	Not known
1883	W. Hickton	Broughton XVIII	Not known
1885	A. Watson	North v. South	£1,101 (record to this date)
1886	R. G. Barlow	Notts	£1,000
1889	R. Pilling	North v. South	£1,500 (record to this date)
1894	J. Briggs	Yorkshire	£1,000
1897	F. H. Sugg	Kent	Not known
1898	G. R. Baker	Yorkshire	'Highly satisfactory'
1902	A. Ward	Yorkshire	£1,739
1903	W. R. Cuttell and C. Smith (joint)	Essex	£657
1906	J. T. Tyldesley	Yorkshire	£3,111
1909	W. E. Howard	Testimonial	£235
1910	J. Sharp	Yorkshire	£1,679
1913	A. G. Paul	Testimonial	£544
1914	W. Huddleston	Surrey	£896
1920	H. Dean	Kent	£2,217
1921	J. S. Heap	Middlesex	£1,804
1922	H. Makepeace	Surrey	£2,110
1922	B. Blomley	Grant	£500
1923	L. Cook	Middlesex	£1,657
1923	James Tyldesley	Testimonial	£421
1924	E. Tyldesley	Middlesex	£2,458
1925	C. H. Parkin	Middlesex	£1,880
1926	W. E. Howard	Notts	£1,609
1928	C. Hallows	Surrey	£2,906
1929	E. A. McDonald	Middlesex	£1,947
1930	R. Tyldesley	Surrey	£2,027
1932	F. Watson	Surrey (no play)	£1,268
1933	E. Tyldesley	Gloucestershire	£802
1934	G. Duckworth	Surrey	£1,257
1936	J. Iddon	Surrey	£1,266
1937	F. M. Sibbles	Middlesex	£1,229
1938	J. L. Hopwood	Surrey	£1,105
1939	W. Farrimond	Middlesex	£1,000
1945	E. Paynter	Grant	£1,078
1948	W. E. Phillipson	Grant and testimonial	£1,750
1948	C. Washbrook	Australia	£14,000 (record)
1949	R. Pollard	Derbyshire	£8,000
1950	W. B. Roberts	Grant and testimonial	£2,623
1951	H. Makepeace	Testimonial	£1,099
1952	W. Place	Middlesex	£6,297
1953	J. T. Ikin	Surrey	£7,175

CHAPTER 28

Old Trafford

Praise from the M.C.C.: 'most desirable'; Comfort, not capacity; Further improvements planned; The pavilion described; There will be an Old Trafford in Elysium

WE BEGAN THIS story against the background of the old Manchester club and the search for the new ground in 1857. We have crossed the years between and come not to the end of the tale, but to the end of a summer, as it were, with many bright years within the promise of a rich future; and it remains only for a last look at Old Trafford, styled by H. D. Davies 'that perfect stretch of cricketing turf within its chaplet of dignified masonry which men know and revere the wide world over'.

Cricketers from home and abroad have paid their tributes; writers have lavished their richest prose on it. But perhaps Old Trafford received its sporting accolade in 1931 in the rather more formal words of the report of the M.C.C. committee appointed to inspect Test-match grounds with a view to judging their fitness for holding the ever-growing crowds of cricket enthusiasts:

'Old Trafford was in every respect most desirable, and in fact the only ground they had visited where no improvement could be suggested.'

Though bombs cruelly damaged Old Trafford a few years afterwards, energetic work has not only repaired the ravages but actually brought the famous ground to a condition far in advance of what it was in pre-war years. Never again, one supposes, will there be a crowd of 46,000 on any one day as there was in 1926, but the present estimated capacity of 35,000 takes full regard for the comfort of all. There is seating accommodation (if the members' pavilion is included) for 20,000, and herein lie the great improvements carried out between 1946 and 1953. In place of the rather dusty embankment near the railway station are now tidy concrete terraces, with their rows of seats, and one of the next big developments in the minds of officials is a comparable extension and improvement of the terracing at the Stretford End. The bookable numbered seats total 5,838.

The ground covers about 27 acres and comprises the actual first-class playing area with its stands and pavilion, two practice grounds with unrivalled net facilities, and a car park which, taking at least 2,500 cars, is the envy of every other county in the championship. Future plans, besides the new terracing at the Stretford End, include the balancing of F and G stands to the line of H stand. One of the last extensions was to B stand on the site of some of the worst of the war damage. There is provision for eventual placing of covers over some of the seating at present open to the sky.

The pavilion, though damaged in the air-raids and thought at one time to call for complete re-building, was temporarily restored beyond original expectations. It may have to be further enlarged, but that must be a long-term view. Accommodation for members must, of course, always be within certain bounds, and the size of the pavilion and the number of seats available controls the number of members; at present membership stands at 6,532 full members, 421 country members, 315 life members, 42 lady life members, 2,117 lady subscribers, 235 school girls, and 754 juniors, a total of 10,416.

Looking at the pavilion from the playing area, on the extreme right is a committee-room; adjoining it is the president's room. The main portion of the ground floor is taken up by the Long Room with its high chairs and its fine collection of pictures. On the left is the junior professionals' dressing-room, and behind are two bars for members. Upstairs are the home and away teams' dressing-rooms, baths, a massage room, the professionals' dining-room, and the committee dining-room. Above all is the balcony offering a splendid panoramic view of the ground. Below the ground floor are catering and storage facilities, the catering manager's office, and members' toilet accommodation. The groundsman, formerly lodged in a corner of the pavilion, war-damaged and as yet unrestored, now has his separate house near the main gate in Warwick Road.

Great cricketers have come and departed, leaving behind their records of runs and wickets and catches. Here are to be found reminders of the great moments of Old Trafford's history, founded on a hard core of county games with splendid interludes for Test matches. One may dwell in that moment in 1893 when Briggs, summoning up all his resource, tossed the ball up for Ulyett to hit and Ward to catch. Or ponder on an even earlier event, the Test of 1884, the first played on the ground, when A. N. Hornby and W. G. Grace went out together to bat first: the former bareheaded, determined, the very picture of a Lancashire and England captain; Grace with his massive head, M.C.C. cap perched atop, already the greatest batsman in the world. Or the mind may span the years to 1902 when Trumper hit his hundred before lunch; when Rhodes and Lockwood bowled so well to pull the game round; when MacLaren hit out with what seemed recklessness and then in justification pointed to the clouds of the gathering storm; when England required but 32 runs to win, with six wickets still to fall; when with one wicket to go and 8 runs still wanted, rain came on to test all nerves in an hour's wait; and when Tate, after hitting just one boundary, was bowled by Saunders. The scores of the games are there in the record books, the tales are handed down, until the very last season of our review, when Washbrook baffled Yorkshire in the Whitsuntide fixture of 1953, and when the Australians in the Test match lost eight wickets for 35 runs.

Test match and Bank-holiday cricket, it may be argued, is not always true cricket; and for many of us the happiest afternoons at Old Trafford are those days when interest is not quite so intense; when Lancashire are meeting one of the other counties, and a medium-sized crowd enjoys the quiet of a scene on the other side of the main road, but so far removed in mood.

The member in the balcony of the pavilion may eye with anxiety a cloud coming across the sky, blown by the prevailing wind over the practice ground; the journalist sitting high above the ladies' stand, in the biggest press-box in England, may grumble that a door, swinging noisily, disturbs the moment; but then each may look out across the turf so green and towards the railway and beyond to the indigo stillness of the Derbyshire hills and his gaze will return to the middle of the ground where

the teams are engaged and the bat wages its eternal conflict
with the ball and he will be sure that somewhere in the Elysian
Fields there will be an Old Trafford.

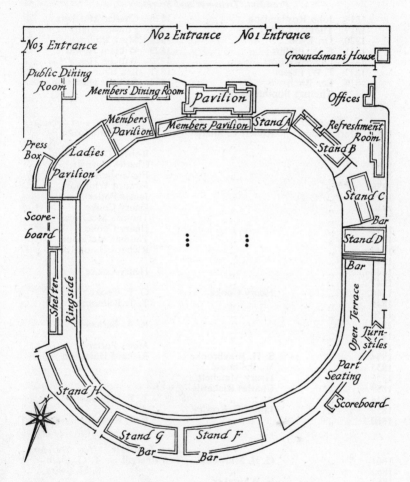

OLD TRAFFORD GROUND, MANCHESTER

APPENDIX I

LIST OF OFFICERS, 1818–1954

President, Treasurer and Secretary

1818	John Rowlandson	1826	Charles Matchett
1819	Thomas Close	1827	Edward Rigby
1820	Dr. Lyon	1828	Mark Philips
1821	F. A. Philips	1829	William Hewitt
1822	Lawrence Fort	1830	William Henry Say
1823	J. W. Fraser	1831	Lea Birch
1824	Lea Birch	1832	Richard Hampson
1825	Thomas Boothman, Jun.		

	President	*Vice-President*	*Hon. Treasurer and Secretary*
1833	Mark Philips	Robert C. Sharp	Richard Hampson
1834	,,	,,	
1835	,,	,,	Robert Garnett, Jun.
1836	,,	,,	Charles Garnett
1837	,,	,,	Frederick Thomas
1838	,,	,,	Edward Whitmore
1839	,,	,,	James Potter
1840	,,	,,	Henry Cooke
1841	,,	,,	Thomas McConnel
1842	,,	,,	Henry Cooke
1843	,,	,,	Thomas McConnel
1844	,,	,,	Richard Hampson
1845	,,	,,	,,
1846	,,	,,	Henry Cooke
1847	,,	,,	,,
1848	,,	Henry Cooke	G. F. Cooke
1849	,,	,,	T. T. Bellhouse
1850	,,	,,	,,
1851	,,	,,	R. A. Barlow
1852	,,	,,	,,
1853	,,	,,	James Potter
1854	,,	S. H. Braybrooke	Richard Hampson
1855	,,	W. Bellhouse	,,
1856	,,	Henry Matchett	,,
1857	,,	Charles Richards	,,
1858	,,	,,	T. T. Bellhouse
1859	,,	James C. Rowley	,,
1860	,,	,,	F. P. Richards

	President	*Vice-President*	*Hon. Treasurer*	*Hon. Secretary*
1861	,,	G. H. Midwood	T. Fothergill	T. G. Blain
1862	,,	,,	,,	S. H. Swire
1863	,,	E. Whittaker	,,	,,
1864	,,	,,	,,	S. H. Swire and A. B. Rowley
1865	,,	A. B. Rowley	,,	S. H. Swire
1866	,,	,,	,,	E. Whittaker
1867	,,	T. T. Bellhouse	R. Heywood	,,
1868	,,	,,	,,	H. W. Barber
1869	,,	O. Whittaker	E. Challender	S. H. Swire
1870	,,	,,	,,	,,
1871	,,	,,	,,	,,

	President	Vice-President	Hon. Treasurer	Hon. Secretary
1872	Mark Philips	John Holt	E. Challender	S. H. Swire
1873	„	„	„	„
1874	A. B. Rowley	„	„	„
1875	„	„	„	„
1876	„	A. H. Wolff	„	„
1877	„	„	„	„
1878	„	„	„	„
1879	„	J. A. Bannerman	„	„
1880	This year the Manchester Club and the County Club were amalgamated.			

	President	Hon. Treasurer	Hon. Secretary
1880	Sir Humphrey de Trafford, Bt.	Dr. Royle	S. H. Swire
1881	„	James MacLaren	„
1882	„	„	„
1883	„	„	„
1884	„	„	„
1885	„	„	„
1886	„	„	„
1887	Sir Humphrey Francis de Trafford	„	„
1888	„	„	„
1889	„	„	„
1890	„	„	„
1891	„	„	„
1892	„	„	„
1893	„	„	„
1894	A. N. Hornby	„	„
1895	„	„	„
1896	„	„	„
1897	„	„	„
1898	„	„	„
1899	„	„	„
1900	„	James Horner	„
1901	„	„	„
1902	„	„	„
1903	„	„	„
1904	„	„	„
1905	„	„	„

	President	Hon. Treasurer	Secretary
1906	„	„	T. J. Matthews
1907	„	„	„
1908	„	„	„
1909	„	„	„
1910	„	Talbot Fair	„
1911	„	„	„
1912	„	„	„
1913	„	„	„
1914	„	„	„
1915	„	„	„
1916	„	„	„
1917	Lord Ellesmere	„	„
1918	„	E. F. Stockton	„
1919	Sir Frank Hollins, Bt.	„	„
1920	„	„	„
1921	Lord Derby	Sir Edwin Stockton	Harry Rylance
1922	„	„	„
1923	O. P. Lancashire	„	„
1924	„	T. A. Higson	„

	President	Hon. Treasurer	Secretary
1925	Sir Edwin Stockton	T. A. Higson	Harry Rylance
1926	"	"	"
1927	Lord Ashton	"	"
1928	"	"	"
1929	Rev. V. F. Royle	"	"
1930	Lord Derby	"	"
1931	"	"	"
1932	Lord Colwyn	A. F. Stockton	R. Howard
1933	"	"	"
1934	Dr. H. H. I. Hitchon	"	"
1935	"	"	"
1936	Myles N. Kenyon	"	"
1937	"	John Boddan	"
1938	Lord Stanley	"	"
1939	Sir Thomas Robinson	"	"
1940	"	"	"
1941	Sir Christopher Needham	"	"
1942	"	"	"
1943	Sir R. Noton Barclay	"	"
1944	"	"	"
1945	R. H. Spooner	"	"
1946	"	J. C. Fallows	"
1947	W. Findlay	"	"
1948	"	"	"
1949	Sir Edward Rhodes	R. A. Boddington	C. G. Howard
1950	"	"	"
1951	Colonel L. Green	"	"
1952	"	"	"
1953	Tom Stone	"	"
1954	"	"	"

Team	1865	1866	1867	1868	1869	1870	1871	1872	1873	1874	1875	1876	1877	1878	1879	1880	1881
MIDDLESEX	W	L															
	W	L															
SURREY			D	D	W	W	W		W							W	
		L	D	L	L	L			W							W	
M.C.C.			L	L	L						L		L	W	L	L	
YORKSHIRE		LL					L	W	L	L	W	L	W	W	W	D	
	L	L					W	W	L	W	L	L	W	D	L	D	W
NOTTINGHAMSHIRE			L								W	L	L	D	L		
			L								L	W	W	D	L		
SUSSEX					W						L	W					
					L						W	W					
HAMPSHIRE						W											
						W											
DERBYSHIRE							L	W	W	L	D	W	L	W	W	W	W
							W	W	W	D	W	W	W	L	W	W	W
KENT							L		L	D	W	W	L	W	W	W	W
							W			L	W	L	L	W	D	W	
LEICESTERSHIRE										W							
										D							
GLOUCESTERSHIRE														D	W	D	
														L	D	L	
AUSTRALIANS														D			
CAMBRIDGE UNIVERSITY																	
SOMERSETSHIRE																	
OXFORD UNIVERSITY																	
CHESHIRE																	
ESSEX																	
NORTHAMPTONSHIRE																	
WARWICKSHIRE																	
DURHAM																	
PHILADELPHIANS																	
WEST INDIANS																	
WORCESTERSHIRE																	
SOUTH AFRICANS																	
LONDON COUNTY																	
AN ENGLAND XI																	
REST OF ENGLAND																	
ALL INDIA																	
GLAMORGAN																	
SCOTLAND																	
NEW ZEALAND																	
WALES																	
MINOR COUNTIES																	
SIR J. CAHN'S XI																	
HOME COUNTIES																	
DEVON																	
LIVERPOOL AND DISTRICT																	
DORSET																	
AUSTRALIAN I.F.																	

A—Abandoned without a ball bein[g]
B—Abandoned owing to the crowd
C—Abandoned owing to the funer[al]
E—No play on the third day owing
F—Verity Memorial Match—Draw[n]
G—Abandoned owing to the death
T—Tie Match.

LANCA[SHIRE]
Mat[ches]
1[8...]

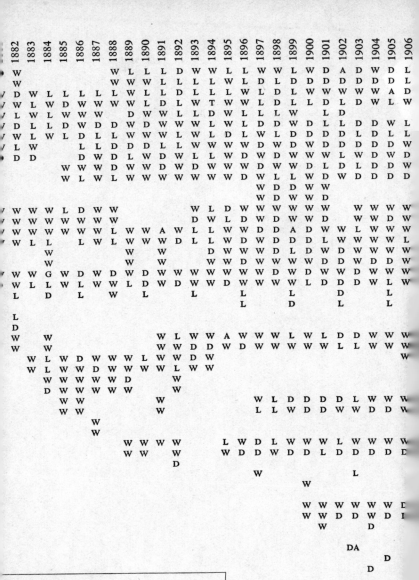

| | 1882 | 1883 | 1884 | 1885 | 1886 | 1887 | 1888 | 1889 | 1890 | 1891 | 1892 | 1893 | 1894 | 1895 | 1896 | 1897 | 1898 | 1899 | 1900 | 1901 | 1902 | 1903 | 1904 | 1905 | 1906 |

bowled owing to rain.
's damaging the pitch.
l of King Edward VII.
to the international crisis.
.
of Mrs. Grace, mother of E. M. and W. G.

SHIRE C.C.C.
ch Results
65-1953

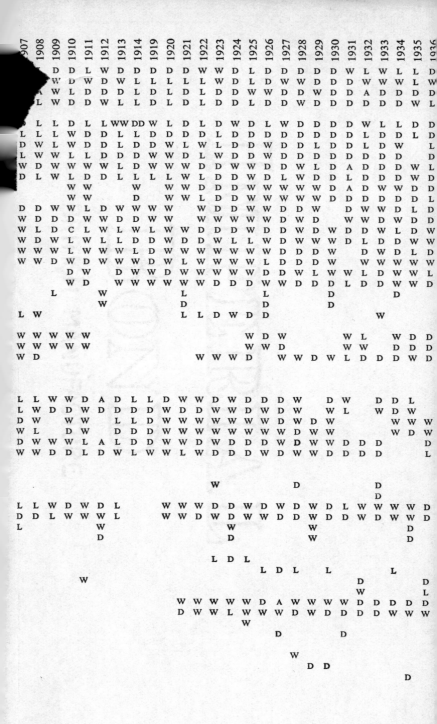

1937	1938	1939	1945	1946	1947	1948	1949	1950	1951	1952	1953	Team
W	W	L		W	W	D	D	L	W	D	D	MIDDLESEX
L	D	D			W	L	W	D	W	D	D	
D	D	L		D	D	L	W	D	D	W	L	SURREY
L	W	E		W	D			D	W			
										W		M.C.C.
L	L	L	F	D	D	D	D	W	D	D	D	YORKSHIRE
W	L	L		D	D	D	D	D	D	D	D	
D	D	D		W	D	W	D	W	D	W	W	NOTTINGHAMSHIRE
W	D	W		D	D	D	D	D	L	W	W	
D	D	A		W	W	W	L	D	W	D	W	SUSSEX
W	W	D		D	W			W	D	L	L	
D	W	W		L	W	D	D	D	L	W	W	HAMPSHIRE
D	W	W		W	T			W	W			
D	L	W		W	W	D	L	D	W	W	L	DERBYSHIRE
D	W	D		W	W	D	D	L	D	D	D	
D	W	W		L	W	L	W	W	W	W	W	KENT
W	L	L			W	L	W	W	W	D		
D	D	D		W	W	W	D	D	D	L	D	LEICESTERSHIRE
D	W			W	W			W	D			
W	D	W		W	W	D	L	W	D	D	W	GLOUCESTERSHIRE
L	L	D				D	D	L	D	D		
	D					D					D	AUSTRALIANS
						D				L	D	
				D	W	D	D	D	D	D	D	CAMBRIDGE UNIVERSITY
D	D	D		W	L	W	W	W	D	D	W	SOMERSETSHIRE
D	L	D				W	W			D	W	
D	W	D		L	D	D	W	W	W	W	D	OXFORD UNIVERSITY
												CHESHIRE
W	W	D		W	D	D	W	W	D	T	D	ESSEX
L	D	D		L	W				D	D	D	
W	W	W		D	W	D	D	D	D	D	D	NORTHAMPTONSHIRE
D	W	W			D	W			W	W	L	
W	W	L		W	D	D	D	W	W	D	D	WARWICKSHIRE
D	D	D		W	D	W	L	D	D	W	D	DURHAM
	D						L					PHILADELPHIANS
	D						L					WEST INDIANS
D	W	W		W	D	D	D	W	D	W	W	WORCESTERSHIRE
D	D	W						W	D			
				D					D			SOUTH AFRICANS
												LONDON COUNTY
												AN ENGLAND XI
												REST OF ENGLAND
				L				L				ALL INDIA
				D								
D	W	D		L	D	D	D	W	D	D	W	GLAMORGAN
D	D	W		D	D	D	D	W	L	W	D	
												SCOTLAND
W						D						NEW ZEALAND
W						L						
												WALES
												MINOR COUNTIES
												SIR J. CAHN'S XI
				W		W						HOME COUNTIES
				W					W	W		DEVON
					D							LIVERPOOL AND DISTRICT
						W						DORSET
												AUSTRALIAN I.F.

APPENDIX II

STATISTICS OF LANCASHIRE COUNTY CRICKET CLUB

1865–1953

The following records refer to all Lancashire first-class matches, except where otherwise stated. The compiler has excluded matches against counties prior to them being regarded as first-class beyond all doubt. It follows that these records may differ in some cases from previous compilations as matches versus Essex, Hampshire, Leicestershire, and Warwickshire prior to 1894 have not been included. Matches versus Somerset prior to 1891 are excluded as are those versus Derbyshire from 1888 to 1893.

C. M. O.

BATTING AND BOWLING AVERAGES
1865–1953

	Born	Died	Played	Matches	Runs	Highest Score	Average	Wickets	Average
Ainscough, T.	1865	1927	1894–1906	2	40	24	13.33	—	—
Ainsworth, J. L.	1877	1923	1899	4	17	11	3.40	18	16.05
Alderson, R.	1920		1948–9	2	55	55	27.50	—	—
Appleby, A.	1843	1902	1866–87	57	948	99	12.31	236	14.32
Arnold, J. F.	—	—	1896	3	94	37	18.80	—	—
Ashworth, J. T.	—	—	1871–3	2	28	19	9.33	—	—
Baker, G. R.	1862	1938	1887–99	227	7,140	186	22.31	136	25.38
Banham, S.	—	—	1939	1	—	—	—	—	—
Barber, H. W.	1841	1924	1866–7	3	41	15	6.83	—	—
Barber, J. H.	—	—	1874–6	3	39	12*	13.00	—	—
Barchard, H. G.	—	—	1888	1	45	40	22.50	—	—
Bardswell, G. R.	1873	1906	1894–9	21	429	56	15.88	8	42.75
Bardsley, R. V.	1890	1952	1910–20	7	46	15	5.75	0	—
Barlow, A.	1915		1947–51	74	707	44	10.55	0	—
Barlow, E. A.	1912	—	1932	7	84	40	10.50	12	32.41
Barlow, R. G.	1850	1919	1871–91	246	7,687	117	20.38	726	13.59
Barnes, J. R.	1897	1945	1919–30	89	3,271	123*	28.69	0	—
Barnes, S. F.	1873	—	1899–1903	46	452	35	11.89	225	19.81
Barron, W.	1917	—	1945	1	3	2	1.50	—	—
Barrell, B.	—	—	1911–23	2	45	25	22.50	9	15.00
Baxter, A. D.	1910	—	1933–4	3	0	0	0.00	16	13.00
Beattie, F. D.	1909	—	1932	5	120	36	15.00	—	—
Bennett, A.	1910	—	1932–3	16	238	51	18.30	24	36.04
Bennett, R.	—	—	1894	1	16	11	8.00	—	—
Benton, C. H.	1869	1918	1892–1901	29	663	68	15.06	—	—
Berry, R.	1926	—	1948–53	86	403	27*	8.57	245	22.51
Biddulph, G. H.	—	—	1885	1	19	18	9.50	0	—
Bigg, G. A.	—	—	1887	1	16	16	16.00	1	13.00
Bird, G. E.	1849	1930	1880	1	0	0	0.00	—	—
Bird, M. C.	1888	1933	1907	5	36	10	3.60	4	21.00
Birley, F. H.	1850	1910	1870–2	2	17	11	5.66	1	32.00
Birtwell, A. J.	1910	—	1937–9	14	103	31	10.30	25	39.96
Blackstock, R.	—	—	1865	1	23	18	11.50	—	—

	Born	Died	Played	Matches	Runs	Highest Score	Average	Wickets	Average
Blake, F.	—	—	1877	1	26	26	26.00	—	—
Bleackley, E. O.	—	—	1919	2	31	21	15.50	—	—
Blomley, B.	1885	—	1903–22	69	313	41	5.69	—	—
Boddington, R. A.	1892	—	1913–24	52	663	58*	11.83	—	—
Boden, R.	—	—	1907	1	8	5	4.00	—	—
Booth, A.	1926	—	1950–1	4	81	49	16.20	—	—
Booth, F. S.	1907	—	1927–37	140	1,330	54	10.07	457	24.46
Boucher, F. W.	—	—	1903	1	12	8	6.00	—	—
Bousfield, E. J.	1838	1895	1865–78	12	279	32	14.68	—	—
Bowden, E.	—	—	1914	4	27	10	4.50	12	37.75
Bower, W. H.	1857	—	1885–6	4	45	23	7.50	—	—
Bowes, J.	1918	—	1938–48	10	106	39	8.83	21	28.66
Boyes, R.	1849	—	1877	1	13	10	13.00	—	—
Bradbury, T.	—	—	1881	1	6	6*	6.00	—	—
Braddock, J.	—	—	1873	1	2	2	2.00	—	—
Brearley, W.	1876	1937	1902–11	106	749	38	6.08	690	18.70
Brierley, T. L.	1910	—	1946–8	46	1,286	116*	23.81	0	—
Briggs, J.	1862	1902	1879–1900	387	10,617	186	18.99	1,688	15.65
Briggs, J.	1916	—	1939	4	0	0*	—	10	39.10
Brocklebank, J. M.	1915	—	1939	4	5	4	1.66	5	55.80
Brooke, F. R. R.	1884	—	1912–13	29	566	61	16.17	—	—
Brooks, A. W.	—	—	1877	1	6	6	6.00	—	—
Broughton, J. J.	1873	—	1901–2	6	153	99	21.85	2	34.50
Brown, W.	—	—	1894	2	17	7	5.66	0	—
Brown, W.	1892	—	1919–22	10	239	39	15.93	22	21.54
Bulcock, L.	—	—	1946	1	1	1	1.00	2	45.00
Bullough, J.	1896	—	1914–19	8	24	17	4.80	13	44.07
Burrows, W.	1844	—	1867–73	14	249	40	9.96	0	—
Butterworth, H. R. W.	1909	—	1931–6	25	584	107	20.13	36	38.66
Butterworth, W. S.	—	—	1876–82	9	73	22	5.61	—	—
Campbell, G. A.	—	—	1866	1	18	10	9.00	—	—
Carlisle, F.	—	—	1869	2	37	18	9.25	—	—
Chadwick, E. L.	1847	1918	1875–81	13	254	42	12.09	—	—
Champion, A.	1851	1909	1886	1	4	4	2.00	—	—
Clarke, J.	—	—	1905	1	0	0	0.00	0	—
Cole, T. G. O.	1877	1944	1904	1	0	0	0.00	—	—
Cook, L.	1885	1933	1907–23	203	2,051	54*	12.28	821	21.36
Cook, W.	1882	1947	1905–7	11	307	46	21.92	51	28.17
Cooper, F.	1921	—	1946	4	96	33*	16.00	—	—
Copeland, W.	—	1917	1885	1	21	21*	21.00	1	23.00
Corlett, S.	1852	—	1871–5	2	6	4	2.00	—	—
Coulthurst, J.	—	—	1919	1					
Coward, C.	1838	1903	1865–76	36	912	85	14.47	0	—
Coward, F.	1842	1905	1867–8	7	35	9	2.91	—	—
Crabtree, H.	—	—	1890–1908	6	117	49	13.00	0	—
Cragg, J. S.	—	—	1908	1	10	9	5.00	—	—
Craig, W. R.	—	—	1874	1	8	7	4.00	—	—
Cranston, K.	1917	—	1947–8	50	1,928	155*	40.16	142	23.00
Crooke, F. J.	—	—	1865	1	55	35	27.50	—	—
Crosfield, S. M.	1861	1908	1883–99	89	1,904	82*	15.11	2	51.50
Crossland, J.	1853	1903	1878–85	69	986	48*	11.46	231	13.16
Cudworth, H.	—	1914	1900	1	4	4	4.00	—	—
Cuttell, W. R.	1864	1929	1896–1906	213	5,389	137	20.41	760	19.59

	Born	Died	Played	Matches	Runs	Highest Score	Average	Wickets	Average
Davies, H. D.	—	—	1924–5	11	260	46	17.33	—	—
Dean, H.	1885	—	1906–21	256	2,452	49*	10.38	1,267	18.01
Deighton, J. H. G.	1920	—	1948–50	7	206	79	25.75	20	25.45
Dewhirst, R.	1851	—	1872–5	13	267	59	12.71	—	—
Dickinson, T. E.	1931	—	1950–1	4	10	9	5.00	3	32.66
Dixon, J.	—	—	1878	1	2	2	1.00	—	—
Dobell, P.	—	—	1886–7	7	96	28	8.72	—	—
Douthwaite, H.	1900	—	1920–1	3	85	29	17.00	—	—
Duckworth, G.	1901	—	1923–38	424	4,174	75	14.14	0	—
Dunlop, G. C.	—	—	1868	1	17	16	8.50	—	—
Durandu, A.	—	—	1887	1	5	5	5.00	—	—
Eccles, A.	1876	1919	1898–1907	123	4,179	139	23.74	0	—
Eccles, H.	—	—	1885–6	5	37	14	5.28	—	—
Eccles, J.	1863	1933	1886–9	47	1,787	184	25.52	0	—
Eckersley, P. T.	1904	1940	1923–35	256	4,588	102*	18.50	1	145.00
Edge, C.	1916	—	1936–8	8	2	1	0.66	25	30.36
Edge, H. E.	—	—	1913	1	3	3	3.00	0	—
Edrich, E. H.	1914	—	1946–8	33	854	121	23.72	—	—
Edrich, G. A.	1918	—	1946–53	226	11,105	162	38.55	2	91.00
Elliott, H.	1904	—	1930	1	4	4	4.00	—	—
Ellis, J.	—	—	1892–8	6	56	26*	7.00	21	11.40
Ellis, S.	—	—	1923–4	8	57	25	9.50	14	18.00
Ellis, W.	1895	—	1920–3	36	846	138*	16.58	—	—
Fairclough, P. M.	1888	—	1911–23	20	140	19	10.76	52	22.26
Fallows, J. A.	1907	—	1946	25	171	35	8.14	—	—
Farnsworth, –.	—	—	1919	1	3	3	1.50	—	—
Farrimond, W.	1903	—	1924–45	134	2,202	63	21.17	0	—
Farrar, H. L.	—	—	1904	1	28	25	14.00	—	—
Findlay, W.	1880	1953	1902–6	58	1,223	81	19.72	0	—
Gaddum, F. D.	1860	1900	1884	1	15	10	7.50	0	—
Garlick, R. G.	1917	—	1938–47	44	753	50	15.36	120	23.30
Garnett, H. G.	1879	1917	1899–1914	144	5,599	139	26.16	8	28.00
Gibson, A. E.	—	—	1887	2	25	16	6.25	—	—
Goodwin, A.	—	—	1894	3	14	10	2.80	0	—
Green, L.	1890	—	1922–35	152	3,575	110*	24.65	9	33.22
Greenhalgh, E.	1910	—	1935–8	14	336	53*	28.15	3	94.00
Greenhough, T.	1931	—	1951–3	3	12	9	4.00	3	43.33
Greenwood, P.	1924	—	1948–52	75	1,270	113	16.49	208	24.47
Gregson, W. R.	1878	—	1906	5	62	26	10.33	24	17.83
Grieves, K.	1925	—	1949–53	150	6,572	150	35.91	176	28.09
Grimshaw, G. H.	—	—	1868	1	11	11	5.50	—	—
Haggas, S.	1856	1926	1884–5	3	59	18	11.80	—	—
Haggas, W.	—	—	1903	1	6	4	3.00	—	—
Haigh, C. H.	—	—	1879–87	23	431	80	14.86	—	—
Hall, A. E.	1896	—	1923–4	9	11	5*	1.83	24	26.25
Hallam, A. W.	1872	—	1895–1900	71	575	31*	8.58	211	19.25
Halliday, T. M.	—	—	1925–9	41	996	109*	22.63	0	—
Hallows, C.	1895	—	1914–32	370	20,142	233*	39.72	19	41.26
Hallows, J.	1875	1910	1898–1907	138	4,997	137*	28.55	279	23.69
Hardcastle, F.	—	1908	1867–9	3	23	11	4.60	—	—
Hardcastle, W.	—	—	1869–73	4	33	9	4.71	—	—
Hargreaves, P. W.	—	—	1881	1	0	0	0.00	—	—
Harper, G.	—	—	1883	1	1	1	1.00	—	—

	Born	Died	Played	Matches	Runs	Highest Score	Average	Wickets	Average
Harrison, F.	—	—	1936	3	4	2*	2.00	4	29.50
Harrop, J.	—	—	1874	1	5	5	2.50	0	—
Harry, F.	1878	1925	1903–8	69	1,528	88	15.95	207	18.33
Hartley, A.	1879	1918	1907–14	112	4,962	234	28.19	1	61.00
Hartley, C. R.	1873	1927	1897–1909	106	3,729	139	23.75	0	—
Hartley, F.	—	—	1924–45	2	2	2	2.00	1	44.00
Hartley, G.	1849	—	1871–2	3	37	24	12.33	—	—
Harwood, B.	—	—	1877	1	0	0*	—	—	—
Hawkwood, C.	1909	—	1931–5	24	596	113	28.38	1	92.00
Head, F. S.	—	—	1868–9	6	75	24	7.50	—	—
Heap, J. G.	—	—	1884	1	0	0	0.00	—	—
Heap, J. S.	1883	1951	1903–21	210	5,146	132*	18.98	410	23.20
Hewitson, J.	—	—	1890	4	99	56	19.80	14	16.78
Hibbard, H.	—	—	1884	1	7	4	3.50	2	27.00
Hibbart	—	—	1867	1	4	2*	4.00	0	—
Hibbert, W. J.	1874	—	1900–1	14	445	79	24.72	3	38.66
Hickmott, W. E.	—	—	1923–4	34	272	31*	10.46	82	24.90
Hickton, W.	1842	1900	1867–71	22	345	55	15.68	126	14.97
Highton, E. F. W.	1924	—	1951	1	6	6	6.00	1	49.00
Higson, P.	1905	—	1928–31	3	22	13*	22.00	—	—
Higson, T. A.	1873	1949	1905–23	5	123	42	20.50	1	58.00
Higson, T. A. (Jnr.)	1911	—	1936–46	20	153	32*	8.05	6	50.33
Hildyard, L. D.	1861	1931	1884–5	7	135	25	12.27	—	—
Hill, R.	—	—	1871	1	8	5	4.00	—	—
Hillkirk, J. R.	1845	—	1871–7	30	596	56*	13.86	—	—
Hilton, J.	1930	—	1952–3	8	99	33	14.14	2	76.00
Hilton, M. J.	1928	—	1946–53	100	1,143	63	12.03	399	19.12
Hird, S. F.	—	—	1939	1					
Hodgson, G.	1904	1951	1928–33	56	244	20	6.77	148	27.75
Holden, C.	1865	1928	1890	3	43	27*	10.75	0	—
Holgate, G.	1839	1895	1866–7	8	281	65	20.07	—	—
Holland, J.	1869	1914	1900–2	12	324	63	19.05	—	—
Hollins, F. H.	1877	—	1902–4	12	290	114	16.11	—	—
Hollins, J. C. H.	1890	—	1914–19	20	454	65	15.13	1	99.00
Holroyd, J.	1907	—	1927–33	11	33	18*	8.25	23	28.34
Holroyd, W.	—	—	1878	1	6	4	3.00	—	—
Hopwood, J. L.	1903	—	1923–39	397	15,519	220	30.05	672	22.18
Hornby, A. H.	1877	1952	1899–1914	283	9,441	129	24.45	1	117.00
Hornby, A. N.	1847	1925	1867–99	286	10,294	188	23.88	3	31.00
Hornby, C. L.	—	—	1877	1	4	4	2.00	1	3.00
Hornby, E. C.	1863	1922	1885–7	9	229	82	19.08	3	32.66
Horridge, L.	1907	—	1927–9	3	33	11*	16.50	3	26.33
Horrocks, R.	1857	—	1880–2	6	116	61	11.60	—	—
Horrocks, W. J.	1905	—	1931–3	15	371	100*	23.18	—	—
Houldsworth, W. H.	1873	—	1893–4	10	156	21	10.40	—	—
Howard, B. J.	1926	—	1947–51	32	996	109	23.95	—	—
Howard, N. D.	1925	—	1946–53	170	5,526	145	28.39	0	—
Howard, R.	1890	—	1922–33	8	166	88*	20.75	0	—
Howe, R.	1853	—	1876–7	3	24	13	4.00	—	—
Hubback, T. R.	—	—	1892	4	63	33	12.60	—	—
Huddleston, W.	1875	—	1899–1914	183	2,765	88	12.28	684	17.55
Hudson, B.	1852	—	1886–8	5	207	98	34.50	3	19.66
Hudson, G. N.	—	—	1936	2	1	1	1.00	0	—
Hulton, C. G.	1846	1919	1869–81	7	75	19	9.37	—	—

	Born	Died	Played	Matches	Runs	Highest Score	Average	Wickets	Average
Hulton, H. A.	—	—	1868	2	13	6	4.33	—	—
I'Anson, J.	1869	1936	1896–1908	57	986	110*	14.71	148	20.75
Iddison, R.	1834	1890	1865–70	16	621	106	23.88	56	15.62
Iddison, W. H.	1841	—	1867–8	4	46	19	5.75	1	95.00
Iddon, J.	1903	1946	1924–45	483	21,975	222	37.05	532	26.68
Ikin, J. T.	1918	—	1939–53	204	10,822	192	41.94	227	30.19
Ingleby, R.	—	—	1899	1	40	29	40.00	0	—
Isherwood, F.	—	—	1881	1	0	0	0.00	—	—
Jackson, E.	1849	—	1871–85	15	104	11	5.47	—	—
Jacques, T.	—	—	1937	2	4	2	2.00	1	70.00
Jervis, Capt.	—	—	1874	1	6	6	3.00	—	—
John, H. C.	—	—	1881	1	15	15*	—	—	—
Jolley, W. T.	—	—	1947	2	21	13	21.00	5	26.40
Jones, C. L.	1853	1904	1876–88	5	52	20*	6.50	1	6.00
Jones, J. L.	1876	—	1910	4	10	7*	10.00	—	—
Jowett, G.	1863	1928	1885–9	19	507	58	16.90	0	—
Kaye, J. L.	—	—	1867	1	21	20	10.50	0	—
Kelly, J.	1922	—	1947–9	6	150	58	18.75	0	—
Kemble, A. T.	1862	1925	1885–94	75	1,049	50	10.70	—	—
Kemp, G. M.	1866	1945	1885–92	18	355	109	11.45	—	—
Kentfield, R. W.	—	1904	1888	2	39	18	9.75	2	47.00
Kenyon, M. N.	1886	—	1919–25	91	1,435	61*	14.79	—	—
Kermode, A.	1876	1934	1902–8	76	631	64*	7.88	321	22.61
Kershaw, J. E.	1854	1903	1877–85	31	554	66	11.30	—	—
Kevan, J. H.	—	—	1875	2	12	12	3.00	—	—
Kewley, E.	—	—	1875	1	3	3	1.50	—	—
King, B. P.	1915	—	1946–7	37	1,505	145	28.39	—	—
Knowles, A.	—	—	1888	1	6	6	3.00	—	—
Lancashire, O. P.	1857	1934	1878–88	95	1,927	76*	13.19	—	—
Lancaster, T.	1863	1935	1894–9	27	554	66	19.10	66	22.06
Landon, C. W.	1850	1903	1874–5	6	121	47	12.10	2	34.50
Latchford, J. R.	1909	—	1930–2	7	154	63	15.40	4	45.25
Lawton, A. E.	1879	—	1912–14	12	269	52	14.15	14	18.50
Lawton, W.	—	—	1948	2	3	3	1.50	1	64.00
Leach, C.	1897	—	1923–4	12	161	79	10.73	—	—
Leach, H.	1862	1928	1881	1	33	33	33.00	—	—
Leach, H. W.	—	—	1866	1	18	17	9.00	—	—
Leach, J.	—	—	1866–77	4	105	34	13.12	—	—
Leach, R.	—	—	1868–76	3	3	3	0.75	—	—
Leach, R. C.	—	—	1885	1	49	39	24.50	—	—
Leach, W. E.	—	—	1885	5	208	56	26.00	0	—
Leese, C. P.	1889	1947	1911	1	16	10	8.00	—	—
Leese, E.	1854	—	1880–4	8	146	62	14.60	—	—
Leese, J. F.	1845	1914	1865–81	23	515	44	12.87	5	18.80
Leigh, J.	1862	1925	1887	1	2	1	1.00	—	—
Leventon, E.	—	—	1867	1	6	6	3.00	2	12.00
Lister, W. H. L.	1911	—	1933–9	158	3,561	104*	18.45	1	74.00
Littlewood, G. H.	1882	1917	1902–4	14	129	42	9.21	58	19.36
Littlewood, G. W.	1858	—	1885	3	28	8*	5.60	—	—
Lloyd, R. A.	1891	—	1921–2	3	100	51	20.00	—	—
Lomax, J. G.	1925	—	1949–53	57	1,137	78	14.96	81	31.09
McDonald, E. A.	1892	1937	1924–31	217	1,868	100*	10.15	1,053	20.96
McIntyre, H.	—	—	1884	1	1	1*	—	—	—
McIntyre, W.	1844	1892	1872–80	72	757	66	8.22	442	11.62
Mackinnon, Lt.	—	—	1871	2	41	22	10.25	5	12.40
MacLaren, A. C.	1871	1944	1890–1914	307	15,735	424	33.26	1	254.00

	Born	Died	Played	Matches	Runs	Highest Score	Average	Wickets	Average
MacLaren, G.	—	—	1902	2	7	3	1.75	2	6.50
MacLaren, J. A.	1870	1952	1891–4	4	9	6	2.25	—	—
MacLeod, K. G.	1888	—	1908–13	75	2,619	131	22.77	81	24.72
McNairy, F.	—	—	1925	1	4	4*	—	1	73.00
Makepeace, H.	1882	1952	1906–30	487	25,207	203	36.37	41	48.07
Makinson, J.	1836	1914	1865–73	5	131	45	14.55	4	18.25
Marchbank, W.	—	—	1869–70	2	1	1	0.25	—	—
Marner, P.	1936	—	1952–3	18	438	72	19.90	3	62.33
Marriott, C. S.	1895	—	1919–21	12	78	16	5.57	34	28.44
Massey, W. N.	—	—	1883	1	6	5	3.00	—	—
Matthews, D. M.	—	—	1936–8	6	128	46	16.00	—	—
Mayall, J.	—	—	1885	1	0	0	0.00	—	—
Melhuish, F.	—	—	1877	3	32	13	5.33	—	—
Melling, J.	1850	—	1874–6	3	39	20	7.80	0	—
Mellor, H.	—	—	1874–5	2	28	17	7.00	—	—
Miller, F. M.	—	—	1904	1	37	37	18.50	—	—
Miller, H.	1859	—	1880–1	5	84	27	10.50	10	19.40
Mills, H.	—	—	1889	1	1	1	1.00	—	—
Mills, W. G.	1852	1902	1871–7	6	57	26	5.70	6	16.16
Mold, A.	1865	1921	1889–1901	259	1,669	57	7.13	1,541	15.13
Moorhouse, E.	—	—	1873–5	5	72	34	12.00	—	—
Moorsom, L.	—	—	1865	1	12	7	6.00	—	—
Mortimer, R. G.	1869	—	1891	1	22	22*	—	—	—
Mugliston, F. H.	1886	1932	1906–8	7	117	35	10.63	—	—
Musson, F. W.	1894	—	1914–21	16	510	75	19.61	—	—
Napier, Rev. J. R.	1859	1939	1888	2	48	37	24.00	11	9.27
Nash, G.	1850	1903	1879–85	52	292	30	5.30	188	12.75
Nelson, J.	—	—	1913	1	7	5	3.50	—	—
Norbury, V.	1887	—	1919–22	14	594	100	25.82	23	19.47
Nutter, A. E.	1913	—	1935–45	70	2,200	109*	29.72	152	29.29
Nutter, E.	—	1903	1885	1	18	18	18.00	—	—
Oakley, W.	1861	—	1893–4	19	131	24	5.95	31	18.96
Oldfield, N.	1911	—	1935–9	151	7,002	147*	35.72	2	42.50
Ollivant, A.	—	—	1873–4	2	35	24*	17.50	—	—
Openshaw, W. E.	1852	1915	1879–82	4	37	16	7.40	—	—
Palmer, S.	—	—	1879–80	6	28	8	3.11	0	—
Parker, W.	—	—	1904	2	66	40	22.00	4	43.75
Parkin, C. H.	1886	1943	1914–26	158	1,959	57	12.09	901	16.12
Parkin, R.	1908	—	1931–9	20	231	60	16.50	23	36.73
Parkinson, H.	—	—	1922–3	15	34	8	2.61	—	—
Parkinson, L. W.	1908	—	1932–6	88	2,132	93	21.53	192	29.44
Parr, H. B.	1845	1930	1872–6	10	167	61	11.13	—	—
Parr, F. D.	1928	—	1951–3	43	460	42	12.43	—	—
Patterson, W. S.	1854	1939	1874–82	7	132	50	13.20	24	10.04
Paul, A. G.	1864	1947	1889–1900	95	2,958	177	21.91	2	73.00
Payne, J. H.	1858	1942	1883	9	158	33	13.16	—	—
Payne, W.	—	—	1898	1	0	0	0.00	0	—
Paynter, E.	1901	—	1926–45	293	16,555	322	41.59	24	52.08
Pennington, H.	—	—	1900	4	41	29*	10.25	—	—
Perry, W.	—	—	1865	1	16	16	8.00	—	—
Pewtress, A. W.	1891	—	1919–25	50	1,483	89	21.80	1	10.00
Phillips, W.	—	—	1904–8	10	109	18	7.26	—	—
Phillipson, W. E.	1910	—	1933–48	158	4,050	113	25.96	545	24.78
Pilkington, C. C.	1876	1950	1895	2	38	18	9.50	3	33.33
Pilling, R.	1855	1891	1877–89	173	1,751	61*	10.36	0	—

	Born	Died	Played	Matches	Runs	Highest Score	Average	Wickets	Average
Pilling, W.	—	1924	1891	1	9	9*	—	—	—
Place, W.	1914	—	1937–53	263	13,625	266*	39.15	1	42.00
Poidevin, L. O. S.	1876	1931	1904–8	105	4,461	168*	29.93	46	38.92
Pollard, R.	1912	—	1933–50	266	3,273	63	13.30	1,015	22.14
Porter, E. H.	1846	—	1874–82	17	301	61	10.75	0	—
Potter, G.	1878	—	1902	10	449	86	28.06	—	—
Potter, T. O.	—	1909	1866	1	39	39	19.50	—	—
Potter, W.	—	—	1870	1	23	12	11.50	—	—
Preston, S.	1905	—	1928–30	5	46	33	15.33	6	35.33
Price, A.	1864	—	1885	1	8	8	4.00	—	—
Price, E. J.	1918	—	1946–7	35	305	54	13.86	115	20.63
Radcliffe, G.	1877	—	1903–6	7	171	60	15.54	—	—
Radcliffe, L.	1871	—	1897–1905	50	277	26	6.15	—	—
Rae, R. B.	—	—	1945	1	74	74	74.00	0	—
Ramsbottom, J.	—	—	1868	1	1	1	0.50	0	—
Ratcliffe, E.	—	—	1884	1	9	7	4.50	0	—
Rawlinson, E. B.	1837	1892	1867	1	15	14	15.00	—	—
Rawlinson, W.	1850	—	1870–1	2	23	10	5.75	—	—
Rawsthorne, G. O.	—	—	1919	1	2	2	2.00	—	—
Reynolds, F. R.	1834	1915	1865–74	36	276	34*	6.57	88	20.37
Rhodes, A.	—	—	1922–4	17	382	70	17.36	15	31.66
Rhodes, C.	—	—	1937–8	8	11	6	1.83	22	28.13
Richmond, W.	—	—	1868	1	1	1	0.50	—	—
Ricketts, J.	1843	1894	1867–77	32	1,015	195*	17.20	12	20.66
Rickman, W.	—	—	1876	1	5	5	5.00	—	—
Ritchie, D. M.	—	—	1924	1	3	3	3.00	—	—
Roberts, R.	—	—	1872–4	10	101	20	6.31	—	—
Roberts, W. B.	1914	1951	1939–49	114	810	51	10.94	382	20.86
Robinson, W.	1851	1919	1880–8	111	3,528	154	20.51	0	—
Rogerson, G.	—	—	1923	12	340	47*	17.89	—	—
Roper, E.	1851	1921	1876–86	28	586	65	12.73	—	—
Rowland, D.	—	—	1868	1	0	0	0.00	0	—
Rowlands, L.	1882	—	1903–10	6	27	9	4.50	16	20.12
Rowley, A. B.	1837	1911	1865–71	11	267	63*	15.70	25	22.04
Rowley, E. B.	1842	1905	1865–80	80	1,622	78	13.29	0	—
Rowley, E. B. (Jnr.)	1870	—	1893–8	15	537	65	28.26	—	—
Royle, Rev. V. P. F. A.	1854	1929	1873–91	71	1,701	81	15.60	2	57.00
Rushton, F.	1906	—	1928–9	6	59	28	11.80	10	36.20
Rutter, F. R.	—	—	1868	2	15	8*	5.00	0	—
Sawyer, C. M.	1856	1921	1884	1	11	11*	—	0	—
Schofield, J.	—	—	1876	4	27	11	6.75	—	—
Scholfield, F. B.	—	—	1911	1	17	17	17.00	—	—
Schultz, S. S.	1857	1937	1877–82	9	215	42*	15.35	0	—
Scott, W.	—	—	1874	1	14	9	14.00	—	—
Seymour, A.	—	—	1869	1	45	25	22.50	—	—
Sharp, J.	1878	1938	1899–1925	518	21,815	211	30.89	433	27.30
Shelmerdine, G. O.	1899	—	1919–25	31	980	105	23.90	0	—
Shore, C.	1859	1912	1886	1	3	3	1.50	0	—
Sibbles, F. M.	1904	—	1925–37	306	3,436	71*	14.87	932	22.11
Silcock, W.	—	—	1899–1902	6	82	43	13.66	5	73.40
Sladen, A. R.	—	—	1903–4	2	8	5	2.66	6	29.16
Slater, R.	—	—	1865	1	0	0	0.00	0	—
Smalley, J.	—	—	1869	2	24	17	6.00	—	—

T

	Born	Died	Played	Matches	Runs	Highest Score	Average	Wickets	Average
Smith, A.	1846	1908	1867–71	4	56	30	9.33	—	—
Smith, A.	1858	—	1886–94	47	1,416	124	20.37	29	17.82
Smith, C.	1861	1925	1893–1902	167	2,251	81	12.16	1	18.00
Smith, C. S.	1932	—	1951–3	11	129	67	18.42	27	22.77
Smith, D. J.	1929	—	1951–2	3	26	14	6.50	4	51.25
Smith, J.	1833	1909	1865–9	6	153	40*	13.90	11	26.36
Smith, R.	1868	—	1893	1	6	6	6.00	0	—
Smith, S.	1929	—	1952	5	127	40	15.87	—	—
Smith, T.	—	—	1867	2	18	12	6.00	1	36.00
Spencer, H.	—	—	1914	2	5	4	2.50	3	46.33
Spooner, A. F.	1886	—	1906–9	18	500	83	15.62	—	—
Spooner, R. H.	1880	—	1899–1921	170	9,889	247	37.17	5	110.80
Stanning, H. D.	1881	1946	1906–8	33	898	86	16.94	0	—
Stanning, J.	1877	1929	1900–3	4	137	62	19.57	—	—
Statham, J. B.	1930	—	1950–3	92	664	54*	9.76	333	16.15
Steel, A. G.	1858	1914	1877–93	47	1,960	105	29.25	238	13.16
Steel, D. Q.	1856	1933	1876–87	22	560	82	16.99	—	—
Steel, E. E.	1864	1941	1884–1904	40	861	69*	15.94	122	21.29
Steel, H. B.	1862	1911	1883–96	22	765	100	22.50	—	—
Stephenson, G. F.	1853	1927	1875–7	2	0	0*	0.00	1	17.00
Stoddart, W. B.	1871	1935	1898–9	15	294	43*	14.00	37	24.29
Stone, D.	1927	—	1949–50	6	86	46	14.33	9	52.44
Storer, E.	1838	—	1865–78	6	46	23	7.66	15	16.33
Sugg, F. H.	1862	1933	1887–99	234	9,546	220	26.37	10	25.90
Swire, S. H.	1839	1905	1865–8	5	93	18*	11.62	0	—
Tattersall, R.	1922	—	1948–53	128	1,049	45	12.05	584	16.84
Taylor, A.	—	—	1898	2	6	6	2.00	2	48.00
Taylor, F.	1855	1936	1874–88	51	1,390	96	17.37	2	21.00
Taylor, F.	—	—	1920–2	15	188	29*	15.66	40	25.65
Taylor, J.	1846	—	1871–3	3	49	33	9.80	0	—
Taylor, M. L.	1904	—	1924–31	95	2,216	107*	22.84	0	—
Teggin, A.	1860	—	1886	6	31	9	3.87	16	10.93
Tennent, H. N.	1842	1904	1865–70	3	48	21	9.60	—	—
Thomas, R.	1871	—	1894–1902	20	60	17	3.52	—	—
Thornber, H.	—	1913	1874	1	0	0	0.00	—	—
Tindall, S. M.	1867	1922	1894–8	42	1,039	86	17.03	1	28.00
Tinsley, A.	1867	1933	1890–5	57	1,310	65	16.17	0	—
Tinsley, H. J.	1865	—	1894–6	4	57	18	9.50	—	—
Trafford, C. E. de	1864	1951	1884	1	0	0	0.00	—	—
Tranter, G.	1842	—	1875–6	3	12	5	2.40	4	27.00
Tyldesley, E.	1889	—	1909–36	573	34,222	256*	45.20	6	55.33
Tyldesley, H.	1893	1935	1914–23	4	63	33*	15.75	3	33.66
Tyldesley, J. D.	1889	1923	1910–22	116	2,875	112*	18.79	309	26.18
Tyldesley, J. T.	1873	1930	1895–1923	507	31,949	295*	41.38	2	85.00
Tyldesley, R. K.	1898	1943	1919–31	374	6,126	105	15.78	1,449	16.65
Tyldesley, W. K.	1887	1918	1908–14	87	2,979	152	22.91	8	47.87
Unsworth, J.	1844	—	1871	2	25	23	8.33	3	25.00
Wadsworth, E.	1850	—	1871–9	7	69	30	5.30	0	—
Walker, R.	1846	1919	1874–5	2	27	19	9.00	—	—
Wall, H.	1852	1914	1877	3	24	15	6.00	—	—
Wall, T.	1841	1875	1868	2	48	37	12.00	0	—
Wall, W.	1854	1922	1877	1	17	17*	17.00	—	—

	Born	Died	Played	Matches	Runs	Highest Score	Average	Wickets	Average
Walsh, G.	—	1904	1874–7	2	16	15	5.33	—	—
Walton, M.	—	—	1867	1	6	6	3.00	—	—
Warburton, L.	—	—	1929–38	6	159	74*	39.75	5	43.40
Ward, A.	1865	1939	1889–1904	329	15,264	185	30.77	65	36.61
Ward, F.	1865	—	1884–96	47	986	145	14.50	27	19.92
Wardle, C.	1837	1907	1867–72	2	19	7*	19.00	0	—
Washbrook, C.	1914	—	1933–53	347	21,021	251*	45.89	3	81.33
Watson, A.	1844	1920	1871–93	279	4,117	74	12.32	1,279	13.47
Watson, F.	1899	—	1920–37	457	22,833	300*	37.06	402	31.86
Webb, S.	1874	1923	1899–1903	73	513	38*	7.65	265	19.72
Webster, F.	—	—	1925–7	2	12	10	6.00	7	17.42
Wharmby, G. H.	1870	—	1894	6	29	11	4.83	8	26.12
Wharton, A.	1923	—	1946–53	185	6,978	139	32.11	111	33.54
Whatmough, T.	1844	—	1871	2	42	28*	21.00	3	26.33
Whewell, J. W.	—	—	1921–7	12	19	12	2.37	—	—
Whitehead, R.	1883	—	1908–14	107	2,571	131*	21.07	300	24.20
Whitehead, T.	—	—	1884	1	8	8	8.00	0	—
Whiteside, J. P.	1861	1946	1888–90	6	25	12	3.12	—	—
Whittaker, D.	1857	1901	1884–8	7	91	26	9.10	0	—
Whittaker, E.	1834	—	1865–8	11	232	39	12.21	1	125.00
Wilkinson, L. L.	1916	—	1937–47	63	296	48	8.00	232	26.25
Wilson, A.	1921	—	1948–53	72	167	13*	3.88	—	—
Winder, G. A.	1850	—	1869	2	23	9	5.75	—	—
Wood, R.	—	—	1880–4	6	166	52	23.71	4	18.00
Woolley, A.	—	—	1926	7	61	24	6.77	11	31.90
Worsley, W.	1869	1918	1903–13	136	628	37*	5.98	—	—
Wright, E. L.	1885	1918	1905–10	4	53	17	6.62	—	—
Wright, Rev. F. W.	1844	1924	1869–75	14	407	120*	22.61	3	52.00
Yates, C.	—	—	1882	1	28	24	14.00	—	—
Yates, G.	1856	—	1885–94	92	1,632	74	13.60	30	31.13

WICKET-KEEPING
(10 or more dismissals)

	Played	Matches	Stumped	Caught	Total
Duckworth, G. ..	1923–38	424	287	634	921
Pilling, R. ..	1877–89	173	149	316	465
Smith, C. ..	1893–1902	167	114	313	427
Farrimond, W. ..	1924–45	134	65	232	297
Worsley, W. ..	1903–13	136	44	236	280
Barlow, A. ..	1947–51	74	46	104	150
Blomley, B. ..	1903–22	69	33	108	141
Wilson, A. ..	1948–53	72	31	110	141
Kemble, A. T. ..	1885–94	75	42	85	127
Findlay, W. ..	1902–6	58	12	101	113
Garnett, H. G.† ..	1899–1914	144	15	87	102
Radcliffe, L. ..	1897–1905	50	34	68	102
Boddington, R. A. ..	1913–24	52	21	72	93
Brierley, T. L. ..	1946–8	46	19	61	80
Parr, F. D. ..	1951–3	43	18	61	79
Brooke, F. R. R. ..	1912–13	29	11	46	57
Edrich, E. H. ..	1946–8	33	14	37	51

† H. G. Garnett did not keep wicket in many of the matches in which he played.

		Played	*Matches Stumped*		*Caught*	*Total*
Jackson, E.	.. ..	1871–85	15	14	20	34
Thomas, R.	.. ..	1894–1902	20	8	21	29
Phillips, W.	.. ..	1904–8	10	4	15	19
Parkinson, H.	.. ..	1922–3	15	3	14	17
Musson, F. W.	.. ..	1914–21	16	4	12	16
Whewell, J. W.	.. ..	1921–7	12	3	13	16
Whiteside, J. P.	..	1888–90	6	7	6	13
Roberts, R.	.. ..	1872–4	10	4	8	12

HIGHEST INNINGS TOTALS

801	v. Somerset (Taunton)	..	..	..	..	..	1895
676—7	v. Hampshire (Old Trafford)	..	..	..	..		1911
640—8	v. Sussex (Hove)	..	..	..	..	..	1937
627	v. Notts (Nottingham)	..	..	..	..		1905
601—8	v. Sussex (Brighton	..	..	..	..	..	1905

HIGHEST INNINGS TOTAL AGAINST EACH COUNTY

546	v. Derbyshire (Old Trafford)	..	..	..	..	1898
510	v. Essex (Clacton)	..	..	..	..	1947
564—9	v. Glamorgan (Old Trafford)	..	..	..	..	1938
474—3	v. Gloucestershire (Liverpool)	..	..	..	..	1903
676—7	v. Hampshire (Old Trafford)	..	..	..	..	1911
531	v. Kent (Old Trafford)	..	..	..	..	1906
590	v. Leicestershire (Leicester)	..	..	..	..	1899
484—8	v. Middlesex (Old Trafford)	..	..	..	..	1926
528—4	v. Northamptonshire (Old Trafford)	..	..	..	1928
627	v. Nottinghamshire (Nottingham)	..	..	..	..	1905
801	v. Somerset (Taunton)	..	..	..	..	1895
588—4	v. Surrey (Old Trafford)	..	..	..	..	1928
640—8	v. Sussex (Hove)	..	..	..	..	1937
526	v. Warwickshire (Birmingham)	..	..	..	..	1920
592—4	v. Worcestershire (Worcester)	..	..	..	..	1929
509—9	v. Yorkshire (Old Trafford)	..	..	..	..	1926

HIGHEST INNINGS TOTALS AGAINST

634	by Surrey (Oval)	..	..	..	..	..	1895
603—8	by Rest of England (Oval)	..	..	..	..	..	1928

HIGHEST INNINGS TOTAL BY EACH COUNTY
AGAINST LANCASHIRE

577	by Derbyshire (Old Trafford)	..	..	..	..	1896
559—9	by Essex (Leyton)	..	..	..	..	1904
425	by Glamorgan (Old Trafford)	..	..	..	..	1938
561	by Gloucestershire (Bristol)	..	..	..	..	1938
487	by Hampshire (Liverpool)	..	..	..	..	1901
479	by Kent (Canterbury)	..	..	..	..	1906
493	by Leicestershire (Leicester)	..	..	..	..	1910
501—3	by Middlesex (Lord's)	..	..	..	..	1914
368	by Northamptonshire (Blackpool)	..	..	..	1939
504—5	by Nottinghamshire (Old Trafford)	..	..	..	1949
561	by Somerset (Bath)	..	..	..	..	1901
634	by Surrey (Oval)	..	..	..	..	1895
485	by Sussex (Old Trafford)	..	..	..	..	1903
532—4	by Warwickshire (Birmingham)	..	..	..	..	1901
492	by Worcestershire (Old Trafford)	..	..	..	..	1906
590	by Yorkshire (Bradford)	..	..	..	..	1887

LOWEST INNINGS TOTALS

25	*v.* Derbyshire (Old Trafford)	1871
28	*v.* Australians (Liverpool)	1896
30	*v.* Yorkshire (Holbeck)	1868

LOWEST INNINGS TOTAL AGAINST EACH COUNTY

25	*v.* Derbyshire (Old Trafford)	1871
83	*v.* Essex (Chelmsford)	1935
49	*v.* Glamorgan (Liverpool)	1924
45	*v.* Gloucestershire (Preston)	1936
54	*v.* Hampshire (Portsmouth)	1937
61	*v.* Kent (Canterbury)	1884
73	*v.* Leicestershire (Leicester)	1935
63	*v.* Middlesex (Lord's)	1891
101	*v.* Northamptonshire (Northampton)	1928
37	*v.* Nottinghamshire (Liverpool)	1907
48	*v.* Somerset (Old Trafford)	1892
35	*v.* Surrey (Old Trafford)	1888
55	*v.* Sussex (Old Trafford)	1892
76	*v.* Warwickshire (Birmingham)	1906
75	*v.* Worcestershire (Worcester)	1932
30	*v.* Yorkshire (Holbeck	1868

LOWEST INNINGS TOTALS AGAINST

22	by Glamorgan (Liverpool)	1924
24	by Sussex (Old Trafford)	1890
30	by M.C.C. (Lord's)	1886

LOWEST INNINGS TOTAL BY EACH COUNTY
AGAINST LANCASHIRE

37	by Derbyshire (Chesterfield)	1922
37	by Derbyshire (Old Trafford)	1923
59	by Essex (Liverpool)	1931
22	by Glamorgan (Liverpool)	1924
33	by Gloucestershire (Liverpool)	1888
37	by Hampshire (Old Trafford)	1900
38	by Kent (Maidstone)	1881
33	by Leicestershire (Leicester)	1925
69	by Middlesex (Lord's)	1933
48	by Northamptonshire (Northampton)	1922
35	by Nottinghamshire (Nottingham)	1895
31	by Somerset (Old Trafford)	1894
33	by Surrey (Oval)	1873
24	by Sussex (Old Trafford)	1890
49	by Warwickshire (Birmingham)	1896
48	by Worcestershire (Worcester)	1910
33	by Yorkshire (Leeds)	1924

TIE MATCHES

Surrey *v.* Lancashire (Oval)	1894
Lancashire *v.* An England XI (Blackpool) (Lancashire had 3 wickets to fall)	1905
Hampshire *v.* Lancashire (Bournemouth)	1947
Essex *v.* Lancashire (Brentwood)	1952

MATCHES COMPLETED IN ONE DAY

v. M.C.C. (Lord's) (won by 6 wickets) 1886
v. Surrey (Old Trafford) (lost by an innings and 25 runs) 1888
v. Somerset (Old Trafford) (won by 8 wickets) 1892
v. Somerset (Old Trafford) (won by an innings and 68 runs) .. 1894
v. Somerset (Old Trafford) (won by 9 wickets) 1925
v. Sussex (Old Trafford) (won by an innings and 87 runs) 1950
v. Somerset (Bath) (won by an innings and 24 runs) 1953

LARGEST ATTENDANCES AT OLD TRAFFORD

107,712   England *v.* Australia (5 days) 1948
78,617   Lancashire *v.* Yorkshire 1926
72,463   England *v.* Australia (Victory Match) 1945
70,492   England *v.* Australia (4 days) 1934
70,000   England *v.* Australia 1926

LARGEST ATTENDANCES AT OLD TRAFFORD ON ONE DAY

46,000   Lancashire *v.* Yorkshire (August Bank Holiday) .. 1926
38,654   England *v.* Australia 1948
31,975   Lancashire *v.* Yorkshire (Whit-Monday) 1925
31,679   Lancashire *v.* Yorkshire (August Bank Holiday) .. 1950
31,116   Lancashire *v.* Yorkshire (August Bank Holiday) .. 1924

HIGHEST INDIVIDUAL SCORES

424   A. C. MacLaren *v.* Somerset (Taunton) 1895
322   E. Paynter *v.* Sussex (Hove) 1937
300*   F. Watson *v.* Surrey (Old Trafford) 1928

INDIVIDUAL CENTURIES

	For Lanca-shire	Total (all first-class)		For Lanca-shire	Total (all first-class)
G. R. Baker	4	4	B. P. King ..	2	6
R. G. Barlow ..	2	4	W. H. L. Lister ..	2	2
J. R. Barnes	3	4	A. C. MacLaren..	30	47
T. L. Brierley ..	1	4	K. G. MacLeod ..	4	6
J. Briggs	9	10	H. Makepeace ..	42	43
H. R. W. Butterworth	1	1	E. A. McDonald	1	1
K. Cranston ..	2	3	V. Norbury ..	1	1
W. R. Cuttell ..	5	5	A. E. Nutter ..	1	1
A. Eccles	4	6	N. Oldfield ..	12	37
J. Eccles	2	2	A. G. Paul ..	4	4
P. T. Eckersley ..	1	1	E. Paynter ..	36	45
E. H. Edrich ..	2	2	W. Place	33	35
G. A. Edrich ..	19	19	W. E. Phillipson..	2	2
W. Ellis	1	1	L. O. S. Poidevin	8	13
H. G. Garnett ..	5	5	J. Ricketts ..	1	1
L. Green	1	1	W. Robinson ..	4	4
P. Greenwood ..	1	1	J. Sharp	36	38
K. Grieves	9	12	G. O. Shelmerdine	1	1
T. M. Halliday ..	1	1	A. Smith	2	2
C. Hallows	52	55	R. H. Spooner ..	25	31
J. Hallows	8	8	A. G. Steel ..	1	7
A. Hartley	6	6	H. B. Steel ..	1	1
C. R. Hartley ..	4	4	F. H. Sugg ..	15	15
C. Hawkwood ..	1	1	M. L. Taylor ..	1	1
J. S. Heap	1	1	E. Tyldesley ..	90	102

	For Lanca- shire	Total (all first- class)		For Lanca- shire	Total (all first- class)
F. H. Hollins	1	1	J. D. Tyldesley	3	3
J. L. Hopwood	27	27	J. T. Tyldesley	73	86
A. H. Hornby	8	8	R. K. Tyldesley	1	1
A. N. Hornby	9	16	W. K. Tyldesley	3	3
W. J. Horrocks	1	2	A. Ward	24	29
B. J. Howard	2	3	F. Ward	1	1
N. D. Howard	3	3	C. Washbrook	51	69
J. I'Anson	1	1	F. Watson	49	50
R. Iddison	1	2	A. Wharton	8	8
J. Iddon	46	46	R. Whitehead	4	4
J. T. Ikin	19	22	Rev. F. W. Wright	1	1
G. M. Kemp	1	3			

CENTURIES ON FIRST APPEARANCE FOR LANCASHIRE

J. Ricketts	195*	v. Surrey (Oval)	1867
A. C. MacLaren	108	v. Sussex (Hove)	1890
R. Whitehead	131*	v. Nottinghamshire (Old Trafford)	1908

A CENTURY IN EACH INNINGS OF A MATCH

J. T. Tyldesley	106 and 100*	v. Warwickshire (Birmingham)	1897
J. T. Tyldesley	136 and 101	v. Hampshire (Old Trafford)	1910
E. Tyldesley	165 and 123*	v. Essex (Leyton)	1921
C. Hallows	112* and 103*	v. Leicestershire (Ashby-de-la-Zouch)	1924
C. Hallows	123 and 101*	v. Warwickshire (Birmingham)	1928
E. Tyldesley	109 and 108*	v. Glamorgan (Cardiff)	1930
E. Paynter	125 and 113*	v. Warwickshire (Birmingham)	1938
W. Place	105 and 132*	v. Nottinghamshire (Old Trafford)	1947
C. Washbrook	176 and 121*	v. Sussex (Eastbourne)	1947

This feat was accomplished by Lancashire players in other first-class matches as follows:

A. C. MacLaren	142 and 100	A. E. Stoddart's XI v. N.S.W. (Sydney)	1897–8
J. T. Tyldesley	121 and 100*	North v. South (Hastings)	1900
E. Paynter	117 and 100	England v. South Africa (Johannesburg)	1938–9

FOUR HUNDREDS IN SUCCESSIVE INNINGS

E. Tyldesley in 1928. 168 v. Middlesex (Old Trafford), 159 v. Kent (Old Trafford), 242 v. Leicestershire (Leicester), 118 v. Sussex (Brighton).

Note: In between the first and second scores, E. Tyldesley made 73 for England v. West Indies (Oval). In 1926 he scored four successive centuries in first-class matches as follows: 131 v. Surrey (Oval), 131 Players v. Gentlemen (Lord's), 106 v. Essex (Nelson), 126 v. Somerset (Taunton).

HIGHEST INDIVIDUAL SCORES AGAINST

315*	T. Hayward for Surrey (Oval)	1898
282*	A. Sandham for Surrey (Old Trafford)	1928

FOUR CENTURIES IN ONE INNINGS

1904. v. Somerset (Old Trafford). *Total:* 580. (A. C. MacLaren 151, A. H. Hornby 114, J. T. Tyldesley 103, W. R. Cuttell, 101.)

AGGREGATES OF 2,000 RUNS IN A SEASON

			For Lancashire		All first-class matches	
			Runs	Average	Runs	Average
G. A. Edrich (1)	..	1952	1,977	41.18	2,067	41.34
C. Hallows (3)	..	1925	2,185	52.02	2,354	52.31
		1927	2,119	73.06	2,343	75.58
		1928	2,564	65.74	2,645	64.51
J. Iddon (1) ..	..	1934	2,381	52.91	2,381	52.91
H. Makepeace (2)	..	1923	2,286	50.80	2,310	49.14
		1926	2,340	48.75	2,340	48.75
E. Paynter (4)	..	1932	1,830	41.59	2,035	37.68
		1936	2,016	45.81	2,016	45.81
		1937	2,626	58.35	2,904	53.77
		1938	2,020	57.71	2,691	58.50
W. Place (1) ..	..	1947	2,408	68.80	2,501	62.52
J. Sharp (1) ..	..	1911	1,959	41.68	2,099	40.36
R. H. Spooner (1)	..	1911	1,743	56.22	2,312	51.37
E. Tyldesley (6)	..	1922	2,070	46.00	2,168	41.69
		1923	1,785	43.53	2,040	37.77
		1926	2,432	62.35	2,826	64.22
		1928	2,467	77.09	3,024	79.57
		1932	2,420	59.02	2,420	59.02
		1934	2,487	57.83	2,487	57.83
J. T. Tyldesley (5)	..	1901	2,633	56.02	3,041	55.29
		1904	2,335	66.71	2,439	62.53
		1906	1,992	47.42	2,270	46.32
		1907	1,710	36.38	2,132	36.75
		1910	1,961	49.02	2,265	46.22
C. Washbrook (2)	..	1946	1,938	71.77	2,400	68.57
		1947	1,950	78.00	2,662	68.25
F. Watson (3)	..	1928	2,541	63.52	2,583	61.05
		1929	2,137	46.45	2,137	46.45
		1930	2,031	45.13	2,031	45.13

AGGREGATES OF 1,000 RUNS IN A SEASON FOR LANCASHIRE

19 times—J. T. Tyldesley.
18 times—E. Tyldesley.
13 times—J. Iddon, H. Makepeace, C. Washbrook.
12 times—F. Watson.
11 times—C. Hallows.
10 times—J. Sharp.
 9 times—E. Paynter, A. Ward.
 8 times—J. T. Ikin, W. Place, J. L. Hopwood.
 7 times—A. C. MacLaren.
 6 times—G. A. Edrich.
 5 times—K. Grieves, N. Oldfield, R. H. Spooner.
 3 times—A. Hartley, F. H. Sugg.
Twice —H. G. Garnett, J. Hallows, A. Wharton.
Once —G. R. Baker, C. R. Hartley, A. H. Hornby, A. N. Hornby, N. D. Howard, B. P. King, K. G. MacLeod, A. E. Nutter, L. O. S. Poidevin.
 Notes: N. Oldfield is the only Lancashire batsman to score 1,000 runs for Lancashire in his first season in first-class cricket (1935). K. Cranston scored 989 in 1947, his first season, and reached the 1,000 in all first-class matches. B. P. King (1946) and K. Grieves (1949) both scored 1,000 in their first season for the county but had previously appeared in first-class cricket for other teams.

1,000 RUNS IN A MONTH IN ALL FIRST-CLASS MATCHES

		Runs	*Average*
May 1928	C. Hallows	1,000	125.00
July 1926	E. Tyldesley	1,024	128.00
July 1946	C. Washbrook	1,079	98.09

FAST SCORING

The fastest century ever scored for Lancashire was by A. H. Hornby, who reached his century in 48 minutes when making 106 *v.* Somerset at Old Trafford in 1905. Hornby shared with W. Findlay in a 9th wicket partnership of 113 in 30 minutes.

K. G. MacLeod hit 8 sixes in his innings of 128 *v.* Somerset at Bath in 1909. N. D. Howard hit J. McConnon for 4 sixes in an over *v.* Glamorgan at Swansea in 1953.

E. Paynter made 322 in 5 hours *v.* Sussex at Hove in 1937, reaching his 100 before lunch. R. H. Spooner reached his century before lunch *v.* Somerset at Bath in 1906.

LARGEST PARTNERSHIPS FOR LANCASHIRE

371 (2nd wicket):
    F. Watson and E. Tyldesley *v.* Surrey (Old Trafford) 1928
368 (1st wicket):
    A. C. MacLaren and R. H. Spooner *v.* Gloucestershire (Liverpool) 1903
363 (2nd wicket):
    A. C. MacLaren and A. G. Paul *v.* Somerset (Taunton) 1895
350* (1st wicket):
    C. Washbrook and W. Place *v.* Sussex (Old Trafford) 1947
336 (2nd wicket):
    F. Watson and E. Tyldesley *v.* Worcestershire (Worcester) .. 1929
327 (2nd wicket):
    F. Watson and E. Tyldesley *v.* India (Old Trafford) 1932
324 (4th wicket):
    A. C. MacLaren and J. T. Tyldesley *v.* Nottinghamshire (Nottingham) 1904
316 (2nd wicket):
    J. L. Hopwood and E. Tyldesley *v.* Gloucestershire (Bristol) .. 1934
306 (2nd wicket):
    F. Watson and E. Tyldesley *v.* Sussex (Brighton) 1928
306 (3rd wicket):
    E. Paynter and N. Oldfield *v.* Hampshire (Southampton) 1938
305 (2nd wicket):
    F. Watson and J. Iddon *v.* Somerset (Taunton) 1934
300 (4th wicket):
    E. Tyldesley and J. Iddon *v.* Leicestershire (Leicester) 1928

C. Washbrook shared with L. Hutton (Yorkshire) in the record first-wicket partnership in test cricket of 359 for England *v.* South Africa at Johannesburg in 1948-9.

RECORD PARTNERSHIP FOR EACH WICKET

1st wicket—368:
    A. C. MacLaren and R. H. Spooner *v.* Gloucestershire (Liverpool) 1903
2nd wicket—371:
    F. Watson and E. Tyldesley *v.* Surrey (Old Trafford) 1928
3rd wicket—306:
    E. Paynter and N. Oldfield *v.* Hampshire (Southampton) 1938
4th wicket—324:
    A. C. MacLaren and J. T. Tyldesley *v.* Nottinghamshire (Nottingham) 1904
5th wicket—235*:
    N. Oldfield and A. E. Nutter *v.* Nottinghamshire (Old Trafford) .. 1939

6th wicket—278:
　　J. Iddon and H. R. W. Butterworth *v*. Sussex (Old Trafford)　　.. 1932
7th wicket—245:
　　A. H. Hornby and J. Sharp *v*. Leicestershire (Old Trafford)　　.. 1912
8th wicket—150:
　　A. Ward and C. R. Hartley *v*. Leicestershire (Leicester)　..　.. 1900
9th wicket—142:
　　L. O. S. Poidevin and A. Kermode *v*. Sussex (Eastbourne)　.. 1907
10th wicket—173:
　　J. Briggs and R. Pilling *v*. Surrey (Aigburth)　　..　..　.. 1885

LARGEST PARTNERSHIPS AGAINST LANCASHIRE

380 (2nd wicket):
　　F. A. Tarrant and J. W. Hearne for Middlesex (Lord's)　..　.. 1914
333 (1st wicket):
　　J. F. Byrne and S. P. Kinneir for Warwickshire (Birmingham)　.. 1905
330 (3rd wicket):
　　A. E. Dipper and W. R. Hammond for Gloucestershire (Old
　　Trafford)　　..　..　..　..　..　..　..　.. 1925
327 (3rd wicket):
　　S. P. Kinneir and W. G. Quaife for Warwickshire (Birmingham)　.. 1901
323 (1st wicket):
　　P. Holmes and H. Sutcliffe for Yorkshire (Sheffield)　..　.. 1931

CENTURY PARTNERSHIPS FOR THE FIRST WICKET
IN BOTH INNINGS

103 and 100:
　　A. Hartley and W. K. Tyldesley *v*. Hampshire (Southampton)　.. 1910
141 and 193:
　　A. H. Hornby and H. Makepeace *v*. Nottinghamshire (Nottingham) 1912
114 and 116:
　　H. Makepeace and C. Hallows *v*. Australians (Liverpool) ..　.. 1926
202 and 107*:
　　C. Hallows and F. Watson *v*. Glamorgan (Old Trafford) ..　.. 1928
108 and 126*:
　　E. Paynter and C. Washbrook *v*. Nottinghamshire (Nottingham) .. 1937
101 and 118:
　　C. Washbrook and J. T. Ikin *v*. Hampshire (Old Trafford) ..　.. 1953
Note: C. Washbrook has also shared in century first-wicket partnerships in
both innings of a match with L. Hutton (Yorkshire) for England *v*. Australia
at Adelaide 1946–7 and again at Leeds 1948.
In 1928 C. Hallows and F. Watson shared in 12 century first-wicket partnerships, 5 of these being of 200 or more.

ALL TEN WICKETS IN AN INNINGS

10—46　　W. Hickton *v*. Hampshire (Old Trafford)　　..　.. 1870
　　　(Some authorities do not recognise this as a first-class match)
10—55　　J. Briggs *v*. Worcestershire (Old Trafford)　　..　.. 1900
10—102　R. Berry *v*. Worcestershire (Blackpool) ..　..　.. 1953

ALL TEN WICKETS IN AN INNINGS AGAINST

10—104　V. E. Walker for Middlesex (Old Trafford)　　..　.. 1865
10—40　　G. O. Allen for Middlesex (Lord's)　　..　..　.. 1929
10—131　A. P. Freeman for Kent (Maidstone)　..　..　.. 1929
10—79　　A. P. Freeman for Kent (Old Trafford)　..　..　.. 1931
10—90　　T. E. Bailey for Essex (Clacton) ..　..　..　.. 1949

NINE WICKETS IN AN INNINGS

9—118	A. Watson v. Derbyshire (Old Trafford)	..	..	..	1874
9—25	A. Appleby v. Sussex (Brighton)	..	..	..	1877
9—63	A. G. Steel v. Yorkshire (Old Trafford)	..	..	..	1878
9—29	J. Briggs v. Derbyshire (Derby)	..	..	..	1885
9—39	R. G. Barlow v. Sussex (Old Trafford)	..	..	..	1886
9—88	J. Briggs v. Sussex (Old Trafford)	..	..	..	1888
9—41	A. Mold v. Yorkshire (Huddersfield)	..	..	..	1890
9—29	A. Mold v. Kent (Tonbridge)	..	..	..	1892
9—62	A. Mold v. Kent (Old Trafford)	..	..	..	1895
9—77	J. Sharp v. Worcestershire (Worcester)	..	..	..	1901
9—37	J. Hallows v. Gloucestershire (Gloucester)	..	..	..	1904
9—47	W. Brearley v. Somerset (Old Trafford)	..	..	..	1905
9—44	F. Harry v. Warwickshire (Old Trafford)	..	..	..	1906
9—36	W. Huddleston v. Nottinghamshire (Liverpool)	..	..	..	1906
9—46	H. Dean v. Derbyshire (Chesterfield)	..	..	..	1907
9—80	W. Brearley v. Yorkshire (Old Trafford)	..	..	..	1909
9—35	H. Dean v. Warwickshire (Liverpool)	..	..	..	1909
9—31	H. Dean v. Somerset (Old Trafford)	..	..	..	1909
9—77	H. Dean v. Somerset (Bath)	..	..	..	1910
9—43	J. S. Heap v. Northamptonshire (Northampton)	..	..	..	1910
9—109	H. Dean v. Leicestershire (Leicester)	..	..	..	1911
9—62	H. Dean v. Yorkshire (Liverpool)	..	..	..	1913
9—32	C. H. Parkin v. Leicestershire (Ashby-de-la-Zouch)	..	..	..	1924
9—33	J. L. Hopwood v. Leicestershire (Old Trafford)	..	..	..	1933
9—69	J. L. Hopwood v. Worcestershire (Blackpool)	..	..	..	1934
9—42	J. Iddon v. Yorkshire (Sheffield)	..	..	..	1937
9—40	R. Tattersall v. Nottinghamshire (Old Trafford)	..	..	..	1953

Nine wickets in an innings has been taken by Lancashire players in other first-class matches as follows:

9—31	J. Briggs—Lord Londesborough's XI v. Australians (Scarborough)	..	..	..	..	..	..	1890
9—103	S. F. Barnes—England v. South Africa (Johannesburg)						..	1913–14
9—85	C. H. Parkin—Players v. Gentlemen (Oval)					..	..	1920

FOURTEEN OR MORE WICKETS IN A MATCH

14—72	W. McIntyre v. Derbyshire (Old Trafford)	..	..	1876
15—47	W. McIntyre v. Derbyshire (Derby)	..	..	1877
14—102	W. S. Patterson v. Nottinghamshire (Nottingham)	..	..	1877
14—112	A. G. Steel v. Yorkshire (Old Trafford)	..	..	1878
15—131	A. Mold v. Somerset (Taunton)	..	..	1891
14—95	A. Mold v. Gloucestershire (Bristol)	..	..	1891
14—122	J. Briggs v. Yorkshire (Old Trafford)	..	..	1891
14—159	A. Mold v. Sussex (Brighton)	..	..	1892
15—87	A. Mold v. Sussex (Brighton)	..	..	1894
16—111	A. Mold v. Kent (Old Trafford)	..	..	1895
15—85	A. Mold v. Nottinghamshire (Nottingham)	..	..	1895
14—59	S. F. Barnes v. Derbyshire (Derby)	..	..	1903
14—70	S. F. Barnes v. Essex (Leyton)	..	..	1903
14—151	W. Brearley v. Essex (Old Trafford)	..	..	1904
17—137	W. Brearley v. Somerset (Old Trafford)	..	..	1905
15—70	F. Harry v. Warwickshire (Old Trafford)	..	..	1906
14—111	W. Brearley v. Essex (Old Trafford)	..	..	1908
14—77	H. Dean v. Somerset (Old Trafford)	..	..	1909
16—103	H. Dean v. Somerset (Bath)	..	..	1910
14—93	J. S. Heap v. Northamptonshire (Northampton)	..	..	1910
14—142	W. Brearley v. Somerset (Liverpool)	..	..	1911
15—108	H. Dean v. Kent (Old Trafford)	..	..	1912
17—91	H. Dean v. Yorkshire (Liverpool)	..	..	1913

14—99	C. H. Parkin v. Leicestershire (Liverpool)	1914
14—123	C. H. Parkin v. Yorkshire (Old Trafford)	1919
14—81	J. S. Heap v. Gloucestershire (Bristol)	1919
14—180	C. H. Parkin v. Hampshire (Liverpool)	1921
14—73	C. H. Parkin v. Derbyshire (Chesterfield)	1922
15—95	C. H. Parkin v. Glamorgan (Blackpool)	1923
15—154	E. A. McDonald v. Kent (Old Trafford)	1928
15—112	J. L. Hopwood v. Worcestershire (Blackpool)	1934
14—216	R. Pollard v. Middlesex (Old Trafford)	1946
14—125	R. Berry v. Worcestershire (Blackpool)	1953
14—73	R. Tattersall v. Nottinghamshire (Old Trafford) ..	1953

Note: C. H. Parkin's 14—99 v. Leicestershire at Liverpool in 1914 was accomplished in his first match for Lancashire.

The following performances by Lancashire players in other first-class matches are noteworthy:

15—28	J. Briggs—England v. South Africa (Cape Town) ..	1888–9
15—57	J. Briggs—Lord Londesborough's XI v. Australians (Scarborough)	1890
17—159	S. F. Barnes—England v. South Africa (Johannesburg) ..	1913–14

150 WICKETS IN A SEASON

		For Lancashire		All first-class matches	
		Wickets	Average	Wickets	Average
W. Brearley (2) ..	1905	133	19.04	181	19.25
	1908	154	15.46	163	16.17
J. Briggs (5)	1888	102	11.57	160	10.49
	1890	78	13.12	158	12.34
	1893	128	13.71	166	15.89
	1896	145	19.06	165	19.71
	1897	155	16.51	155	16.51
L. Cook (2)	1920	150	14.96	156	14.88
	1921	148	22.91	151	22.99
H. Dean (2)	1911	179	17.48	183	17.43
	1912	136	12.51	162	13.67
E. A. McDonald (4)	1925	198	18.55	205	18.67
	1926	175	20.23	175	20.23
	1927	150	23.90	150	23.90
	1928	190	19.75	190	19.75
A. Mold (4)	1893	142	15.07	166	16.96
	1894	187	11.60	207	12.30
	1895	192	13.73	213	15.96
	1896	137	17.62	150	18.12
C. H. Parkin (4) ..	1922	181	16.44	189	17.46
	1923	186	16.06	209	16.94
	1924	194	13.38	200	13.67
	1925	150	19.38	152	19.30
A. G. Steel (1) ..	1878	55	8.10	164	9.40
R. Tattersall (2) ..	1950	171	13.29	193	13.59
	1953	135	16.45	164	18.13
R. K. Tyldesley (2) ..	1924	167	13.32	184	13.98
	1929	154	15.57	154	15.57
L. L. Wilkinson (1) ..	1938	145	22.97	151	23.38

100 WICKETS IN A SEASON FOR LANCASHIRE

11 times—J. Briggs.
10 times—R. K. Tyldesley.
 8 times—H. Dean.
 7 times—A. Mold.

6 times—E. A. McDonald, R. Pollard.
4 times—W. R. Cuttell, C. H. Parkin.
3 times—W. Brearley, L. Cook, R. Tattersall.
Twice   —M. J. Hilton, J. L. Hopwood, W. E. Phillipson, F. M. Sibbles.
Once   —S. F. Barnes, F. S. Booth, J. Hallows, W. Huddleston, A. Kermode,
          W. B. Roberts, J. Sharp, J. B. Statham, A. Watson, S. Webb, L. L.
          Wilkinson.

Note: A. Mold took 102 wickets in 1889, his first season in first-class cricket,
92 of them for Lancashire. He completed 100 wickets in a season in all first-
class matches in his first 8 successive seasons, 1889–96.

OUTSTANDING INNINGS BOWLING ANALYSES

5—3	R. G. Barlow *v.* Kent (Old Trafford)	1878
6—3	R. G. Barlow *v.* Derbyshire (Derby)	1881
5—5	J. Crossland *v.* Kent (Old Trafford)	1883
4—0	Rev. J. R. Napier *v.* Yorkshire (Sheffield)	1888
7—8	L. Cook *v.* Derbyshire (Chesterfield)	1920
6—6	C. H. Parkin *v.* Glamorgan (Liverpool)	1924
5—0	R. K. Tyldesley *v.* Leicestershire (Old Trafford)	1924
7—6	R. K. Tyldesley *v.* Northamptonshire (Liverpool)	1924

GOOD BOWLING SPELLS

7 wickets in 19 balls.	R. Tattersall *v.* Nottinghamshire (Old Trafford)	1953
7 wickets in 20 balls.	A. Mold *v.* Somerset (Old Trafford)	1894
5 wickets in 7 balls.	J. Briggs *v.* Sussex (Old Trafford)	1890

FOUR WICKETS IN FOUR BALLS

A. Mold	*v.* Nottinghamshire (Nottingham)	.. ..	1895
W. Brearley	*v.* Somerset (Old Trafford)	..	1905
R. K. Tyldesley	*v.* Derbyshire (Derby) (not all in same innings) ..		1929

'HAT-TRICKS'

The following list is in addition to the above cases of 4 wickets in 4 balls.

J. Crossland	*v.* Surrey (Oval)	1881
R. G. Barlow	*v.* Derbyshire (Derby)	1881
A. Mold	*v.* Somerset (Old Trafford)	1894
W. R. Gregson	*v.* Leicestershire (Blackpool)	1906
R. Whitehead	*v.* Surrey (Old Trafford)	1912
J. Bullough	*v.* Derbyshire (Derby)	1914
J. D. Tyldesley	*v.* Derbyshire (Old Trafford)	1920
J. D. Tyldesley	*v.* Worcestershire (Old Trafford)	1922
E. A. McDonald	*v.* Sussex (Brighton)	1925
E. A. McDonald	*v.* Kent (Dover)	1926
E. A. McDonald	*v.* Warwickshire (Birmingham)	1930
L. L. Wilkinson	*v.* Sussex (Hove)	1938
R. Pollard	*v.* Glamorgan (Preston)	1939
R. Pollard	*v.* Warwickshire (Blackpool)	1947
J. T. Ikin	*v.* Somerset (Taunton)	1949
R. Tattersall	*v.* Nottinghamshire (Old Trafford)	1953

'Hat-tricks' were performed by Lancashire players in other first-class
matches as follows:

A. G. Steel	Cambridge University *v.* Oxford University (Lord's)	1879
R. G. Barlow	Players *v.* Gentlemen (Oval)	1884
J. Briggs	North *v.* South (Scarborough)	1891
J. Briggs	England *v.* Australia (Sydney)	1891–2
S. F. Barnes	Players *v.* Gentlemen (Lord's)	1909
S. F. Barnes	England *v.* The Rest (Oval)	1912

THE CRICKETER'S DOUBLE
1,000 RUNS AND 100 WICKETS IN A SEASON

For Lancashire   *All First-Class Matches*

		Runs	Average	Wickets	Average	Runs	Average	Wickets	Average
W. R. Cuttell	1898	952	27.20	109	20.69	1,003	25.71	114	21.21
J. Hallows	1904	1,071	39.66	108	19.37	1,071	39.66	108	19.37
J. L. Hopwood	1934	1,660	39.52	111	19.29	1,672	38.00	111	20.69
J. L. Hopwood	1935	1,538	33.43	103	20.55	1,538	33.43	103	20.55

The following instances of 800 runs and 80 wickets in a season have been recorded:

A. G. Steel	1881	353	50.42	42	10.78	848	29.24	139	12.56
R. G. Barlow	1882	795	31.80	67	9.97	1,077	27.61	85	11.22
R. G. Barlow	1883	555	25.22	83	13.98	847	22.89	106	15.69
J. Briggs	1887	736	27.25	102	16.90	819	28.24	114	17.70
J. Briggs	1888	648	25.92	102	11.57	872	21.26	160	10.49
J. Briggs	1893	698	20.52	128	13.71	921	19.59	166	15.89
W. R. Cuttell	1899	983	25.86	87	21.16	1,054	26.35	90	21.78
J. Briggs	1900	761	20.66	120	17.45	817	20.94	127	17.74
W. R. Cuttell	1900	787	21.86	109	19.11	804	21.72	109	19.65
J. Sharp	1901	884	23.89	113	22.66	884	23.89	113	22.66
J. D. Tyldesley	1921	852	23.66	83	28.22	852	23.66	83	28.22
J. L. Hopwood	1930	1,066	28.81	80	19.02	1,083	28.50	81	19.40
J. Iddon	1932	1,427	34.80	77	17.88	1,451	34.54	80	17.72
J. L. Hopwood	1936	1,602	33.37	83	22.98	1,602	33.37	83	22.98
W. E. Phillipson	1937	866	29.86	131	23.62	866	29.86	131	23.62
A. E. Nutter	1938	1,156	32.11	91	24.64	1,156	32.11	91	24.64
W. E. Phillipson	1946	842	27.16	80	23.98	855	26.71	80	24.12
K. Cranston	1947	989	41.20	69	21.33	1,228	33.18	83	22.81

Note: K. Cranston's feat of scoring 1,228 runs and taking 83 wickets in all first-class matches in his first season represents the best all-round début by a Lancashire player. A. E. Nutter scored 1,156 runs and took 91 wickets in his first full season after playing in only 11 previous matches for the county.

100 RUNS AND 10 WICKETS IN A MATCH

R. G. Barlow, 71, 39* and 10—119	*v.* Surrey (Old Trafford)	..	..	1883
J. Briggs, 129* and 10—41	*v.* Sussex (Old Trafford)	..	..	1890
J. Briggs, 115 and 13—209	*v.* Yorkshire (Old Trafford)	..	1892
J. Briggs, 112 and 11—115	*v.* Surrey (Oval)	..	..	..	1893
J. L. Hopwood, 110, 45 and 10—53	*v.* Leicestershire (Old Trafford)	..	1933
J. T. Ikin, 67, 85* and 11—119	*v.* Nottinghamshire (Old Trafford)	1947

Notes: J. Briggs also scored 1 and 126* and took 9—88 in the only innings in which he bowled *v.* Sussex (Old Trafford) in 1888.

R. G. Barlow scored 10 and 101* and took 10—48 for North of England *v.* Australians at Nottingham in 1884.

10,000 RUNS AND 1,000 WICKETS FOR LANCASHIRE

J. Briggs is the only cricketer who has scored 10,000 runs and taken 1,000 wickets for Lancashire. He scored 10,617 runs and took 1,688 wickets for the county and in all first-class matches scored 13,983 runs and took 2,201 wickets.

10,000 RUNS FOR LANCASHIRE

		For Lancashire		All First-class Matches	
		Runs	Average	Runs	Average
E. Tyldesley ..	..	34,222	45.20	38,874	45.46
J. T. Tyldesley	..	31,949	41.38	37,897	40.66
H. Makepeace	..	25,207	36.37	25,799	36.23
F. Watson ..	..	22,833	37.06	23.596	36.98
J. Iddon ..	..	21,975	37.05	22,681	36.76
J. Sharp ..	..	21,815	30.89	22,715	31.11
C. Washbrook	..	21,021	45.89	26,977	46.11
C. Hallows ..	..	20,142	39.72	20,926	40.24
E. Paynter ..	..	16,555	41.59	20,023	42.24
A. C. MacLaren	..	15,735	33.26	21,959	34.04
J. L. Hopwood	..	15,519	30.05	15,548	29.90
A. Ward ..	..	15,264	30.77	17,783	30.08
W. Place ..	..	13,625	39.15	14,629	37.70
G. A. Edrich	..	11,105	38.55	11,334	38.29
J. T. Ikin ..	..	10,822	41.94	14.047	39.68
J. Briggs ..	..	10,617	18.99	13,983	18.19
A. N. Hornby	..	10,294	23.88	15,798	23.72

500 WICKETS FOR LANCASHIRE

		For Lancashire		All First-class Matches	
		Wickets	Average	Wickets	Average
J. Briggs ..	..	1,688	15.65	2,201	15.99
A. Mold ..	..	1,541	15.13	1,673	15.54
R. K. Tyldesley	..	1,449	16.65	1,509	17.21
A. Watson ..	..	1,279	13.47	1,338	13.46
H. Dean ..	..	1,267	18.01	1,301	18.14
E. A. McDonald	..	1,053	20.96	1,347	20.66
R. Pollard ..	..	1,015	22.14	1,122	22.56
F. M. Sibbles	..	932	22.11	940	22.43
C. H. Parkin ..	..	901	16.12	1,048	17.58
L. Cook ..	..	821	21.36	839	21.20
W. R. Cuttell	..	760	19.59	792	19.59
R. G. Barlow	..	726	13.59	933	14.52
W. Brearley ..	..	690	18.70	844	19.31
W. Huddleston	..	684	17.55	685	17.57
J. L. Hopwood	..	672	22.18	673	22.45
R. Tattersall ..	..	584	16.84	756	17.96
W. E. Phillipson	..	545	24.78	555	24.72
J. Iddon ..	..	532	26.68	550	26.91

WICKET-KEEPING

Most Dismissals in an Innings

7	W. Farrimond	(st. 1, ct. 6)	*v.* Kent (Old Trafford)	1930
		(equals World Record)		
6	H. G. Garnett	(st. 0, ct. 6)	*v.* Warwickshire (Birmingham)	1914
6	G. Duckworth	(st. 1, ct. 5)	*v.* Kent (Dover)	1926
6	G. Duckworth	(st. 1, ct. 5)	*v.* Worcestershire (Worcester) ..	1936

Most Dismissals in a Match

8	G. Duckworth	(st. 3, ct. 5)	*v.* Kent (Maidstone)	1928
8	G. Duckworth	(st. 5, ct. 3)	*v.* Warwickshire (Old Trafford)	1936

Most Dismissals in a Season (70 or more)

		For Lancashire			All First-class Matches		
		Stumped	*Caught*	*Total*	*Stumped*	*Caught*	*Total*
C. Smith	1895	25	51	76	25	51	76
G. Duckworth	1928	28	69	97	30	77	107
G. Duckworth	1929	26	44	70	37	58	95
G. Duckworth	1930	23	37	60	28	53	81
G. Duckworth	1934	25	54	79	26	60	86
G. Duckworth	1936	21	48	69	26	57	83
W. Farrimond	1938	15	69	84	15	70	85
W. Farrimond	1939	10	62	72	10	62	72

FIELDING

Most Catches in an Innings

| 6 | R. K. Tyldesley | *v.* Hampshire (Liverpool) .. | .. | .. | 1921 |
| 6 | K. Grieves | *v.* Sussex (Old Trafford) .. | .. | .. | 1951 |

Most Catches in a Match

| 8 | K. Grieves | *v.* Sussex (Old Trafford) .. | .. | .. | 1951 |

Most Catches in a Season (50 or more)

		For Lancashire	All First-class Matches
K. Grieves	1950	63	63
J. T. Ikin	1946	45	55
K. Grieves	1953	54	54

LANCASHIRE *v.* YORKSHIRE

	Lancashire	*Yorkshire*
Highest Innings Total	509—9	590
Lowest Innings Total	30	33
Number of Centuries	41	46
Most Runs	E. Tyldesley, 1,844	H. Sutcliffe, 3,006
Highest Individual Score ..	R. H. Spooner, 200*	M. Leyland, 211*
Most Wickets	J. Briggs, 170	W. Rhodes, 237
Best Bowling in an Innings ..	A. Mold, 9—41	G. H. Hirst 9—23